Advanced Spanish

Edited by
Enrique Montes

www.livinglanguage.com

Editor: Suzanne McQuade
Production Editor: Carolyn Roth
Production Manager: Tom Marshall
Interior Design: Sophie Chin
Illustrations: Sophie Chin

First Edition

Library of Congress Cataloging-in-Publication Data

Advanced Spanish / edited by Enrique Montes. -- 1st ed.
    p. cm.
  ISBN 978-0-307-97164-7
1. Spanish language--Textbooks for foreign speakers--English. 2.
Spanish language--Grammar. 3. Spanish language--Spoken Spanish. I.
Montes, Enrique.
  PC4129.E5A38 2011
  468.2'421--dc23
                      2011021882

PRINTED IN THE UNITED STATES OF AMERICA

10 9 8 7 6 5 4

Acknowledgments

Thanks to the Living Language team: Amanda D'Acierno, Christopher Warnasch, Suzanne McQuade, Laura Riggio, Erin Quirk, Amanda Munoz, Fabrizio LaRocca, Siobhan O'Hare, Sophie Chin, Sue Daulton, Alison Skrabek, Carolyn Roth, Ciara Robinson, and Tom Marshall.

How to Use This Course 8

O U T L I N E

COURSE

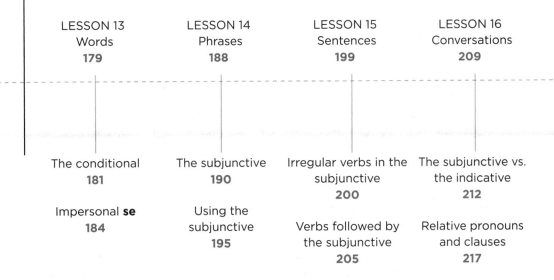
OUTLINE

How to Use This Course

¡Bienvenidos! Welcome to *Living Language Advanced Spanish*!

Before we begin, let's take a quick look at what you'll see in this course.

CONTENT

Advanced Spanish is a continuation of *Intermediate Spanish*. Now that you've mastered the basics with *Essential* and *Intermediate Spanish*, you'll take your Spanish even further with a comprehensive look at irregular verbs, advanced verb tenses, and complex sentences.

UNITS

There are four units in this course. Each unit has four lessons arranged in a "building block" structure: the first lesson will present essential *words*, the second will introduce longer *phrases*, the third will teach *sentences*, and the fourth will show how everything works together in everyday *conversations*.

At the beginning of each unit is an introduction highlighting what you'll learn in that unit. At the end of each unit you'll find the Unit Essentials, which reviews the key information from that unit, and a self-graded Unit Quiz, which tests what you've learned.

LESSONS

There are four lessons per unit for a total of 16 lessons in the course. Each lesson has the following components:

- **Introduction** outlining what you will cover in the lesson.

- **Word Builder 1** (first lesson of the unit) presenting key words and phrases.

- **Phrase Builder 1** (second lesson of the unit) introducing longer phrases and expressions.

- **Sentence Builder 1** (third lesson of the unit) teaching sentences.

- **Conversation 1** (fourth lesson of the unit) for a natural dialogue that brings together important vocabulary and grammar from the unit.

- **Take It Further** providing extra information about the new vocabulary you just saw, expanding on certain grammar points, or introducing additional words and phrases.

- **Word/Phrase/Sentence/Conversation Practice 1** practicing what you learned in Word Builder 1, Phrase Builder 1, Sentence Builder 1, or Conversation 1.

- **Grammar Builder 1** guiding you through important Spanish grammar that you need to know.

- **Work Out 1** for a comprehensive practice of what you saw in Grammar Builder 1.

- **Word Builder 2/Phrase Builder 2/Sentence Builder 2/Conversation 2** for more key words, phrases, or sentences, or a second dialogue.

- **Take It Further** for expansion on what you've seen so far and additional vocabulary.

- **Word/Phrase/Sentence/Conversation Practice 2** practicing what you learned in Word Builder 2, Phrase Builder 2, Sentence Builder 2, or Conversation 2.

- **Grammar Builder 2** for more information on Spanish grammar.

- **Work Out 2** for a comprehensive practice of what you saw in Grammar Builder 2.

- **Tip** or **Culture Note** for a helpful language tip or useful cultural information related to the lesson or unit.

- **Drive It Home** reviewing important grammar and vocabulary from the lesson.

- **How Did You Do?** outlining what you learned in the lesson.

UNIT ESSENTIALS

You will see the **Unit Essentials** at the end of every unit. This section summarizes and reviews the key information from the unit, but with missing vocabulary information for you to fill in. In other words, each Unit Essentials works as both a study guide and a blank "cheat sheet." Once you complete it, you'll have your very own reference for the most essential vocabulary and grammar from the unit.

UNIT QUIZ

After each Unit Essentials, you'll see a **Unit Quiz**. The quizzes are self-graded so it's easy for you to test your progress and see if you should go back and review.

PROGRESS BAR

You will see a **Progress Bar** on each page that has course material. It indicates your current position within the unit and lets you know how much progress you're making. Each line in the bar represents a Grammar Builder section.

AUDIO

Look for the symbol ⏵ to help guide you through the audio as you're reading the book. It will tell you which track to listen to for each section that has audio. When you see the symbol, select the indicated track and start listening! If you don't see the symbol, then there isn't any audio for that section. You'll also see ⏸, which will tell you where that track ends.

The audio can be used on its own—in other words, without the book—when you're on the go. Whether in your car or at the gym, you can listen to the audio on its own to brush up on your pronunciation or review what you've learned in the book.

PRONUNCIATION GUIDE, GRAMMAR SUMMARY, GLOSSARY

At the back of this book you will find a **Pronunciation Guide**, **Grammar Summary**, and **Glossary**. The Pronunciation Guide provides information on Spanish pronunciation and the phonetics system used in this course. The Grammar Summary contains a helpful, brief overview of key points in the Spanish grammar system. The Glossary (Spanish–English and English–Spanish) includes all of the essential words from the four units of *Advanced Spanish*, as well as some additional vocabulary.

FREE ONLINE TOOLS

Go to **www.livinglanguage.com/languagelab** to access your free online tools. The tools are organized around the units in this course, with audiovisual flashcards, as well as interactive games and quizzes for each unit. These tools will help you to review and practice the vocabulary and grammar that you've seen in the units, as well as provide some bonus words and phrases related to the unit's topic.

Unit 1:
Shopping

In this unit, you'll learn vocabulary related to clothing and colors, as well as some useful shopping expressions. You'll also learn how to make comparisons and how to talk about future plans. By the end of this unit, you should be able to:

☐ Name articles of clothing and talk about shopping

☐ Conjugate common stem-changing verbs

☐ Compare things using adjectives and adverbs

☐ Describe how clothing fits and looks

☐ Use direct object pronouns

☐ Talk about the near future

☐ Conjugate reflexive verbs

☐ Use reflexive pronouns

Lesson 1: Words

By the end of this lesson, you will be able to:

☐ Understand how to conjugate common stem-changing verbs

☐ Name articles of clothing

Word Builder 1

▶ 1A Word Builder 1 (CD 7, Track 1)

el cinturón	*belt*
los pantalones	*pants*
el traje	*suit*
la camisa	*shirt*
la corbata	*tie*
los calcetines	*socks*
los vaqueros	*jeans*
la camiseta	*T-shirt*
la gabardina	*raincoat*
el saco/la chaqueta	*jacket*
el jersey/el suéter	*sweater*
los zapatos	*shoes*
la falda	*skirt*

⏸

✎ Word Practice 1

1. _____

2. _____

3. _____

4. _____

Identify the correct items on the clothesline.

ANSWER KEY
1. la camisa/la camiseta; 2. los calcetines; 3. la falda; 4. los zapatos

Grammar Builder 1
STEM-CHANGING VERBS

▶ 1B Grammar Builder 1 (CD 7, Track 2)

In previous units in both *Essential Spanish* and *Intermediate Spanish*, you learned the conjugations of a few irregular verbs. Remember stem-changing verbs from Lesson 10 of *Essential Spanish*? Let's take another look at these verbs. The first group includes verbs in which the **o** of the infinitive changes to **ue**, as in almorzar (*to have lunch*). Notice that this change happens in all the forms except **nosotros** and **vosotros**.

ALMORZAR *(TO HAVE LUNCH)*	
yo almuerzo	nosotros/as almorzamos
tú almuerzas	vosotros/as almorzáis
él/ella/usted almuerza	ellos/ellas/ustedes almuerzan

Here are a few more common **o** to **ue** verbs.

costar	*to cost*
dormir	*to sleep*
encontrar	*to find, to meet*
morir	*to die*
mostrar	*to show*
volver	*to return*
volar	*to fly*
oler	*to smell*
recordar	*to remember*
soñar	*to dream*
mover	*to move*
poder	*can, to be able*

Notice that **h-** is added to **oler** (*to smell*) in the forms where the vowel changes.

OLER *(TO SMELL)*	
yo huelo	nosotros/as olemos
tú hueles	vosotros/as oléis
él/ella/usted huele	ellos/ellas/ustedes huelen

A second common stem change is -e to -ie, as in pensar (*to think*). Again, the nosotros and vosotros forms are not affected.

PENSAR *(TO THINK)*	
yo pienso	nosotros/as pensamos
tú piensas	vosotros/as pensáis
él/ella/usted piensa	ellos/ellas/ustedes piensan

Here are some other e to ie verbs.

mentir	*to lie, to tell lies*
entender	*to understand*
sentir	*to feel*
cerrar	*to close*
comenzar	*to begin*
despertarse	*to wake up*
sentarse	*to sit down*

¿Cuánto cuesta esa camisa?
How much does that shirt cost?

Ellos sueñan con tener mucho dinero.
They dream of having a lot of money.

La clase comienza en veinte minutos.
The class begins in twenty minutes.

No entiendo lo que estás dicendo.
I don't understand what you are saying.

✎ Work Out 1

Complete the following sentences with one of the following verbs: pensar,
dormir, sentir, costar, comenzar, cerrar, encontrar, entender, mostrar, volar.

1. Yo _____ dolor en la espalda.

2. Yo no _____. ¿Puede hablar más despacio por favor?

3. Las tiendas abren a las nueve y media de la mañana y _____

   a las ocho de la noche.

4. Ella _____ las camisetas de algodón al cliente.

5. ¿Cuánto _____ esa blusa roja?

6. Tú no _____ una corbata que combine con la camisa.

7. Mi bebita _____ once horas todas las noches.

8. Nosotros siempre _____ con la misma aerolínea.

9. La película _____ a las cinco.

10. Tú _____ demasiado en tus problemas.

ANSWER KEY
1. siento; 2. entiendo; 3. cierran; 4. muestra; 5. cuesta; 6. encuentras; 7. duerme; 8. volamos;
9. comienza; 10. piensas

Word Builder 2

⏵ 1C Word Builder 2 (CD 7, Track 3)

el vestido	*dress*
el abrigo	*overcoat*
la blusa	*blouse*
el bolso	*handbag*

el traje de baño/el bañador	bathing suit
la bata	robe
las sandalias	sandals
la bufanda	scarf
los guantes	gloves
las medias	stockings

✎ Word Practice 2

Match the Spanish word with its appropriate English translation.

1. las medias   a. *gloves*

2. el bolso   b. *dress*

3. el vestido   c. *blouse*

4. los guantes   d. *stockings*

5. el abrigo   e. *handbag*

6. la blusa   f. *overcoat*

ANSWER KEY
1. d; 2. e; 3. b; 4. a; 5. f; 6. c

Grammar Builder 2
MORE STEM-CHANGING VERBS

▶ 1D Grammar Builder 2 (CD 7, Track 4)

There is another group of verbs with stems that change from **-e** to **-i**. **Pedir** (*to ask for*) is one example.

PEDIR *(TO ASK FOR)*	
yo pido	nosotros/as pedimos

PEDIR *(TO ASK FOR)*	
tú pides	vosotros/as pedís
él/ella/usted pide	ellos/ellas/ustedes piden

Here are some other common **-e** to-**i** verbs.

conseguir	*to find, to obtain, to get*
medir	*to measure*
reír	*to laugh*
repetir	*to repeat*
servir	*to serve*
impedir	*to prevent*
sonreír	*to smile*

Take a look at **sonreír** (*to smile*), which is just like **reír** (*to laugh*). Notice where the accent goes.

SONREÍR *(TO SMILE)*	
yo sonrío	nosotros/as sonreímos
tú sonríes	vosotros/as sonreís
él/ella/usted sonríe	ellos/ellas/ustedes sonríen

Finally, some verbs ending in **-cer** or **-cir** have the irregularity of adding a **-z** before the ending in the first person singular. Take **agradecer** (*to be thankful, to thank*) as an example.

AGRADECER *(TO BE THANKFUL, TO THANK)*	
yo agradezco	nosotros/as agradecemos
tú agradeces	vosotros/as agradecéis
él/ella/usted agradece	ellos/ellas/ustedes agradecen

Other common examples include the following.

ofrecer	to offer
producir	to produce
conducir	to drive
traducir	to translate

Verbs ending in **-ger** and **-gir** change the **-g** to **-j** in the first person singular. One example is escoger (*to choose*).

ESCOGER *(TO CHOOSE)*	
yo escojo	nosotros/as escogemos
tú escoges	vosotros/as escogéis
él/ella/usted escoge	ellos/ellas/ustedes escogen

Here are some other examples.

elegir	to choose
exigir	to demand
proteger	to protect
dirigir	to direct

Él no consigue trabajo.
He doesn't find work.

Tú sonríes poco.
You don't smile a lot.

Yo conduzco un auto verde.
I drive a green car.

Yo exijo una explicación.
I demand an explanation.

✎ Work Out 2

Conjugate the verb in parentheses.

1. La maestra _____ las oraciones varias veces. (repetir)

2. Yo _____ un auto viejo. (conducir)

3. El presidente _____ la reunión. (dirigir)

4. Ella siempre _____ películas extranjeras. (escoger)

5. Tú _____ demasiado de tus empleados. (exigir)

6. Ellos _____ la mesa. (medir)

7. La estación de televisión _____ siete series cada año. (producir)

8. Ellos _____ una película de cine. (escoger)

ANSWER KEY
1. repite; 2. conduzco; 3. dirige; 4. escoge; 5. exiges; 6. miden; 7. produce; 8. escogen

---

Take It Further

There will be times when you're speaking to a native Spanish speaker when you will simply not understand what he or she has just said. The best thing you can do in such circumstances is to let the person know that you are having a bit of trouble. Here are a few phrases—some you already know, and some are new—that can help you.

Disculpe, ¿puede repetir lo que acaba de decir, por favor?
Sorry, could you please repeat what you just said?

No entiendo.
I don't understand.

¿Qué significa … ?
What does … mean?

Disculpe, ¿cómo dijo?
Sorry, what did you say?

✎ Drive It Home

Write the correct form of the verb in parentheses.

1. Tú _____ la lección. (entender)

2. Ella _____ la lección. (entender)

3. Nosotros _____ la lección. (entender)

4. Ellos _____ la lección. (entender)

5. Yo _____ en mi familia. (pensar)

6. Ustedes _____ en su familia. (pensar)

7. Usted _____ en su familia. (pensar)

8. Vosotros _____ en vuestra familia. (pensar)

ANSWER KEY
1. entiendes; 2. entiende; 3. entendemos; 4. entienden; 5. pienso; 6. piensan; 7. piensa; 8. pensáis

How Did You Do?

By now, you should be able to:

☐ Understand how to conjugate common stem-changing verbs
(Still unsure? Jump back to pages 14 and 18.)

☐ Name articles of clothing (Still unsure? Jump back to pages 13 and 17.)

Lesson 2: Phrases

By the end of this lesson, you should be able to:

- ☐ Talk about shopping
- ☐ Compare things using *more/-er* or *less than*
- ☐ Compare two people or things that are equal
- ☐ Use superlatives like *the best*, and *the worst*

Phrase Builder 1

▶ 2A Phrase Builder 1 (CD 7, Track 5)

ir de compras	to go shopping
llevar una prenda puesta	to wear something
ir de escaparates	to go window-shopping
buscar gangas	to look for bargains
comprar en rebaja	to buy on sale
comprar en el mercadillo	to buy at the flea market
probarse algo	to try something on
hacer a la medida	to custom sew
lavar en seco	to dry-clean
lavar a mano	to hand wash

Ⅱ

✎ Phrase Practice 1

Match the Spanish with its appropriate English translation.

1. lavar en seco   a. *to buy on sale*
2. lavar a mano   b. *to dry-clean*
3. ir de escaparates   c. *to look for bargains*
4. ir de compras   d. *to hand wash*
5. buscar gangas   e. *to go shopping*
6. comprar en rebaja   f. *to go window-shopping*

ANSWER KEY
1. b; 2. d; 3. f; 4. e; 5. c; 6. a

Grammar Builder 1
COMPARATIVES

▶ 2B Grammar Builder 1 (CD 7, Track 6)

In English, you can compare things with the formula *more/-er* or *less* + adjective/adverb/noun + *than*. In Spanish, the *more* comparative formula is:

más + adjective/adverb/noun + que

Mi hermana es más alta que mi madre.
My sister is taller than my mother.

Juan tiene más camisas que su hermano.
Juan has more shirts than his brother.

But just like in English, there are a few exceptions. The following adjectives have a different form for the comparative.

ADJECTIVE		COMPARATIVE	
bueno/a	*good*	mejor	*better*
malo/a	*bad*	peor	*worse*
grande	*big*	mayor	*bigger/older*
pequeño/a	*small*	menor	*smaller/younger*

Esta camisa me queda mejor que la azul.
This shirt fits me better than the blue one.

Esta corbata se ve peor que la otra.
This tie looks worse than the other.

Ella es mayor que nuestra hija.
She is older than our daughter.

Mi hermana es dos años menor que yo.
My sister is two years younger than I (am).

When you want to show inferiority, you will use the following formula:

menos + adjective/adverb/noun + **que**

Yo soy menos tímida que mi amiga Rocío.
I am less shy than my friend Rocío.

Nosotros vamos al cine menos frecuentemente que vosotros.
We go to the movies less often than you (do).

Pedro tiene menos dinero que su esposa.
Pedro has less money than his wife.

✎ Work Out 1

Fill in the blank with the appropriate Spanish translation of the words in parentheses.

1. Yo trabajo _____ tú. (*fewer hours than*)

2. Vosotros viajáis _____ nosotros.
   (*more frequently than*)

3. Esa película es _____ la de las once y media.
   (*longer than*)

4. Este bolso es _____ el negro. (*more expensive than*)

5. Tú lees _____ yo. (*fewer books than*)

6. Ellos tienen _____ sus padres.
   (*more problems than*)

7. Esta chaqueta es _____ la otra.
   (*more elegant than*)

8. Carlos es _____ su esposa.
   (*ten years older than*)

ANSWER KEY

1. menos horas que; 2. más frecuentemente que; 3. más larga que; 4. más costoso que; 5. menos libros que; 6. más problemas que; 7. más elegante que; 8. diez años mayor que

Direct Object Pronouns   Reflexive Verbs

The Future with **ir a**
(going to)   Colors, Patterns,
and Fabrics

Phrase Builder 2

 2C Phrase Builder 2 (CD 7, Track 7)

¿Qué desea?	*What would you like?*
¿De qué color?	*What color?*
¿Cuánto vale?	*How much is it?*
¿Algo más?	*Anything else?*
No, gracias, eso es todo.	*No, thanks; that's all.*
Me queda mal.	*It doesn't fit me.*
Te quedan bien.	*They fit you well.*
¡Qué elegante!	*How elegant!*
Me lo llevo.	*I'll take it.*
Es muy costoso.	*It's very expensive.*

Phrase Practice 2

Match the Spanish with its appropriate English translation.

1. Me lo llevo.

2. Me queda mal.

3. ¿De qué color?

4. ¿Cuánto vale?

5. ¿Qué desea?

6. ¿Algo más?

a. *What color?*

b. *How much is it?*

c. *I'll take it.*

d. *What would you like?*

e. *Anything else?*

f. *It doesn't fit me.*

ANSWER KEY

1. c; 2. f; 3. a; 4. b; 5. d; 6. e

Grammar Builder 2
EQUAL COMPARISONS AND SUPERLATIVES

▷ 2D Grammar Builder 2 (CD 7, Track 8)

There will be times when you want to compare two people or things that are equal. In this case, you will use the following formula:

tan + adjective/adverb + como

Madrid es tan interesante como Nueva York.
Madrid is as interesting as New York.

La vida en Madrid es tan rápida como en Nueva York.
Life in Madrid is as fast as in New York.

To compare two phrases, you need to use tanto, which will agree in gender and number with the noun it precedes.

Carmen tiene tanta paciencia como tú.
Carmen has as much patience as you (do).

Ella tiene tanto dinero como su padre.
She has as much money as her father (does).

Ella tiene tantos gastos como ustedes.
She has as many expenses as you (do).

Ella tiene tantas sandalias como yo.
She has as many sandals as I (do).

When you use expressions like *the biggest, the worst, the most exciting*, and *the least difficult*, you are using superlatives. Forming superlatives in Spanish is very easy: simply add the corresponding definite article (el, la, los, las) to the patterns you've already learned, and use the preposition de when you want to express *in/of*.

Este vestido es el más costoso (de todo).
This dress is the most expensive (of all).

La falda roja es la más fea.
The red skirt is the ugliest.

Marta es la menos extrovertida de la familia.
Marta is the least extroverted in the family.

Ellos son los menos puntuales de todos mis amigos.
They are the least punctual of all my friends.

Mis hermanas son las más altas de la clase.
My sisters are the tallest in the class.

Ese edificio es el más alto.
That building is the highest.

Ⅱ

✎ Work Out 2

Fill in the blanks with the Spanish equivalents of the words in parentheses.

1. **Mi oficina es** _____ **la tuya.** (*as big as*)

2. **Estos tiquetes son** _____ . (*the least expensive*)

3. **Nuestra habitación es** _____ **las tres.**

   (the smallest of)

4. **Es** _____ **película del año.** *(the worst)*

5. **Ella lleva el vestido** _____ **.** *(the prettiest)*

6. **Los zapatos de color café son** _____ **.** *(the most comfortable)*

7. **Me gusta el chocolate** _____ **a ti.** *(as much as)*

8. **Él tiene** _____ **trabajo del mundo.** *(the best)*

ANSWER KEY

1. tan grande como; 2. los menos costosos; 3. la más pequeña de; 4. la peor; 5. más bonito; 6. los más cómodos; 7. tanto como; 8. el mejor

☀ Tip!

A good way to improve your Spanish vocabulary is to read short passages from newspapers or magazines, many of which you can, of course, find online. Before you begin to read an article, it is important that you focus on the title of the article and look at any pictures that are attached to it. Skim quickly over the entire text, looking for information that will help you get the gist of the content. In this way, you can familiarize yourself with the topic and begin to anticipate the information that you'll read. Read the text only a couple of times, and don't focus on each individual word. It's more important that you get the overall picture. Trying to understand and learn each little word will only cause you to give up and feel frustrated. For now, focus on the big picture, and then move on to something else. Soon enough, you'll be able to worry about all the little details! To find some practice material, go to your favorite search engine and type in **revistas en español** (*magazines in Spanish*) or **periódicos en español** (*newspapers in Spanish*).

✎ Drive It Home

Make comparative sentences using the adjective in parentheses. Follow the model
by saying that the first person is more of the quality mentioned than the second one.

example: **María (inteligente) Jorge**
María es más inteligente que Jorge.

1. **Mi hermana (tímida) mi prima.** _____

   _____

2. **Mi hermana (alta) mi prima.** _____

   _____

3. **Mi hermana (morena) mi prima.** _____

   _____

4. **Mi hermana (elegante) mi prima.** _____

   _____

5. **La comedia (buena) el drama.** _____

   _____

6. **La comedia (malo) el drama.** _____

   _____

ANSWER KEY
1. Mi hermana es más tímida que mi prima. 2. Mi hermana es más alta que mi prima. 3. Mi hermana
es más morena que mi prima. 4. Mi hermana es más elegante que mi prima. 5. La comedia es mejor
que el drama. 6. La comedia es peor que el drama.

How Did You Do?

By now, you should be able to:

☐ Talk about shopping (Still unsure? Jump back to page 23.)

☐ Compare things using *more/-er* or *less than* (Still unsure? Jump back to page 24.)

☐ Compare two people or things that are equal
(Still unsure? Jump back to page 28.)

☐ Use superlatives like *the best*, and *the worst* (Still unsure? Jump back to page 29.)

Lesson 3: Sentences

By the end of this lesson, you should be able to:

☐ Talk about what size you wear

☐ Describe how clothing fits and looks

☐ Use direct object pronouns

☐ Talk about things you are planning to do in the near future

Sentence Builder 1

▶ 3A Sentence Builder 1 (CD 7, Track 9)

¿Qué número calza?	What shoe size do you wear?
Calzo el número treinta y siete.	I wear shoe size 37.
¿Qué talla lleva usted?	What size do you wear?
No estoy seguro/a.	I'm not sure.
Mi talla es cuarenta.	I wear size 40.

¿Le gustaría probarse este suéter?	*Would you like to try this sweater on?*
¿Ya lo atendieron?	*Has someone helped you? (lit., Have you been helped?)*
Gracias, sólo estoy mirando.	*Thanks, I'm just looking.*
¿Dónde está el probador?	*Where is the dressing room?*
Estoy buscando un vestido de noche informal.	*I'm looking for a casual evening dress.*

✎ Sentence Practice 1

Fill in the blanks in each sentence based on the English translation.

1. ¿Qué talla _____ usted? *What size do you wear?*

2. No estoy _____ . *I'm not sure.*

3. _____ es cuarenta. *I wear size 40.*

4. Gracias, _____ . *Thanks, I'm just looking.*

5. Estoy buscando _____ . *I'm looking for a casual evening dress.*

6. ¿Dónde está _____ ? *Where is the dressing room?*

ANSWER KEY
1. lleva; 2. seguro/a; 3. Mi talla; 4. sólo estoy mirando; 5. un vestido de noche informal; 6. el probador

Grammar Builder 1
DIRECT OBJECT PRONOUNS

▶ 3B Grammar Builder 1 (CD 7, Track 10)

A direct object is a noun (or pronoun) that shows you what the verb is acting on.
For example, in the sentence *Manuel is buying a sweater*, the direct object is the

noun *sweater*—it's the answer to the question *what is Manuel buying?* A direct object can also be a person, as in *Manuel sees the salesperson,* in answer to the question *who does Manuel see?*

Direct object pronouns are the pronouns used to replace direct object nouns, such as *sweater* or *salesperson* in our examples above. In English, there are some different pronouns used as direct objects: *me* instead of *I, her* instead of *she, him* instead of *he,* etc. Spanish is no different. Let's look at the direct object pronouns in Spanish.

DIRECT OBJECT PRONOUNS			
me	*me*	nos	*us*
te	*you (infml.)*	os	*all of you (infml.)*
lo	*him, it, you (fml.)*	los	*them, you*
la	*her, it, you (fml.)*	las	*them, you*

Don't forget that nouns in Spanish can be feminine or masculine, even if they're inanimate. So, lo can mean *he* or *it* for a masculine noun, and la can mean *she* or *it* for a feminine noun. The same is true of los and las, in the plural. The direct object pronouns that correspond to usted are lo and la, and the ones that correspond to ustedes are los and las. The difference depends on whether you are talking to a man or a woman.

Yo amo a María.
I love María.

Yo la amo.
I love her.

Manuela llama a Pedro.
Manuela calls Pedro.

Direct Object Pronouns

Reflexive Verbs

The Future with **ir a**
(*going to*)

Colors, Patterns,
and Fabrics

Manuela lo llama.
Manuela calls him.

Ellos visitan a María y Clara.
They visit María and Clara.

Ellos las visitan.
They visit them.

Now let's look at how direct object pronouns are used. In Spanish, as you saw in the examples above, they come right before the verb.

Carlos no te conoce.
Carlos doesn't know you.

Los oigo pero no los veo.
I hear them, but I don't see them.

Nosotros no la olvidamos.
We don't forget her.

However, if the main verb appears in the infinitive form (ending in -ar, -er, or -ir), the direct object pronoun can come either before the verbal phrase or after the infinitive, in which case the pronoun is attached to it.

Carlos te quiere conocer.
Carlos wants to meet you.

Carlos quiere conocerte.
Carlos wants to meet you.

Los puedo oír, pero no los puedo ver.
I can hear them, but I can't see them.

Puedo oírlos, pero no puedo verlos.
I can hear them, but I can't see them.

Nosotros no queremos olvidarla.
We don't want to forget her.

Nosotros no la queremos olvidar.
We don't want to forget her.

A similar thing happens with the present participle (**-ando, -iendo**) form. Notice the use of the accent mark, which ensures that the stress remains on the same syllable as it would if there were no participial ending.

Te estoy ayudando.
I am helping you.

Estoy ayudándote.
I am helping you.

Ⓘ

✎ Work Out 1

Replace the direct object noun with a pronoun.

1. **La señorita atiende al cliente.** _____

_____

2. Ella está comprando unos zapatos. _____

_____

3. Mis hijas van a dar una fiesta el viernes. _____

_____

4. Yo voy a traer unas flores. _____

_____

5. Vais a escribir una carta. _____

_____

6. Estoy enviando un mensaje a Roberto. _____

_____

7. Manuel conoce a tu familia. _____

_____

8. Mis amigos llaman a María todos los días. _____

_____

ANSWER KEY
1. La señorita lo atiende. 2. Ella los está comprando./Ella está comprándolos. 3. Mis hijas la van a dar el viernes. 4. Yo las voy a traer./Yo voy a traerlas. 5. Vais a escribirla./La vais a escribir. 6. Estoy enviándolo a Roberto./Lo estoy enviando a Roberto. 7. Manuel la conoce. 8. Mis amigos la llaman todos los días.

Sentence Builder 2
▶ 3C Sentence Builder 2 (CD 7, Track 11)

¿Puedo probarme esta falda?	*Can I try this skirt on?*
¿Me puede hacer un descuento?	*Can you give me a discount?*
¿Está rebajado?	*Is it reduced/on sale?*

¿Cómo le quedan?	How do they fit?
Me quedan un poco cortos.	They are a bit short.
Ese color es el último grito de la moda.	That color is very trendy right now.
¿Cuánto cuesta la cartera negra de cuero?	How much is the black leather handbag?
¿Dónde se encuentran chaquetas para caballero?	Where can I find men's jackets?
La chaqueta no combina bien con los pantalones.	The jacket doesn't go well with the pants.

⑪

✎ Sentence Practice 2

Fill in the blanks in each sentence based on the English translation.

1. ¿Puedo _____ esta falda? *Can I try this skirt on?*

2. ¿Me puede _____? *Can you give me a discount?*

3. ¿Está _____? *Is it reduced/on sale?*

4. Me quedan _____. *They are a bit short.*

5. ¿Cuánto cuesta _____ ?

   How much is the black leather handbag?

6. La chaqueta _____ los pantalones.

   The jacket doesn't go well with the pants.

ANSWER KEY

1. probarme; 2. hacer un descuento; 3. rebajado; 4. un poco cortos; 5. la cartera negra de cuero;
6. no combina bien con

Direct Object Pronouns

Reflexive Verbs

The Future with **ir a**
(*going to*)

Colors, Patterns,
and Fabrics

Grammar Builder 2
THE FUTURE WITH IR A (*GOING TO*)

▶ 3D Grammar Builder 2 (CD 7, Track 12)

Now let's take a look at how we can talk about things we are planning on doing tomorrow or in the near future. In Spanish, there is a very simple formula:

ir (*to go*) + a (*to*) + verb in the infinitive

This is the equivalent of *going to* in English.

Yo voy a comprar un traje.
I am going to buy a suit.

Tú vas a ir de compras por la tarde.
You are going to go shopping in the afternoon.

Ella va a estrenar su chaqueta el martes.
She is going to wear her jacket for the first time on Tuesday.

Usted va a viajar a España.
You are going to travel to Spain.

Nosotros vamos a mirar escaparates.
We are going to go window-shopping.

Vosotros vais a buscar zapatos.
You are going to look for shoes.

Ustedes van a descansar.
You are going to rest.

Here are some useful time expressions that you can use to show a time in the future.

hoy	today
hoy por la tarde	today in the afternoon
hoy por la noche	today in the evening
mañana	tomorrow
mañana por la mañana	tomorrow morning
mañana por la tarde	tomorrow afternoon
mañana por la noche	tomorrow evening
más tarde	later
esta tarde	this afternoon
esta noche	this evening
la semana que viene	next week
el mes que viene	next month
el año que viene	next year

✎ Work Out 2

Answer the following questions using the information in parentheses.

1. ¿Cuándo van a ir a Los Ángeles? (ellos, en diciembre) _____

_____

2. ¿Qué vas a comprar? (yo, unos pantalones y unos zapatos) _____

_____

3. ¿Adónde vais de vacaciones? (nosotros, Costa Rica) _____

_____

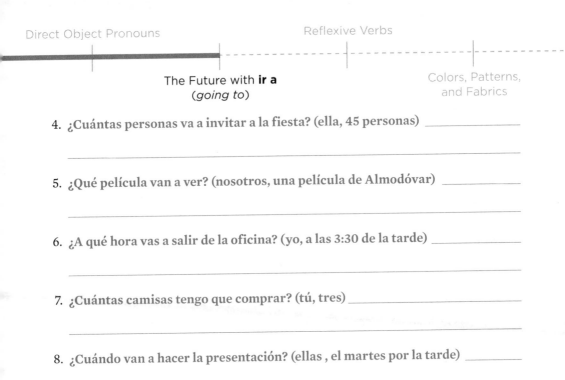

4. ¿Cuántas personas va a invitar a la fiesta? (ella, 45 personas) _____

5. ¿Qué película van a ver? (nosotros, una película de Almodóvar) _____

6. ¿A qué hora vas a salir de la oficina? (yo, a las 3:30 de la tarde) _____

7. ¿Cuántas camisas tengo que comprar? (tú, tres) _____

8. ¿Cuándo van a hacer la presentación? (ellas , el martes por la tarde) _____

ANSWER KEY

1. Ellos van a ir en diciembre. 2. Voy a comprar unos pantalones y unos zapatos. 3. Vamos a ir
a Costa Rica. 4. Ella va a invitar a cuarenta y cinco personas. 5. Vamos a ver una película de
Almodóvar. 6. Voy a salir a las tres y media de la tarde. 7. Tienes que comprar tres camisas. 8. Ellas
van a hacer la presentación el martes por la tarde.

Take It Further

You're probably going to need a few more adjectives to describe the way clothes
and shoes fit. Here is a very useful list.

ajustado/a	*tight*
suelto/a	*loose, flowing*
escotado/a	*low-cut*
ancho/a	*baggy, wide*
enterizo/a	*one-piece*
de dos piezas	*two-piece*
cómodo/a	*comfortable*
incómodo/a	*uncomfortable*

| suave | soft |
| duro/a | hard |

Los vestidos sueltos y escotados son perfectos para noches de verano.
Loose and low-cut dresses are perfect for summer nights.

Estos zapatos no son tan suaves como los negros.
These shoes are not as soft as the black ones.

Los trajes de baño enterizos son más cómodos que los de dos piezas.
One-piece bathing suits are more comfortable than two-piece ones.

Estos pantalones están muy ajustados.
These pants are very tight.

✎ Drive It Home

A. Change each sentence by replacing **el helado** with the object pronoun **lo**.

1. **Yo pruebo el helado.** _____

2. **Ella prueba el helado.** _____

3. **Tú pruebas el helado.** _____

4. **Nosotros probamos el helado.** _____

B. Now rewrite the sentences that you created above using the future with **ir a**.

1. _____

2. _____

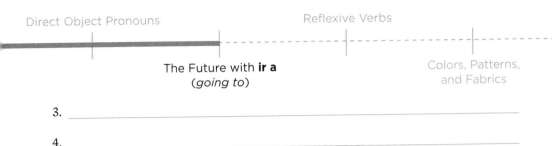

Direct Object Pronouns   Reflexive Verbs

The Future with **ir a**
(*going to*)   Colors, Patterns,
and Fabrics

3. _____

4. _____

ANSWER KEY
A. 1. Yo lo pruebo. 2. Ella lo prueba. 3. Tú lo pruebas. 4. Nosotros lo probamos.
B. 1. Yo lo voy a probar./Yo voy a probarlo. 2. Ella lo va a probar./Ella va a probarlo. 3. Tú lo vas a probar./Tú vas a probarlo. 4. Nosotros lo vamos a probar./Nosotros vamos a probarlo.

How Did You Do?

By now, you should be able to:

☐ Talk about what size you wear (Still unsure? Jump back to page 32.)

☐ Describe how clothing fits and looks (Still unsure? Jump back to page 41.)

☐ Use direct object pronouns (Still unsure? Jump back to page 33.)

☐ Talk about things you are planning to do in the near future
(Still unsure? Jump back to page 39.)

Lesson 4: Conversations

By the end of this lesson, you should be able to:

☐ Conjugate reflexive verbs

☐ Use reflexive pronouns

☐ Talk about colors, patterns, and fabrics

Conversation 1

▶ 4A Conversation 1 (CD 7, Track 13 - Spanish Only; Track 14 - Spanish and English)

Juan is at a men's shop trying on some clothes, because he is going on vacation
with his girlfriend next week and he needs a few things.

Vendedora:	¿Qué tal le quedan los pantalones, señor?
Juan:	Estos vaqueros azul claro son muy anchos y estos negros son demasiado ajustados. ¿Tiene una talla intermedia?
Vendedora:	Espere un momento. Voy a buscar a ver qué encuentro. Y las camisetas, ¿qué tal?
Juan:	La anaranjada parece ser de un material más ligero que la verde, ¿no es verdad?
Vendedora:	Sí, la anaranjada es cien por ciento de algodón. El color es el último grito de la moda y le queda mejor que la verde. Claro, es también más costosa.
Juan:	¿Tiene más en mi talla?
Vendedora:	Sí, creo que sí. ¿Tiene algún color en mente?
Juan:	Me gustaría llevar dos blancas, una azul oscura y otra en amarillo o rojo.
Vendedora:	Si gusta esperar un momento, voy a buscar los vaqueros y otras camisetas. Ya regreso.
Juan:	Mientras espero, voy a mirar por ahí a ver qué más encuentro.
Vendedora:	Muy bien. Hay pantalones cortos y bañadores en descuento allá enfrente.

Saleswoman:	Do the pants fit, sir?
Juan:	These light blue jeans are too loose, and these black ones are too tight. Do you have something in between?
Saleswoman:	Wait a moment. I'll take a look and see what I can find. What about the T-shirts?
Juan:	The orange one seems to be made of a lighter material than the green one, right?
Saleswoman:	Yes, the orange one is one hundred percent cotton. The color is very trendy nowadays, and it suits you better than the green one. Of course, it's more expensive.
Juan:	Do you have more in my size?
Saleswoman:	Yes, I think so. Do you have a color in mind?

The Future with **ir a**
(*going to*)

Juan:	*I'd like to take two white ones, a dark blue one, and another one in yellow or red.*
Saleswoman:	*If you'd like to wait a moment, I'll go get the jeans and the T-shirts. I'll be back soon.*
Juan:	*While I wait, I'll take a look over there to see what else I find.*
Saleswoman:	*Very well. There are shorts and bathing suits on sale over there in the front.*

Take It Further

When it comes to clothes, you'll find that in the Spanish-speaking world, there are different words for the same thing. In Latin America, for example, blue jeans are los jeans, sweater is un suéter, and jacket is una chaqueta, un saco, or una americana. But in Spain, a pair of blue jeans is unos vaqueros, a sweater is un suéter or un jersey, and a jacket may be referred to as una chaqueta. And when it comes to talking about underwear, no one seems to agree: women's underwear can be bragas, bombachas, calzoncitos, or pantis, and men's undergarments are calzones or calzoncillos. Stockings are medias or pantymedias, and socks are calcetines or medias. Slippers are known as zapatillas, pantuflas, or chinelas, and a robe as bata, albornoz, or deshabillé. So, what to do? When in Rome, do as the Romans, and simply use the words people use where you are!

✎ Conversation Practice 1

Fill in the blank with the correct word from the conversation.

1. **Estos vaqueros** _____ **son muy anchos y estos negros son**

   demasiado _____ . *These light blue jeans are too loose, and these*

   black ones are too tight.

2. _____ buscar a ver qué encuentro. *I'll take a look and see what I can find.*

3. Sí, la anaranjada es cien por ciento de _____. *Yes, the orange one is one hundred percent cotton.*

4. Claro, también es más _____. *Of course, it's more expensive.*

5. _____ llevar dos blancas, una azul oscura y otra en amarillo o rojo. *I'd like to take two white ones, a dark blue one, and another one in yellow or red.*

6. Si gusta esperar un momento, voy a buscar los _____ y otras _____. *If you'd like to wait a moment, I'll go get the jeans and the T-shirts. I'll be back soon.*

ANSWER KEY
1. azul claro/ajustados; 2. Voy a; 3. algodón; 4. costosa; 5. Me gustaría 6. vaqueros/camisetas

Grammar Builder 1
REFLEXIVE VERBS

▶ 4B Grammar Builder 1 (CD 7, Track 15)

Reflexive verbs are verbs in which the subject performs the action on him- or herself. Spanish reflexive verbs often correspond to English verbs that use reflexive pronouns, like *to wash oneself, to dress oneself,* and so on. But there are also many verbs that are reflexive in Spanish but are not reflexive in English. Spanish reflexive verbs are conjugated following the same rules as -ar, -er, -ir, or irregular verbs, but their infinitives always end in -se. When reflexive verbs are conjugated, they always take the following reflexive pronouns.

REFLEXIVE PRONOUNS	
me *(myself)*	nos *(ourselves)*

REFLEXIVE PRONOUNS	
te (*yourself*)	os (*yourselves*)
se (*himself, herself, itself, yourself*)	se (*themselves, yourselves*)

These pronouns come before the conjugated verb. Let's take a look at levantarse, which means *to get up*.

LEVANTARSE *(TO GET UP)*			
(yo) me levanto	*I get up*	(nosotros/as) nos levantamos	*we get up*
(tú) te levantas	*you get up*	(vosotros/as) os levantáis	*you get up*
(él/ella/usted) se levanta	*he/she/it gets up*	(ellos/ellas/ ustedes) se levantan	*they/you get up*

When a reflexive verb is used with other verbs, like in the present continuous with estar or the immediate future with ir, the reflexive pronoun can be placed either before the verb phrase or after it. If it comes after, it's attached to the end of the main verb.

(Yo) me levanto a las seis todos los días.
I get up at six every day.

En este momento me estoy levantando.
Right now, I am getting up.

En este momento estoy levantándome.
Right now, I am getting up.

Mañana me voy a levantar tarde.
Tomorrow I'm going to get up late.

Mañana voy a levantarme tarde.
Tomorrow I'm going to get up late.

Here are some more common reflexive verbs in Spanish. Again, notice that some of them can be translated reflexively in English, but not all of them.

REFLEXIVE VERBS	
acostarse	*to go to bed*
llamarse	*to be called*
vestirse	*to get dressed*
ponerse	*to put (something) on*
divertirse	*to have fun*
ducharse	*to shower*
bañarse	*to bathe*
sentarse	*to sit down*
sentirse	*to feel*
despedirse	*to say good-bye*

You've probably noticed that if you take off the -se ending of the reflexive infinitive, you're left with another, non-reflexive verb. Our first example, levantarse, is like this. **Levantarse** means *to get up, to rise,* or *to lift oneself from a seated or reclining position,* but **levantar** simply means *to lift* or *to raise (something else).* Similar pairs are **llamar** (*to call*) and **llamarse** (*to call oneself, to be called*), **vestir** (*to dress [someone else]*) and **vestirse** (*to get dressed, to dress oneself*), and so on. Here are some more examples of reflexive verbs.

Me siento muy feliz.
I feel very happy.

Ella se va a despedir de su familia esta tarde.
She's going to say good-bye to her family this afternoon.

Ellos se están vistiendo para la fiesta.
They are getting dressed for the party.

Also note that reflexives can have a reciprocal sense. In the plural form, the reflexive pronoun can sometimes mean *each other* or *one another*, as in these sentences.

Nos miramos.
We look at each other.

Ellos se están besando.
They are kissing each other.

Los perros se huelen.
The dogs smell one another.

Ⅱ

✎ Work Out 1

Combine the following words to form sentences, conjugating the verbs as necessary.

1. **Yo/llamarse/Pedro Campos.** _____

_____

2. **Ellos/ir a divertirse/en la fiesta de esta noche.** _____

_____

3. **Él/ir a sentarse/a leer el periódico.** _____

_____

4. En este momento yo/estar probándose/el vestido. _____

_____

5. ¿A qué hora/levantarse/usted todos los días? _____

_____

6. Ellos/acostarse/muy tarde los fines de semana. _____

_____

7. ¿Vosotros/estar mirando/en el espejo ahora? _____

_____

8. Después de/trotar/ella/ir a bañarse. _____

_____

ANSWER KEY

1. Yo me llamo Pedro Campos. 2. Ellos van a divertirse/se van a divertir en la fiesta de esta noche. 3. Él se va a sentar/va a sentarse a leer el periódico. 4. En este momento me estoy probando/estoy probándome el vestido. 5. ¿A qué hora se levanta usted todos los días? 6. Ellos se acuestan muy tarde los fines de semana. 7. ¿Os estáis mirando en el espejo ahora? 8. Después de trotar, ella se va a bañar/va a bañarse.

🎧 Conversation 2

▶ 4C Conversation 2 (CD 7, Track 16 - Spanish Only; Track 17 - Spanish and English)

Now listen in as Sara, Juan's girlfriend, does some shopping of her own.

Vendedora:	¿Ya la atendieron?
Sara:	Gracias. ¿Cuánto cuesta la cartera negra de cuero? No tiene una etiqueta con el precio.
Vendedora:	Vamos a ver … Tiene razón. Estos bolsos están rebajados y tienen un treinta por ciento de descuento.
Sara:	¡Es una ganga! Me lo llevo. También me gustaría probarme unos zapatos.

Vendedora:	¿Qué número calza?
Sara:	Treinta y siete.
Vendedora:	La talla treinta y siete está en esta sección. ¿Busca algún color en particular?
Sara:	Sí, quiero unos zapatos que vayan con el bolso negro.
Vendedora:	Aquí hay unos muy bonitos y con un tacón no muy alto. Son muy cómodos. ¿Le gustan?
Sara:	A ver … me los voy a probar. ¡Me quedan como anillo al dedo! ¡Me los llevo! ¿Están también rebajados?
Vendedora:	Soñar no cuesta nada, ¿verdad? Desafortunadamente, no.
Sara:	Bueno, no importa. Son bonitos y me quedan bien.

Saleswoman:	*Is someone helping you?*
Sara:	*Thank you. How much is the black leather bag? It doesn't have a price tag.*
Saleswoman:	*Let's see … You're right. These handbags are on sale, and they are thirty percent off.*
Sara:	*That's a bargain! I'll take it. I'd also like to try on some shoes.*
Saleswoman:	*What size do you wear?*
Sara:	*Thirty-seven.*
Saleswoman:	*Size thirty-seven is in this section. Are you looking for any particular color?*
Sara:	*Yes, I'd like a pair of shoes that go with the black bag.*
Saleswoman:	*Here are some very pretty ones with a not-so-high heel. They are very comfortable. Do you like them?*
Sara:	*Let's see … I'm going to try them on. They fit me like a glove! I'll take them! Are they also on sale?*
Saleswoman:	*It doesn't hurt to ask! (lit., "To dream doesn't cost anything, right?") Unfortunately, no …*
Sara:	*Well, it doesn't matter. They're pretty and they fit me well.*

Ⓘ

Take It Further

As you learn Spanish, you'll see that there's a saying for just about anything and everything. There are two sayings in the above dialogue. The first one, **Me queda como anillo al dedo**, is equivalent of the English saying *It fits me like a glove*. The second one, **Soñar no cuesta nada**, literally means *To dream doesn't cost anything*, but in this context, you can translate it as *It doesn't hurt to ask.*

✎ Conversation Practice 2

Unscramble the Spanish sentences below from the dialogue above. The English sentence is unscrambled.

1. ¿la/atendieron/ya? *Is someone helping you?* _____

   _____

2. ¿cuero/cuesta/la/cuánto/negra/cartera/de? *How much is the black leather bag?*

   _____

3. ¿calza/número/qué? *What size do you wear?* _____

   _____

4. probarme/gustaría/zapatos/unos/me/también. *I'd also like to try on some shoes.*

   _____

5. no/nada/¿verdad?/soñar/cuesta *It doesn't hurt to ask!* (lit., "To dream doesn't cost anything, right?") _____

   _____

6. bonitos/son/me/y/bien/quedan. *They're pretty and they fit me well.* _____

   _____

Grammar Builder 2
COLORS, PATTERNS, AND FABRICS

▶ 4D Grammar Builder 2 (CD 7, Track 18)

Here are the colors in Spanish.

amarillo	yellow
azul	blue
celeste	sky blue
azul marino	navy blue
rojo	red
verde	green
marrón/café	brown
negro	black
blanco	white
gris	gray
naranja/anaranjado	orange
morado	purple
rosa/rosado	pink
dorado	gold
plateado	silver

Remember that most colors have to agree in gender and number with the noun they modify. Exceptions are those ending in -e or in a consonant like, **verde**, **azul**, **marrón**, **café**, and **celeste**, which only have to agree in number.

Este vestido plateado no combina con esos zapatos rojos.
This silver dress doesn't match those red shoes.

Las camisas amarillas son más costosas que las azules.
The yellow shirts are more expensive than the blue ones.

Los zapatos café no me gustan.
I don't like the brown shoes.

Here are a few more adjectives you can use with colors to describe clothes.

a rayas	striped
a cuadros	plaid
estampado	with a pattern, patterned
de lunares	polka-dotted
oscuro	dark
claro	light

And here are some types of fabric.

algodón	cotton
lana	wool
lino	linen
seda	silk
cuero	leather
plástico	plastic
gamuza	suede
poliéster	polyester

Me gusta la camisa de algodón de rayas azules y grises.
I like the blue and gray striped cotton shirt.

Direct Object Pronouns   Reflexive Verbs

The Future with **ir a**
(*going to*)   Colors, Patterns,
and Fabrics

Quiero una chaqueta de gamuza café.
I want a brown suede jacket.

La falda roja a cuadros de lana es muy costosa.
The red plaid wool skirt is very expensive.

✎ Work Out 2

Answer using complete sentences. ¿De qué color son estas cosas?

1. las naranjas _____

2. el océano _____

3. la luna _____

4. los limones _____

5. el sol _____

6. la sangre _____

7. el césped _____

8. el carbón _____

ANSWER KEY
1. Las naranjas son anaranjadas. 2. El océano es azul. 3. La luna es blanca. 4. Los limones son amarillos. 5. El sol es amarillo. 6. La sangre es roja. 7. El césped es verde. 8. El carbón es negro.

Take It Further

Just like in English, there are many idiomatic expressions in Spanish using colors. Here are a few.

ponerse rojo como un tomate	to be embarrassed (lit., to turn red like a tomato)
ponerse colorado	to be embarrassed (lit., to turn red)
estar rojo de la ira	to be very angry (lit., to be red with fury)
contar un chiste verde	to tell an obscene joke (lit., to tell a green joke)
ver todo negro	to be a pessimist (lit., to see everything as black)
ver todo color de rosa	to be an optimist, to wear rose-colored glasses (lit., to see everything pink)
ir de punta en blanco	to be dressed to the nines (lit., to go from the tip in white)
ser de sangre azul	to have blue blood (lit., to be of blue blood)
estar negro de la risa	to laugh very hard (lit., to turn black with laughter)

✎ Drive It Home

Give the complete conjugation of the following reflexive verbs:

DUCHARSE *(TO SHOWER)*	
yo _____	nosotros/as _____
tú _____	vosotros _____
él/ella/Ud. _____	ellos/ellas/Uds. _____

PONERSE *(TO PUT ON)*	
yo _____	nosotros/as _____
tú _____	vosotros_____
él/ella/Ud._____	ellos/ellas/Uds._____

ANSWER KEY

ducharse: me ducho, te duchas, se ducha, nos duchamos, os ducháis, se duchan

ponerse: me pongo, te pones, se pone, nos ponemos, os ponéis, se ponen

How Did You Do?

By now, you should be able to:

☐ Conjugate reflexive verbs (Still unsure? Jump back to page 46.)

☐ Use reflexive pronouns (Still unsure? Jump back to page 46.)

☐ Talk about colors, patterns, and fabrics (Still unsure? Jump back to page 53.)

Don't forget to practice and reinforce what you've learned by visiting **www.livinglanguage.com/languagelab** for flashcards, games, and quizzes for Unit 1!

Unit 1 Essentials

Vocabulary Essentials

ITEMS OF CLOTHING

	belt
	jacket
	pants
	suit
	shirt
	tie
	socks
	jeans
	T-shirt
	raincoat
	jacket
	sweater
	shoes
	skirt
	dress
	overcoat
	blouse
	handbag
	bathing suit
	robe

Advanced Spanish

	sandals
	scarf
	gloves
	stockings

[Pgs. 13 and 17]

CLOTHING VERBS

	to go shopping
	to wear something
	to go window-shopping
	to look for bargains
	to buy on sale
	to buy at the flea market
	to try something on
	to custom sew
	to dry-clean
	to hand wash

[Pg. 23]

SHOPPING EXPRESSIONS

	What would you like?
	What color?
	How much is it?
	Anything else?
	No, thanks; that's all.
	It doesn't fit me.

	They fit you well.
	How elegant!
	I'll take it.
	It's very expensive.
	What shoe size do you wear?
	I wear shoe size 37.
	What size do you wear?
	I'm not sure.
	I wear size 40.
	Would you like to try this sweater on?
	Is someone helping you?
	Thanks, I'm just looking.
	Where is the dressing room?
	I'm looking for a casual evening dress.
	Can I try this skirt on?
	Can you give me a discount?
	Is it reduced/on sale?
	How do they fit?
	They are a bit short.
	That color is very trendy right now.
	How much is the black leather handbag?
	Where can I find men's jackets?
	The jacket doesn't go well with the pants.

[Pgs. 27, 32, and 37]

FUTURE TIME EXPRESSIONS

	today
	today in the afternoon
	today in the evening
	tomorrow
	tomorrow morning
	tomorrow afternoon
	tomorrow evening
	later
	this afternoon
	this evening
	next week
	next month
	next year

[Pg. 40]

CLOTHING ADJECTIVES

	tight
	loose/flowing
	low-cut
	baggy/wide
	one-piece
	two-piece
	comfortable
	uncomfortable
	soft

	hard

[Pg. 41]

COLORS

	yellow
	blue
	sky blue
	navy blue
	red
	green
	brown
	black
	white
	gray
	orange
	purple
	pink
	gold
	silver

[Pg. 53]

PATTERNS

	striped
	plaid
	with a pattern, patterned
	polka-dotted

Advanced Spanish

| | dark |
| | light |

[Pg. 54]

FABRICS

	cotton
	wool
	linen
	silk
	leather
	plastic
	suede
	polyester

[Pg. 54]

IDIOMATIC EXPRESSIONS USING COLORS

	to be embarrassed (lit., to turn red like a tomato)
	to be embarrassed (lit., to turn red)
	to be very angry (lit., to be red with fury)
	to tell an obscene joke (lit., to tell a green joke)
	to be a pessimist (lit., to see everything as black)
	to be an optimist, to wear rose-colored glasses (lit., to see everything pink)

	to be dressed to the nines (lit., to go from the tip in white)
	to have blue blood (lit., to be of blue blood)
	to laugh very hard (lit., to turn black with laughter)

[Pg. 56]

Grammar Essentials

O TO UE STEM-CHANGING VERBS

ALMORZAR *(TO HAVE LUNCH)*	
yo almuerzo	nosotros/as almorzamos
tú almuerzas	vosotros/as almorzáis
él/ella/usted almuerza	ellos/ellas/ustedes almuerzan

Similar verbs: costar (*to cost*), dormir (*to sleep*), encontrar (*to find, to meet*), morir (*to die*), mostrar (*to show*), volver (*to return*), volar (*to fly*), oler (*to smell*), recordar (*to remember*), soñar (*to dream*), mover (*to move*), poder (*can, to be able*)

E TO IE STEM-CHANGING VERBS

PENSAR *(TO THINK)*	
yo pienso	nosotros/as pensamos
tú piensas	vosotros/as pensáis
él/ella/usted piensa	ellos/ellas/ustedes piensan

Similar verbs: mentir (*to lie, to tell lies*), entender (*to understand*), sentir (*to feel*), cerrar (*to close*), comenzar (*to begin*), despertarse (*to wake up*), sentarse (*to sit down*)

E TO I STEM-CHANGING VERBS

PEDIR *(TO ASK FOR)*	
yo pido	nosotros/as pedimos
tú pides	vosotros/as pedís
él/ella/usted pide	ellos/ellas/ustedes piden
Similar verbs: **conseguir** *(to find)*, **medir** *(to measure)*, **reír** *(to laugh)*, **repetir** *(to repeat)*, **servir** *(to serve)*, **impedir** *(to prevent)*, **sonreír** *(to smile)*	

CER VERBS ADDING Z IN FIRST PERSON SINGULAR

AGRADECER *(TO BE THANKFUL)*	
yo agradezco	nosotros/as agradecemos
tú agradeces	vosotros/as agradecéis
él/ella/usted agradece	ellos/ellas/ustedes agradecen
Similar verbs: **ofrecer** *(to offer)*, **producir** *(to produce)*, **conducir** *(to drive)*, **traducir** *(to translate)*, **conocer** *(to know)*	

GER AND GIR VERBS ADDING J IN FIRST PERSON SINGULAR

ESCOGER *(TO CHOOSE)*	
yo escojo	nosotros/as escogemos
tú escoges	vosotros/as escogéis
él/ella/usted escoge	ellos/ellas/ustedes escogen
Similar verbs: **elegir** *(to choose)*, **exigir** *(to demand)*, **proteger** *(to protect)*, **dirigir** *(to direct)*	

COMPARATIVES AND SUPERLATIVES

To form a comparative:

más + adjective/adverb/noun + que

Some adjectives have irregular comparatives.

ADJECTIVE		COMPARATIVE	
bueno/a	*good*	mejor	*better*
malo/a	*bad*	peor	*worse*
grande	*big*	mayor*	*bigger/older*
pequeño/a	*small*	menor	*smaller/younger*
* Note that mayor can also mean *older*, and menor can also mean *younger*.			

To make equal comparisons:

tan + adjective/adverb + como

To form the superlative:

el/la/los/las + comparative adjective/adverb

DIRECT OBJECT PRONOUNS

DIRECT OBJECT PRONOUNS			
me	*me*	nos	*us*
te	*you (infml.)*	os	*all of you (infml.)*
lo	*him, it, you (fml.)*	los	*them, you*
la	*her, it, you (fml.)*	las	*them, you*

Remember that direct pronouns come right before the verb, unless the verb appears in the infinitive, in which case the direct object pronoun can come before the verbal phrase, or after the infinitive, in which case the pronoun is attached to the infinitive.

FUTURE WITH IR A (*TO GO TO*)

ir (*to go*) + a (*to*) + verb in the infinitive

REFLEXIVE PRONOUNS

REFLEXIVE PRONOUNS	
me *(myself)*	nos *(ourselves)*
te *(yourself)*	os *(yourselves)*
se *(himself, herself, itself, yourself)*	se *(themselves, yourselves)*

REFLEXIVE VERBS

LEVANTARSE *(TO GET UP)*	
(yo) me levanto	(nosotros/as) nos levantamos
(tú) te levantas	(vosotros/as) os levantáis
(él/ella/usted) se levanta	(ellos/ellas/ustedes) se levantan
Similar verbs: acostarse *(to go to bed)*, llamarse *(to be called)*, vestirse *(to get dressed)*, ponerse *(to put something on)*, divertirse *(to have fun)*, ducharse *(to shower)*, bañarse *(to bathe)*, sentarse *(to sit down)*, sentirse *(to feel)*, despedirse *(to say good-bye)*	

VERBS

AGRADECER *(TO BE THANKFUL)*	
yo agradezco	nosotros/as agradecemos
tú agradeces	vosotros/as agradecéis
él/ella/usted agradece	ellos/ellas/ustedes agradecen

ALMORZAR *(TO HAVE LUNCH)*	
yo almuerzo	nosotros/as almorzamos
tú almuerzas	vosotros/as almorzáis
él/ella/usted almuerza	ellos/ellas/ustedes almuerzan

ESCOGER *(TO CHOOSE)*	
yo escojo	nosotros/as escogemos
tú escoges	vosotros/as escogéis
él/ella/usted escoge	ellos/ellas/ustedes escogen

LEVANTARSE *(TO GET UP)*

(yo) me levanto	(nosotros/as) nos levantamos
(tú) te levantas	(vosotros/as) os levantáis
(él/ella/usted) se levanta	(ellos/ellas/ustedes) se levantan

OLER *(TO SMELL)*

yo huelo	nosotros/as olemos
tú hueles	vosotros/as oléis
él/ella/usted huele	ellos/ellas/ustedes huelen

PEDIR *(TO ASK FOR)*

yo pido	nosotros/as pedimos
tú pides	vosotros/as pedís
él/ella/usted pide	ellos/ellas/ustedes piden

PENSAR *(TO THINK)*

yo pienso	nosotros/as pensamos
tú piensas	vosotros/as pensáis
él/ella/usted piensa	ellos/ellas/ustedes piensan

SONREÍR *(TO SMILE)*

yo sonrío	nosotros/as sonreímos
tú sonríes	vosotros/as sonreís
él/ella/usted sonríe	ellos/ellas/ustedes sonríen

Unit 1 Quiz

A. Fill in the blanks by conjugating the verb in parentheses.

1. Ella _____ hablar varios idiomas. (poder)

2. El estudiante le _____ a la profesora. (mentir)

3. Yo _____ un dolor de cabeza muy fuerte. (tener)

4. Los niños _____ cuando están contentos. (sonreír)

5. Nosotros _____ mucho los fines de semana. (dormir)

6. Los camareros _____ la comida. (servir)

7. Ustedes _____ un carro muy rápido. (conducir)

8. Usted _____ al trabajo en una semana. (volver)

B. Match the column on the left with the English word on the right.

1. la corbata	a. *worse*
2. la falda	b. *to try on*
3. probar	c. *wide*
4. la bufanda	d. *tie*
5. ajustado	e. *tight*
6. ancho	f. *shoe*
7. peor	g. *skirt*
8. el zapato	h. *scarf*

C. Fill in the blanks with the Spanish equivalents of the words in parentheses.

1. Tu casa es _____ la mía. (bigger than)

2. Esta ciudad es _____ . (the most expensive)

3. Esta película es _____ del año. (the best)

4. Mi trabajo es _____ el tuyo. (as good as)

5. Estos pantalones son _____ los otros pantalones. (uglier)

6. Este restaurante es _____ el otro. (better than)

7. Mi padre es _____ yo. (taller)

8. Esta blusa es _____ . (the least expensive)

D. Choose the vocabulary word that fits the sentence.

1. Ella se (ducha/pone) ropa muy elegante.

2. El (algodón/marrón) es un color muy bonito.

3. Nosotros llamamos a Clarisa y Mirna pero no (la/las) visitamos.

4. Tú te (acuestas/llamas) en una cama muy cómoda.

5. La comedia es mejor (como/que) el drama.

6. La comedia es tan buena (como/que) el drama.

7. ¿Cuánto (comienza/cuesta) esta camiseta?

8. Yo me (acuesto/levanto) temprano por la mañana.

ANSWER KEY
A. 1. puede; 2. miente; 3. tengo; 4. sonríen; 5. dormimos; 6. sirven; 7. conducen; 8. vuelve
B. 1. d; 2. g; 3. b; 4. h; 5. e; 6. c. 7. a; 8. f
C. 1. más grande que; 2. la más cara; 3. la mejor; 4. tan bueno como; 5. más feos que; 6. mejor que; 7. más alto que; 8. la menos cara
D. 1. pone; 2. marrón; 3. las; 4. acuestas; 5. que; 6. como; 7. cuesta; 8. levanto

How Did You Do?

Give yourself a point for every correct answer, then use the following key to determine whether or not you're ready to move on:

0–7 points: It's probably best to go back and study the lessons again to make sure you understood everything completely. Take your time; it's not a race! Make sure you spend time reviewing vocabulary with the flashcards and reading through each grammar note carefully.

8–16 points: If the questions you missed were in sections A or B, you may want to review the vocabulary again; if you missed answers mostly in sections C or D, check the unit essentials to make sure you have your conjugations and other grammar basics down.

17–20 points: Feel free to move on to the next unit! You're doing a great job.

 **points**

Unit 2:
Let's Eat!

In this unit, you'll learn how to order food at a restaurant and how to do some grocery shopping in Spanish. You will also learn how to talk about things that happened in the past. By the end of this unit, you should be able to:

☐ Name and describe types of food

☐ Use indirect object pronouns

☐ Form adverbs by adding **-mente**

☐ Order food in a restaurant

☐ Use expressions of quantity

☐ Talk about things that happened in the past

☐ Shop for food in a grocery store

☐ Conjugate the past tense of irregular verbs

Lesson 5: Words

By the end of this lesson, you should be able to:

☐ Name and describe types of food

☐ Use indirect object pronouns

☐ Form adverbs

Word Builder 1

▶ 5A Word Builder 1 (CD 7, Track 19)

el desayuno	breakfast
el almuerzo	lunch
la merienda	snack time
la cena	dinner
la comida	food, dinner
la cuchara	spoon
el tenedor	fork
el cuchillo	knife
el vaso	glass
la copa	wineglass
la taza	cup
el plato	plate, dish
la servilleta	napkin
la carta/el menu	menu
la cuenta	bill, check
la propina	tip

(II)

✎ Word Practice 1

Match each Spanish word below to its appropriate English translation.

1. el desayuno   a. *lunch*

2. la cuenta   b. *dinner*

3. la copa   c. *menu*

4. la carta   d. *bill, check*

5. la cena

6. el almuerzo

e. breakfast

f. wineglass

ANSWER KEY
1. e; 2. d; 3. f; 4. c; 5. b; 6. a

Grammar Builder 1
INDIRECT OBJECT PRONOUNS

▶ 5B Grammar Builder 1 (CD 7, Track 20)

Take a look at this sentence: *I gave him the book.* You already know that *the book* is the thing given; it's the direct object. But there's a second type of object in that sentence, too. *Him* is an indirect object pronoun. It could also be expressed as *to him*, as in *I gave the book to him.* Indirect object pronouns tell us to whom or for whom an action is done. Let's take a look at them in Spanish.

INDIRECT OBJECT PRONOUNS			
me	*(to/for) me*	nos	*(to/for) us*
te	*(to/for) you (infml. sg.)*	os	*(to/for) you (infml. pl.)*
le	*(to/for) him, her, it, you (fml. sg.)*	les	*(to/for) them, you (fml. pl.)*

Indirect object pronouns can be used to replace indirect object nouns.

¿Qué les vas a ofrecer a tus invitados?
What are you going to offer your guests?

Les voy a ofrecer champaña.
I'm going to offer them champagne.

¿Qué le vas a regalar a Pablo?
What are you going to give Pablo?

The Preterite of **-er**
and **-ir** Verbs

Spelling Changes
in the Preterite

The Preterite of **ser**, **ir**,
tener, and **hacer**

Irregular Verbs in
the Preterite

Le voy a regalar una guitarra.
I'm going to give him a guitar.

Notice that since le and les can refer to several things, you can also use them
along with a phrase like a él, a ella, a usted, a ellos, a ellas, or a ustedes to avoid
misunderstanding.

No les voy a comprar nada a ellos.
I'm not going to buy anything for them.

Le dijimos la verdad a él.
We told him the truth.

In addition, you'll see that Spanish speakers often like to emphasize the indirect
object pronoun by using a mí, a ti, a nosotros/as, a vosotros/as, and so on, even
when these expressions are not necessary for clarification.

Ellas nos dan la receta a nosotros.
They give us the recipe.

Tú me escribes una carta a mí.
You write a letter to me.

¿Qué nos vas a comprar a nosotros?
What are you going to buy for us?

Les voy a enviar unas tarjetas a mis primos.
I'm going to send some cards to my cousins.

Just like direct object pronouns, indirect object pronouns are placed before a
single conjugated verb or verb phrase; or attached to the end of a verbal phrase.

Margarita le da el plato a Laura.
Margarita gives Laura the dish.

Margarita le está dando el plato a Laura.
Margarita is giving Laura the dish.

Margarita está dándole el plato a Laura.
Margarita is giving Laura the dish.

Margarita le va a dar el plato a Laura.
Margarita is going to give Laura the dish.

Margarita va a darle el plato a Laura.
Margarita is going to give Laura the dish.

With commands, the indirect object pronoun is attached to affirmative commands, but placed before negative ones.

Por favor, póngame tres kilos de limones.
Please give me three kilos of lemons.

No nos dé leche en polvo.
Do not give us powdered milk.

Tráigame una servilleta.
Bring me a napkin.

No me sirva el almuerzo frío.
Don't serve me a cold lunch.

The Preterite of -er
and -ir Verbs

Spelling Changes
in the Preterite

The Preterite of **ser**, **ir**,
tener, and **hacer**

Irregular Verbs in
the Preterite

✏ Work Out 1

Fill in the blank with the appropriate indirect object pronoun.

1. Ella _____ sirve la comida a él.

2. Él _____ regala unas flores a ella.

3. Voy a escribir _____ una carta a ellas.

4. El mesero _____ trae la carta a nosotras.

5. Ella _____ trae un regalo a ustedes.

6. Tú _____ das los dos litros de leche a mí.

7. _____ vamos a enviar una invitación muy especial a vosotros.

8. Por favor, traiga _____ un cuchillo a nosotros.

ANSWER KEY
1. le; 2. le; 3. (escribir)les; 4. nos; 5. les; 6. me; 7. Os; 8. (tráiga)nos

Word Builder 2

▶ 5C Word Builder 1 (CD 7, Track 21)

Here is some more useful vocabulary you can use to talk about food.

la comida	food
el pan	bread
la carne	meat
el pollo	chicken
el cerdo	pork
el vegetal	vegetable
el tomate	tomato
el fríjol	bean

la mantequilla	butter
el jugo	juice
el arroz	rice
duro/a	hard
sobrecocido/a	overcooked
quemado/a	burnt
picante	spicy
podrido/a	bad, rotten
pasado/a	spoiled
agrio/a	sour
dulce	sweet
salado/a	salty
amargo/a	bitter
a la parrilla	grilled
frito/a	fried
ahumado/a	smoked

⏸

✎ Word Practice 2

Match the Spanish adjective on the left with its appropriate English translation on the right.

1. amargo/a   a. sour

2. agrio/a   b. bitter

3. ahumado/a   c. spoiled

4. duro/a   d. smoked

5. podrido/a   e. hard

6. pasado/a   f. bad, rotten

ANSWER KEY
1. b; 2. a; 3. d; 4. e; 5. f; 6. c

Grammar Builder 2
ADVERBS

▶ 5D Grammar Builder 2 (CD 7, Track 22)

Adverbs are words that are used to describe a verb, an adjective, or another adverb, like the word *happily*. In English, a lot of adverbs are formed by adding -*ly* to the end of an adjective, as in *happy–happily*. Similarly, in Spanish, adverbs are formed by adding -mente to the feminine form of adjectives ending in -o and to the final -e or consonant of any other adjective. Here are a few adjective-adverb pairs.

feliz	*happy*	felizmente	*happily*
triste	*sad*	tristemente	*sadly*
lento	*slow*	lentamente	*slowly*
rápido	*quick*	rápidamente/ rápido	*quickly*
nuevo	*new*	nuevamente	*once again, anew*
frecuente	*frequent*	frecuentemente	*frequently*
normal	*normal*	normalmente	*normally*

When an adverb is describing a verb, telling you how something is done, it's placed after the verb, regardless of whether it is a single verb or a verb phrase.

Ella come lentamente.
She eats slowly.

Ellos trabajan rápidamente.
They work quickly.

Nosotros vamos a comer rápidamente.
We're going to eat quickly.

But an adverb can also come at the beginning of a sentence if it describes a characteristic of, or expresses an attitude toward, the whole sentence.

Normalmente trabajo ocho horas diarias.
I normally work eight hours a day.

Tristemente no podemos viajar el mes entrante.
Sadly, we won't be able to travel next month.

When an adverb describes an adjective or another adverb, it's placed in front of the word it is modifying.

Sus respuestas son completamente absurdas.
Your answers are completely absurd.

Yo duermo muy bien.
I sleep very well.

Tienes que trabajar más rápidamente.
You need to work more quickly.

When using two or more adverbs in a series, the suffix **-mente** is dropped from all except the very last one.

Ella trabaja rápida, diligente y eficientemente.
She works quickly, diligently, and efficiently.

La serpiente se mueve lenta y silenciosamente.
The snake moves slowly and quietly.

(II)

✎ Work Out 2

Fill in the blank with the appropriate adverb.

1. Necesito el informe (inmediato). _____

2. Marcos hace su trabajo (rápido y eficiente). _____

   _____

3. (Frecuente) corremos por las mañanas en el parque. _____

4. Marta habla (lento y claro). _____

5. Ella no contesta el teléfono (rápido). _____

6. (Nuevo) tenemos un problema con la computadora. _____

7. El problema se va a resolver (fácil). _____

8. Vosotros (normal) vais al cine los sábados por la tarde. _____

ANSWER KEY
1. inmediatamente; 2. rápida y eficientemente; 3. Frecuentemente; 4. lenta y claramente;
5. rápidamente; 6. Nuevamente; 7. fácilmente; 8. normalmente

Take It Further

Watch out for those false cognates! False cognates are words that look the same or similar in English and in Spanish but actually have very different meanings. Here are three examples of adverbs that look the same but mean different things (immediately after each is the English equivalent of the Spanish word).

actualmente	*at the present time*
efectivamente/realmente	*actually*
en absoluto	*absolutely not*

totalmente	absolutely
sensiblemente	perceptibly
sensatamente	sensibly

Here are a few other words that are false cognates.

embarazada	pregnant
el delito	crime
contestar	to answer
atender	to take care of
asistir	to be present; to attend
éxito	success
suceso	an event or happening

✎ Drive It Home

Replace the indirect object pronoun me with the indirect object pronoun indicated on each line.

A. Carlita me da la servilleta.

1. *to you (infml.)* _____

   _____

2. *to him/to her/to you (fml.)* _____

   _____

3. *to us* _____

   _____

The Preterite of **-er**
and **-ir** Verbs

Spelling Changes
in the Preterite

The Preterite of **ser**, **ir**,
tener, and **hacer**

Irregular Verbs in
the Preterite

4. *to them* _____

_____

B. **Juan me ofrece una copa de vino.**

1. *to you (infml.)* _____

_____

2. *to him/to her/to you (fml.)* _____

_____

3. *to us* _____

_____

4. *to them* _____

_____

ANSWER KEY
A. 1. Carlita te da la servilleta. 2. Carlita le da la servilleta. 3. Carlita nos da la servilleta. 4. Carlita
les da la servilleta.
B. 1. Juan te ofrece una copa de vino. 2. Juan le ofrece una copa de vino. 3. Juan nos ofrece una
copa de vino. 4. Juan les ofrece una copa de vino.

How Did You Do?

By now, you should be able to:

☐ Name and describe types of food (Still unsure? Jump back to page 77.)

☐ Use indirect object pronouns (Still unsure? Jump back to page 74.)

☐ Form adverbs (Still unsure? Jump back to page 79.)

Indirect Object Pronouns
More on Adverbs
Adverbs
The Preterite of -ar
Verbs and estar

Lesson 6: Phrases

By the end of this lesson, you should be able to:

☐ Describe how food tastes

☐ Use expressions of quantity

☐ Form adverbs that don't end in -mente

☐ Talk about things that happened in the past

Phrase Builder 1

▶ 6A Phrase Builder 1 (CD 8, Track 1)

Me gustaría …	I would like …
Me puede traer …	Could you bring me …
Tengo ganas de …	I feel like …
No huele bien.	It doesn't smell good.
Huele mal.	It smells bad.
Sabe a vinagre.	It tastes like vinegar.
La leche está cortada.	The milk is sour.
¿Algo más?	Anything else?
No, nada más, gracias.	No, nothing else, thanks.
Las papayas tienen buena pinta.	The papayas look good.
¿Cuánto es?	How much is it?

Ⓘ

The Preterite of **-er**
and **-ir** Verbs

Spelling Changes
in the Preterite

The Preterite of **ser**, **ir**,
tener, and **hacer**

Irregular Verbs in
the Preterite

✎ Phrase Practice 1

Match the Spanish phrase on the left with its appropriate English translation on the right.

1. ¿Algo más?
2. ¿Cuánto es?
3. Tengo ganas de …
4. Me gustaría …
5. Me puede traer …
6. Huele mal.

a. *How much is it?*
b. *Could you bring me …*
c. *It smells bad.*
d. *I feel like …*
e. *Anything else?*
f. *I would like …*

ANSWER KEY
1. e; 2. a; 3. d; 4. f; 5. b; 6. c

Grammar Builder 1
MORE ON ADVERBS

▶ 6B Grammar Builder 1 (CD 8, Track 2)

There are, of course, a few adverbs that do not follow the pattern described in the previous lesson. Let's break them down into groups, starting with adverbs of quantity or degree.

bastante	*quite, enough*
poco	*a few, a little*
mucho	*a lot*
demasiado	*too much*
muy	*very*
tanto	*as much, as many*
más	*more*
menos	*less*
nada	*nothing*

| algo | somewhat |

And here are adverbs of time that don't end in -mente.

ahora	now
ya	already, now
tarde	late
temprano	early
pronto	soon
por fin	finally

And finally, here are adverbs of manner that don't end in -mente.

bien	well
mal	badly, poorly
mejor	better
peor	worse

Ella siempre se sirve demasiada comida.
She always serves herself too much food.

La comida está muy condimentada.
The food is very spicy.

Tengo poco tiempo para almorzar.
I have little time for lunch.

Yo desayuno temprano.
I have an early breakfast.

⏸

✎ Work Out 1

Give the adverb that means the opposite of each of the adverbs below.

1. mal _____

2. felizmente _____

3. poco _____

4. lentamente _____

5. temprano _____

6. algo _____

7. más _____

8. mejor _____

ANSWER KEY
1. bien; 2. tristemente; 3. mucho; 4. rápidamente; 5. tarde; 6. nada; 7. menos; 8. peor

Phrase Builder 2

▶ 6C Phrase Builder 2 (CD 8, Track 3)

la lata de atún	can of tuna
la tajada de jamón	slice of ham
la pieza de pollo	piece of chicken
la bolsa de papas	sack of potatoes
la botella de agua mineral	bottle of mineral water
el cartón de jugo	carton of juice
el racimo de uvas	bunch of grapes
el frasco de mermelada	jar of jam
el manojo de zanahorias	handful of carrots

el paquete de galletas	*package of cookies*
la rebanada de pan	*slice of bread*
un litro de leche	*a liter of milk*
dos kilos de naranjas	*two kilos of oranges*

✎ Phrase Practice 2

Fill in the blanks in each phrase based on the English translation.

1. la _____ de atún *can of tuna*

2. la _____ de jamón *slice of ham*

3. la _____ de pollo *piece of chicken*

4. la _____ de papas *sack of potatoes*

5. la _____ de agua mineral *bottle of mineral water*

6. el _____ de uvas *bunch of grapes*

7. el _____ de mermelada *jar of jam*

8. el _____ de zanahorias *handful of carrots*

9. el _____ de galletas *package of cookies*

10. la _____ de pan *slice of bread*

ANSWER KEY

1. lata; 2. tajada; 3. pieza; 4. bolsa; 5. botella; 6. racimo; 7. frasco; 8. manojo; 9. paquete; 10. rebanada

Grammar Builder 2
THE PRETERITE OF -AR VERBS AND ESTAR

▶ 6D Grammar Builder 2 (CD 8, Track 4)

Now that you're able to talk about things that are happening in the present and discuss plans for the future, it's time to learn how to talk about things that happened in the past. To do this, you will be using what's called the preterite tense. As with the present tense, in the preterite, Spanish verbs follow a pattern according to whether they end in -ar, -er, or -ir. Let's first take a look at regular verbs ending in -ar, like estudiar. To form the preterite, take the root of the verb and add the following endings.

PRETERITE ENDINGS OF REGULAR -AR VERBS	
yo -é	nosotros/as -amos
tú -aste	vosotros/as -asteis
él/ella/usted -ó	ellos/ellas/ustedes -aron

ESTUDIAR *(TO STUDY)* - PRETERITE	
yo estudié	nosotros/as estudiamos
tú estudiaste	vosotros/as estudiasteis
él/ella/usted estudió	ellos/ellas/ustedes estudiaron

You might have noticed that the conjugation of -ar verbs in the first person plural (nosotros/as) is the same in the present and in the preterite. Thus, estudiamos can mean *we speak* or *we spoke*; the context should always make it clear whether it is present or past.

Ayer hablé con mis padres por teléfono.
Yesterday, I spoke to my parents over the phone.

La semana pasada viajamos a París.
Last week we traveled to Paris.

Viajamos a las Bahamas para nuestras vacaciones.
We're traveling to the Bahamas on our vacation.

Ella terminó el informe anoche.
She finished the report last night.

Here are some useful time expressions you can use with the preterite.

ayer	*yesterday*
anoche	*last night*
la semana pasada	*last week*
el mes pasado	*last month*
el año pasado	*last year*
luego	*then*
entonces	*then*
después	*afterwards*
más tarde	*later*
una vez	*once*

Hablamos por teléfono y después tomamos un café.
We talked on the phone and then had a cup of coffee.

Caminamos por el parque y luego desayunamos en el hotel.
We walked through the park and then had breakfast at the hotel.

The Preterite of **-er**
and **-ir** Verbs

Spelling Changes
in the Preterite

The Preterite of **ser**, **ir**,
tener, and **hacer**

Irregular Verbs in
the Preterite

Even though the verb estar is an -ar verb, it follows an irregular pattern.

ESTAR *(TO BE)* - PRETERITE			
yo estuve	*I was*	nosotros/as estuvimos	*we were*
tú estuviste	*you were*	vosotros/as estuvisteis	*you were*
él/ella/usted estuvo	*he/she was, you were*	ellos/ellas/ustedes estuvieron	*they/you were*

(II)

✎ Work Out 2

Change the following sentences to the preterite.

1. Tú caminas mucho. _____

_____

2. Ella saborea el vino tinto. _____

_____

3. Ella toca el piano. _____

_____

4. Ustedes hablan por teléfono con su jefe. _____

_____

5. Vosotros escucháis música clásica. _____

_____

6. Él está en Nueva York. _____

_____

7. Hoy estamos en un restaurante italiano. _____

_____

8. Esta semana contestamos sus preguntas. _____

_____

ANSWER KEY

1. Tú caminaste mucho. 2. Ella saboreó el vino tinto. 3. Ella tocó el piano. 4. Ustedes hablaron por teléfono con su jefe. 5. Vosotros escuchasteis música clásica. 6. Él estuvo en Nueva York. 7. Ayer estuvimos en un restaurante italiano. 8. La semana pasada contestamos sus preguntas.

Take It Further

Shopping for food can sometimes be an adventure, for not in every country will you find **supermercados** (*supermarkets*) like in the United States. Many times you will find that there are **plazas de mercado** (*outdoor markets*) where you can find just about anything from fruits and vegetables to cleaning products and even clothes. Going to the market is not only about buying; it's about socializing and interacting with other people. Of course, there are also food stores, and many of them tend to be smaller stores that specialize in a particular category of food.

la panadería	bread bakery
la pastelería	bakery (*for pastries, etc.*)
la lechería	dairy store
la carnicería	butcher shop
la pescadería	fish shop, fish market
la tienda	convenience store
la charcutería	delicatessen (*for cold cuts, etc.*)

✏ Drive It Home

Let's practice the preterite of **-ar** verbs. Change the sentences below according to the subject indicated on each line.

A. Yo viajé el mes pasado.

1. Tú _____

2. Usted _____

3. Él _____

4. Nosotros _____

B. Yo hablé por teléfono anoche.

1. Tú _____

2. Usted _____

3. Ella _____

4. Ellos _____

ANSWER KEY
A. 1. Tú viajaste el mes pasado. 2. Usted viajó el mes pasado. 3. Él viajó el mes pasado. 4. Nosotros viajamos el mes pasado.
B. 1. Tú hablaste por teléfono anoche. 2. Usted habló por teléfono anoche. 3. Ella habló por teléfono anoche. 4. Ellos hablaron por teléfono anoche.

How Did You Do?

By now, you should be able to:

☐ Describe how food tastes (Still unsure? Jump back to page 84.)

☐ Use expressions of quantity (Still unsure? Jump back to page 87.)

☐ Form adverbs that don't end in -mente (Still unsure? Jump back to page 85.)

☐ Talk about things that happened in the past (Still unsure? Jump back to page 89.)

Lesson 7: Sentences

By the end of this lesson, you should be able to:

☐ Order food in a restaurant

☐ Shop for food in a grocery store

☐ Talk about things that happened in the past, using -er and -ir verbs

☐ Conjugate the past tense of irregular verbs

Sentence Builder 1

▶ 7A Sentence Builder 1 (CD 8, Track 5)

¿Cuál es el plato del día?	*What is the special of the day?*
¿Qué desea (usted) pedir?	*What would you like to order?*
¿Qué me recomienda?	*What do you recommend?*
¿Me podría traer la cuenta, por favor?	*Could you please bring me the check?*
¿Está incluida la propina en la cuenta?	*Is the tip included in the bill?*
¿Qué ingredientes tiene este plato?	*What ingredients are in this dish?*
¿Cómo quiere la carne?	*How would you like the meat?*
La quiero término medio, por favor.	*I want it medium-rare, please.*
La quiero término tres cuartos, por favor.	*I want it medium, please.*
La quiero bien asada, por favor.	*I want it well-done, please.*

⏸

✎ Sentence Practice 1

Fill in the blanks in each sentence based on the English translation.

1. ¿Cuál es _____ ? *What is the special of the day?*

2. ¿_____ (usted) pedir? *What would you like to order?*

3. ¿Qué me _____ ? *What do you recommend?*

4. La quiero _____, por favor. *I want it medium-rare, please.*

5. La quiero _____, por favor. *I want it medium, please.*

6. La quiero _____, por favor. *I want it well-done, please.*

ANSWER KEY
1. el plato del día; 2. Qué desea; 3. recomienda; 4. término medio; 5. término tres cuartos; 6. bien asada

Grammar Builder 1
THE PRETERITE OF -ER AND -IR VERBS

▶ 7B Grammar Builder 1 (CD 8, Track 6)

Now let's look at the preterite of -er and -ir verbs, which follow the same pattern.

PRETERITE ENDINGS OF REGULAR -ER/-IR VERBS	
yo -í	nosotros/as -imos
tú -iste	vosotros/as -isteis
él/ella/usted -ió	ellos/ellas/ustedes -ieron

COMER *(TO EAT)* - PRETERITE	
yo comí	nosotros/as comimos
tú comiste	vosotros/as comisteis
él/ella/usted comió	ellos/ellas/ustedes comieron

ESCRIBIR *(TO WRITE)* - PRETERITE	
yo escribí	nosotros/as escribimos
tú escribiste	vosotros/as escribisteis
él/ella/usted escribió	ellos/ellas/ustedes escribieron

Take a look at how the verb oír (*to hear*) is conjugated in the preterite.

OÍR *(TO HEAR)* - PRETERITE	
yo oí	nosotros/as oímos
tú oíste	vosotros/as oísteis
él/ella/usted oyó	ellos/ellas/ustedes oyeron

You already know that there are several verbs that are irregular in the present tense, and, in fact, you've already learned the conjugation of estar in the preterite, which is also irregular. We'll take a look at a few irregular verbs in the preterite over the next couple of lessons. Just keep in mind that a verb's being irregular in the present does not necessarily mean that it will be irregular in the preterite. The verbs despertar(se), volver, almorzar, and salir are examples of this. They have some irregularity in the present, but they're perfectly regular in the preterite.

Yo me despierto a las ocho todos los días.
I get up at eight every day.

Yo me desperté a las nueve ayer.
Yesterday, I got up at nine.

Ellos vuelven esta tarde.
They come back this afternoon.

Ellos volvieron ayer por la noche.
They came back yesterday evening.

Tú almuerzas a la misma hora siempre.
You always have lunch at the same time.

Tú almorzaste más temprano ayer.
You had lunch earlier yesterday.

Yo salgo de la oficina a las tres.
I leave the office at three.

Ayer salí a las cinco.
Yesterday, I left at five.

(II)

✎ Work Out 1

Rewrite the following sentences in the preterite. Use the clues given in parentheses when necessary.

1. Yo bebo café y jugo de naranja con el desayuno. _____

   _____

2. Ella te escribe una carta todos los días. (ayer) _____

   _____

3. Vosotros coméis tostadas con mermelada. _____

   _____

4. Mañana vamos a salir tarde de la oficina. (ayer) _____

   _____

5. Ella come chocolate todo el día. _____

_____

6. Yo no oigo nada. _____

_____

7. Ellas parten para México. _____

_____

ANSWER KEY

1. Yo bebí café y jugo de naranja con el desayuno. 2. Ella te escribió una carta ayer. 3. Vosotros comisteis tostadas con mermelada. 4. Ayer salimos tarde de la oficina. 5. Ella comió chocolate todo el día. 6. Yo no oí nada. 7. Ellas partieron para México.

Sentence Builder 2

▶ 7C Sentence Builder 2 (CD 8, Track 7)

¿En qué puedo servirle?	*How may I help you?*
Necesito un litro de leche.	*I need a liter of milk.*
¿Me puede dar un kilo de patatas?	*Could you give me a kilo of potatoes?*
¿Cuántas naranjas quiere?	*How many oranges do you want?*
Póngame dos chuletas de cordero, por favor.	*Give me two lamb chops, please.*
¿Quiere usted algo más?	*Would you like anything else?*
Eso es todo.	*That's all.*
¿Cuánto pesan las chuletas?	*How much do the chops weigh?*
¿Cómo están las papayas?	*How are the papayas?*
Deme tres botellas de vino tinto.	*Give me three bottles of red wine.*
¿Cuánto le debo?	*How much do I owe you?*

⏸

The Preterite of **-er**
and **-ir** Verbs

Spelling Changes
in the Preterite

The Preterite of **ser**, **ir**,
tener, and **hacer**

Irregular Verbs in
the Preterite

✎ Sentence Practice 2

Fill in the blanks in each sentence based on the English translation.

1. Necesito _____. *I need a liter of milk.*

2. _____. *That's all.*

3. ¿_____ las chuletas? *How much do the chops weigh?*

4. _____ de vino tinto.

   Give me three bottles of red wine.

5. _____ , por favor.

   Give me two lamb chops, please.

6. ¿_____? *How much do I owe you?*

   ANSWER KEY
   1. un litro de leche; 2. Eso es todo; 3. Cuánto pesan; 4. Deme tres botellas; 5. Póngame dos chuletas
   de cordero; 6. Cuánto le debo

Grammar Builder 2
THE PRETERITE OF SER, IR, TENER, AND HACER

▶ 7D Grammar Builder 2 (CD 8, Track 8)

As we mentioned before, there are a few verbs that are irregular in the preterite.
The verbs ser (*to be*) and ir (*to go*) take identical forms in the preterite.

SER *(TO BE)*/IR *(TO GO)* - PRETERITE	
yo fui	nosotros/as fuimos
tú fuiste	vosotros/as fuisteis
él/ella/usted fue	ellos/ellas/ustedes fueron

It is easy to distinguish ser from ir by context.

Ella fue profesora de inglés. (ser)
She was an English teacher.

Ella fue a Chile de vacaciones. (ir)
She went to Chile on vacation.

The verbs **tener** and **hacer** are also irregular in the preterite.

TENER *(TO HAVE)* - PRETERITE	
yo tuve	nosotros/as tuvimos
tú tuviste	vosotros/as tuvisteis
él/ella/usted tuvo	ellos/ellas/ustedes tuvieron

HACER *(TO DO, TO MAKE)* - PRETERITE	
yo hice	nosotros/as hicimos
tú hiciste	vosotros/as hicisteis
él/ella/usted hizo	ellos/ellas/ustedes hicieron

Tuvimos que esperar cuatro horas en el aeropuerto.
We had to wait four hours at the airport.

Yo hice un viaje muy largo.
I took (lit., made) a very long trip.

(II)

✎ Work Out 2

Fill in the blanks with the correct form of the preterite of **ser**, **hacer**, **ir**, or **tener**.

1. Yo _____ al supermercado esta mañana.

2. Tú _____ una familia pequeña.

3. Ellos _____ una presentación muy buena.

4. Ella _____ una cantante famosa.

5. Él _____ una llamada por teléfono al exterior.

6. Ellos _____ felices.

7. Ustedes _____ un apartamento en Nueva York.

8. Vosotros _____ a Costa Rica de vacaciones.

ANSWER KEY
1. fui; 2. tuviste; 3. hicieron; 4. fue; 5. hizo; 6. fueron; 7. tuvieron; 8. fuisteis

⊕ Culture Note

In the Spanish-speaking world, eating habits are a bit different from those in the United States. In most countries, people follow the European way of eating; that is, they don't switch the fork from the left to the right hand when eating; the right hand is not kept on the lap, but rather on the table; and people usually wish each other ¡Buen provecho! (*Enjoy your meal!*) before beginning to eat. Another custom is known as la sobremesa, or *after-dinner conversation*. Usually people stay seated around the table after lunch or dinner to chat while having a drink or a cup of coffee.

Let's practice the preterite of -er and -ir verbs. Change the sentence below according to the subject indicated on each line.

A. Yo bebí una limonada ayer.

1. Tú _____

2. Usted _____

3. Él _____

4. Nosotros _____

B. Yo viví en España el año pasado.

1. Tú _____

2. Usted _____

3. Ella _____

4. Ellos _____

ANSWER KEY

A. 1. Tú bebiste una limonada ayer. 2. Usted bebió una limonada ayer. 3. Él bebió una limonada ayer. 4. Nosotros bebimos una limonada ayer.

B. 1. Tú viviste en España el año pasado. 2. Usted vivió en España el año pasado. 3. Ella vivió en España el año pasado. 4. Ellos vivieron en España el año pasado.

How Did You Do?

By now, you should be able to:

☐ Order food in a restaurant (Still unsure? Jump back to page 94.)

☐ Shop for food in a grocery store (Still unsure? Jump back to page 98.)

☐ Talk about things that happened in the past using -er and -ir verbs (Still unsure? Jump back to page 95.)

☐ Conjugate the past tense of irregular verbs (Still unsure? Jump back to page 99.)

Lesson 8: Conversations

By the end of this lesson, you should be able to:

- ☐ Confidently make spelling changes in the preterite

- ☐ Conjugate irregular verbs in the preterite

⟲ Conversation 1

▶ 8A Conversation 1 (CD 8, Track 9 - Spanish Only; Track 10 - Spanish and English)

Roberto is travelling through Colombia. He is now in Villa de Leyva, at a local restaurant, ordering something for lunch.

Mesero:	Buenas tardes, ¿qúe desea pedir?
Roberto:	¿Cuál es el plato del día?
Mesero:	Como entrada tenemos un ceviche de pescado; el plato principal es ajiaco con pollo, y de postre le podemos ofrecer arroz con leche, natilla o cuajada con melado.
Roberto:	¿Qué ingredientes tiene el ajiaco?
Mesero:	El ajiaco es una sopa espesa a base de pollo, diferentes tipos de papa y guascas, una hierba típica de la región. Se sirve con mazorca y aguacate.
Roberto:	Bueno, suena muy bien. Tráigame el ajiaco solamente.
Mesero:	¿Y de postre?
Roberto:	¿Cuál me recomienda?
Mesero:	La cuajada con melado está muy buena.
Roberto:	Muy bien.
Mesero:	¿Algo más?
Roberto:	Una cerveza, por favor.

Waiter:	*Good afternoon, what would you like to order?*
Roberto:	*What's the special of the day?*
Waiter:	*As an appetizer we have ceviche de pescado; the main dish is ajiaco con pollo, and as a dessert we can offer you arroz con leche, natilla, or cuajada con melado.*
Roberto:	*What are the ingredients in ajiaco?*
Waiter:	*Ajiaco is a type of thick soup with chicken, different kinds of potatoes, and guascas, a typical herb of the region. It's served with corn and avocado.*
Roberto:	*Well, it sounds good. Bring me the ajiaco by itself.*
Waiter:	*And for dessert?*
Roberto:	*Which one do you recommend?*
Waiter:	*The cuajada con melado is very good.*
Roberto:	*Very good.*
Waiter:	*Anything else?*
Roberto:	*A beer, please.*

Culture Note

Villa de Leyva is probably one of the finest colonial towns in Colombia. It is located in Boyacá, a department in the center of the country. Founded in 1572, Villa de Leyva has a very small population—not more than 4,500 inhabitants—and is considered a national monument to colonial architecture. It is a popular recreational destination for people living in Bogotá because it is only a couple of hours away by car.

Conversation Practice 1

Fill in the blanks below with the appropriate word based on the English translations and the dialogue above.

The Preterite of **-er**
and **-ir** Verbs

Spelling Changes
in the Preterite

The Preterite of **ser**, **ir**,
tener, and **hacer**

Irregular Verbs in
the Preterite

1. De postre _____ arroz con leche, natilla o cuajada con melado.

   As a dessert we can offer you arroz con leche, natilla, or cuajada con melado.

2. ¿Qué _____ tiene el ajiaco? *What are the ingredients in ajiaco?*

3. _____ con mazorca y aguacate. *It's served with corn and avocado.*

4. Bueno, _____ muy bien. *Well, it sounds good.*

5. ¿Cuál _____ ? *Which one do you recommend?*

ANSWER KEY
1. le podemos ofrecer; 2. ingredientes; 3. Se sirve; 4. suena; 5. me recomienda

Grammar Builder 1
SPELLING CHANGES IN THE PRETERITE

▶ 8B Grammar Builder 1 (CD 8, Track 11)

Most of the time, irregularities in the preterite have to do with spelling changes.
For example, verbs ending in **-car** change the **c** to **qu** before **e**; verbs ending in **-gar**
change the **g** to **gu** before **e**; and verbs ending in **-zar** change the **z** to **c** before **e**.

SACAR *(TO TAKE OUT)* - PRETERITE	
yo saqué	nosotros/as sacamos
tú sacaste	vosotros/as sacasteis
él/ella/usted sacó	ellos/ellas/ustedes sacaron

LLEGAR *(TO ARRIVE)* - PRETERITE	
yo llegué	nosotros/as llegamos
tú llegaste	vosotros/as llegasteis
él/ella/usted llegó	ellos/ellas/ustedes llegaron

EMPEZAR *(TO BEGIN)* - PRETERITE	
yo empecé	nosotros/as empezamos
tú empezaste	vosotros/as empezasteis
él/ella/usted empezó	ellos/ellas/ustedes empezaron

Often, i is changed to y.

LEER *(TO READ)* - PRETERITE	
yo leí	nosotros/as leímos
tú leíste	vosotros/as leísteis
él/ella/usted leyó	ellos/ellas/ustedes leyeron

CREER *(TO BELIEVE)* - PRETERITE	
yo creí	nosotros/as creímos
tú creíste	vosotros/as creísteis
él/ella/usted creyó	ellos/ellas/ustedes creyeron

The verbs decir (*to say*) and traer (*to bring*) take a j between the vowels.

DECIR *(TO SAY)* - PRETERITE	
yo dije	nosotros/as dijimos
tú dijiste	vosotros/as dijisteis
él/ella/usted dijo	ellos/ellas/ustedes dijeron

TRAER *(TO BRING)* - PRETERITE	
yo traje	nosotros/as trajimos
tú trajiste	vosotros/as trajisteis
él/ella/usted trajo	ellos/ellas/ustedes trajeron

¿Llegaste a tiempo a tu cita?
Did you get to your appointment on time?

Leyó el periódico y se marchó al trabajo.
She/He read the newspaper and left for work.

Le dije la verdad a él.
I told him the truth.

Nos trajeron un vino excelente.
They brought us an excellent wine.

Work Out 1

Change the sentence using the pronoun given in parentheses.

1. Marqué las cajas con nuestros nombres y dirección. (usted) _____

_____

2. No creí lo que dijo. (vosotros) _____

_____

3. Ellas dijeron la verdad. (nosotras) _____

_____

4. Pagamos la cuenta. (yo) _____

_____

5. ¿Trajeron lápiz y papel para tomar nota? (usted) _____

_____

6. **Él apagó la luz muy tarde. (ellas)** _____

_____

7. **Ustedes comenzaron a estudiar italiano. (él)** _____

_____

8. **No leísteis el periódico esta mañana. (tú)** _____

_____

ANSWER KEY

1. Usted marcó las cajas con nuestros nombres y dirección. **2.** No creísteis lo que dijo. **3.** Nosotras dijimos la verdad. **4.** Pagué la cuenta. **5.** ¿Trajo lápiz y papel para tomar nota? **6.** Ellas apagaron la luz muy tarde. **7.** Él comenzó a estudiar italiano. **8.** No leíste el periódico esta mañana.

Conversation 2

8C Conversation 2 (CD 8, Track 12 - Spanish Only; Track 13 - Spanish and English)

Roberto has decided to help his friend Marisa, who is busy working, with grocery shopping. He's at a local grocery store, getting a few things.

Tendero:	¿En qué puedo servirle?
Roberto:	Necesito dos litros de leche.
Tendero:	¿Entera o descremada?
Roberto:	Entera. También quiero un kilo de naranjas, una lata de atún, una bolsa de papas y un manojo de zanahorias.
Tendero:	¿Algo más?
Roberto:	Las papayas tienen buena pinta.
Tendero:	Sí, están muy dulces. ¿Quiere llevar una?
Roberto:	Sí, pero no muy grande.
Tendero:	¿Qué le parece ésta?
Roberto:	Sí, se ve bien. ¿Cuánto le debo?
Tendero:	Son diez mil trescientos pesos.
Roberto:	Aquí tiene. Muchas gracias. Hasta luego.

Shopkeeper:	How may I help you?
Roberto:	I need two liters of milk.
Shopkeeper:	Whole or skim milk?
Roberto:	Whole. I also want a kilo of oranges, a can of tuna, a bag of potatoes, and a handful of carrots.
Shopkeeper:	Anything else?
Roberto:	The papayas look good.
Shopkeeper:	Yes, they're very sweet. Would you like to take one?
Roberto:	Yes, but not a very big one.
Shopkeeper:	How about this one?
Roberto:	Yes, it looks good. How much do I owe you?
Shopkeeper:	That's ten thousand, three hundred pesos.
Roberto:	Here you are. Thanks. Good-bye.

Take It Further

The metric system is almost always used in the Spanish-speaking world. So you will hear people buying things like:

cuatro onzas de queso	four ounces of cheese
media libra de naranjas	a half pound of oranges
dos litros de leche	two liters of milk
cien gramos de crema	a hundred grams of cream
una libra de arroz	a pound of rice
un kilo de patatas	a kilo of potatoes

✎ Conversation Practice 2

Fill in the blanks below with the appropriate word based on the English translations and the dialogue above.

1. ¿En qué _____? *How may I help you?*

2. También quiero _____, una lata de

   atún, _____ y un manojo de zanahorias. *I*

   also want a kilo of oranges, a can of tuna, a bag of potatoes, and a handful of carrots.

3. Las papayas tienen _____. *The papayas look good.*

4. ¿Qué _____ ésta? *How about this one?*

5. Sí, _____ bien. *Yes, it looks good.*

   ANSWER KEY
   1. puedo servirle; 2. un kilo de naranjas/una bolsa de papas; 3. buena pinta; 4. le parece; 5. se ve

Grammar Builder 2
IRREGULAR VERBS IN THE PRETERITE

▶ 8D Grammar Builder 2 (CD 8, Track 14)

The following verbs follow a slightly different pattern of conjugation in the preterite.

PODER *(TO BE ABLE)* - PRETERITE	
yo pude	nosotros/as pudimos
tú pudiste	vosotros/as pudisteis
él/ella/usted pudo	ellos/ellas/ustedes pudieron

The Preterite of **-er**
and **-ir** Verbs

Spelling Changes
in the Preterite

The Preterite of **ser**, **ir**,
tener, and **hacer**

Irregular Verbs in
the Preterite

PONER *(TO PUT)* - PRETERITE	
yo puse	nosotros/as pusimos
tú pusiste	vosotros/as pusisteis
él/ella/usted puso	ellos/ellas/ustedes pusieron

SABER *(TO KNOW)* - PRETERITE	
yo supe	nosotros/as supimos
tú supiste	vosotros/as supisteis
él/ella/usted supo	ellos/ellas/ustedes supieron

QUERER *(TO WANT)* - PRETERITE	
yo quise	nosotros/as quisimos
tú quisiste	vosotros/as quisisteis
él/ella/usted quiso	ellos/ellas/ustedes quisieron

ANDAR *(TO WALK)* - PRETERITE	
yo anduve	nosotros/as anduvimos
tú anduviste	vosotros/as anduvisteis
él/ella/usted anduvo	ellos/ellas/ustedes anduvieron

VENIR *(TO COME)* - PRETERITE	
yo vine	nosotros/as vinimos
tú viniste	vosotros/as vinisteis
él/ella/usted vino	ellos/ellas/ustedes vinieron

Él no pudo comer.

He couldn't eat.

Ella puso el pollo en agua caliente.
She put the chicken in hot water.

Ayer supimos la noticia.
Yesterday we learned the news.

Note that saber used in the preterite changes its meaning: *to learn, to find out.*

Nosotros no quisimos pagar la cuenta.
We didn't want to pay the bill.

Anduviste por todo el museo.
You walked through the entire museum.

Mi esposo vino a casa tarde.
My husband came home late.

Ⓜ

✎ Work Out 2

Fill in the blanks with the correct Spanish preterite form of the English verb in parentheses.

1. ¿Dónde _____ él mi suéter? (*to put*)

2. Ella no _____ llamar a sus padres. (*to want*)

3. Usted no _____ completar el cuestionario. (*to be able*)

4. Él _____ de Argentina. (*to come*)

5. Yo no _____ comer en ese restaurante. (*to be able*)

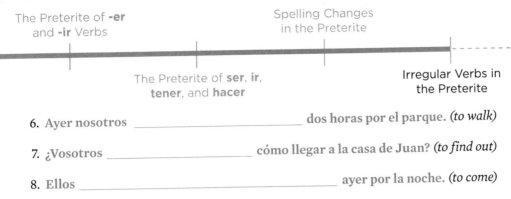

6. Ayer nosotros _____ dos horas por el parque. (*to walk*)

7. ¿Vosotros _____ cómo llegar a la casa de Juan? (*to find out*)

8. Ellos _____ ayer por la noche. (*to come*)

ANSWER KEY
1. puso; 2. quiso; 3. pudo; 4. vino; 5. pude; 6. anduvimos; 7. supisteis; 8. vinieron

⊕ Culture Note

Many people think that food in all of the Spanish-speaking world is hot and spicy. Well, that is perhaps the case in Mexico and a few other countries in Central America. But the truth is, the cuisines of Spanish-speaking countries are as varied as the people who enjoy them. In Spain, you will find paella (a saffron-spiced rice with different kinds of meat and seafood) and the traditional tortilla de patatas (potato omelet). Argentina is known for the excellent quality of its beef; steaks are usually served with chimichurri, a green sauce of herbs and chilies, and empanadas (meat and cheese pastries) are very popular for lunch. In Venezuela and Colombia, arepas (baked cornmeal cakes) are traditionally served with breakfast, and, on the Caribbean coast, arroz con coco (coconut rice) is a typical side dish. Popular desserts in Colombia are arroz con leche (rice pudding), cuajada con melado (soft cheese with melted sugar), and natilla (soft custard). And in Peru, ceviche (raw fish marinated in lime juice) is one of the country's staple dishes.

✎ Drive It Home

Give the preterite yo form of the following irregular verbs:

1. poder _____

2. poner _____

3. saber _____

4. querer _____

5. andar _____

6. venir _____

ANSWER KEY
1. Yo pude. 2. Yo puse. 3. Yo supe. 4. Yo quise. 5. Yo anduve. 6. Yo vine.

How Did You Do?

By now, you should be able to:

☐ Confidently make spelling changes in the preterite
(Still unsure? Jump back to page 105.)

☐ Conjugate irregular verbs in the preterite
(Still unsure? Jump back to page 110.)

Don't forget to practice and reinforce what you've learned by visiting **www.livinglanguage.com/ languagelab** for flashcards, games, and quizzes for Unit 2!

Unit 2 Essentials

Vocabulary Essentials

MEALS AND UTENSILS

	breakfast
	lunch
	snack time
	dinner
	food, dinner
	spoon
	fork
	knife
	glass
	wineglass
	cup
	plate, dish
	napkin
	menu
	bill, check
	tip

[Pg. 73]

FOOD VOCABULARY

	food
	bread
	meat
	chicken
	pork
	vegetable
	tomato
	bean
	butter
	juice
	rice
	hard
	overcooked
	burnt
	spicy
	bad, rotten
	spoiled
	sour
	sweet
	salty
	bitter
	grilled
	fried
	smoked

[Pg. 77]

FOOD EXPRESSIONS

	I would like …
	Could you bring me …
	I feel like …
	It doesn't smell good.
	It smells bad.
	It tastes like vinegar.
	The milk is sour.
	Anything else?
	No, nothing else, thanks.
	The papayas look good.
	How much is it?

[Pg. 84]

FOOD QUANTITY EXPRESSIONS

	can of tuna
	slice of ham
	piece of chicken
	sack of potatoes
	bottle of mineral water
	carton of juice
	bunch of grapes
	jar of jam
	handful of carrots
	package of cookies
	slice of bread

	a liter of milk
	two kilos of oranges
	four ounces of cheese
	a half pound of oranges
	two liters of milk
	a hundred grams of cream
	a pound of rice
	a kilo of potatoes

[Pgs. 87 and 109]

FOOD VENDORS

	bread bakery
	bakery (for pastries, etc.)
	dairy store
	butcher shop
	fish shop, fish market
	convenience store
	delicatessen

[Pg. 92]

RESTAURANT EXPRESSIONS

	What is the special of the day?
	What would you like to order?
	What do you recommend?
	Could you please bring me the check?
	Is the tip included in the bill?

	What ingredients are in this dish?
	How would you like the meat?
	I want it medium-rare, please.
	I want it medium, please.
	I want it well-done, please.

[Pg. 94]

FOOD SHOPPING EXPRESSIONS

	How may I help you?
	I need a liter of milk.
	Could you give me a kilo of potatoes?
	How many oranges do you want?
	Give me two lamb chops, please.
	Would you like anything else?
	That's all.
	How much do the chops weigh?
	How are the papayas?
	Give me three bottles of red wine.
	How much do I owe you?

[Pg. 98]

ADVERBS ENDING IN -MENTE

	happily
	sadly
	slowly
	quickly

	anew, once again
	frequently
	normally
	at the present time
	actually
	absolutely
	perceptibly
	sensibly

[Pgs. 79 and 81]

ADVERBS NOT ENDING IN -MENTE

	quite, enough
	a few, a little
	a lot
	too much
	very
	as much/as many
	more
	less
	very
	nothing
	somewhat
	now
	already, now
	late
	early

	soon
	finally
	well
	badly, poorly
	better
	worse

[Pg. 85]

TIME EXPRESSIONS USED TO TALK ABOUT THE PAST

	yesterday
	last night
	last week
	last month
	last year
	then
	then
	afterwards
	later
	once

[Pg. 90]

Grammar Essentials

INDIRECT OBJECT PRONOUNS			
me	*(to/for) me*	nos	*(to/for) us*
te	*(to/for) you (infml. sg.)*	os	*(to/for) you (infml. pl.)*
le	*(to/for) him, her, it, you (fml. sg.)*	les	*(to/for) them, you (fml. pl.)*

Indirect object pronouns are placed before a single conjugated verb or verb phrase, or attached to the end of a verbal phrase.

Indirect object pronouns are attached to affirmative commands, but placed before negative ones.

ADVERBS

Adverbs are formed by adding -mente to the feminine form of adjectives ending in -o and to the final -e or consonant of any other adjective.

When used to describe a verb, adverbs come after the verb they modify.

When used to describe an adjective or another adverb, adverbs come in front of the word they modify.

An adverb can come at the beginning of a sentence if it describes a characteristic of, or expresses an attitude toward, the whole sentence.

When using two or more adverbs in a series, the suffix -mente is dropped from all except the very last one.

THE PRETERITE

The preterite is used to describe actions in the past. To form the preterite, take the root of the verb and add the following endings.

PRETERITE ENDINGS OF REGULAR -AR VERBS	
yo -é	nosotros/as -amos
tú -aste	vosotros/as -asteis
él/ella/usted -ó	ellos/ellas/ustedes -aron

PRETERITE ENDINGS OF REGULAR -ER/-IR VERBS	
yo -í	nosotros/as -imos
tú -iste	vosotros/as -isteis
él/ella/usted -ió	ellos/ellas/ustedes -ieron

VERBS

ANDAR *(TO WALK)* - PRETERITE

yo anduve	nosotros/as anduvimos
tú anduviste	vosotros/as anduvisteis
él/ella/usted anduvo	ellos/ellas/ustedes anduvieron

COMER *(TO EAT)* - PRETERITE

yo comí	nosotros/as comimos
tú comiste	vosotros/as comisteis
él/ella/usted comió	ellos/ellas/ustedes comieron

CREER *(TO BELIEVE)* - PRETERITE

yo creí	nosotros/as creímos
tú creíste	vosotros/as creísteis
él/ella/usted creyó	ellos/ellas/ustedes creyeron

DECIR *(TO SAY)* - PRETERITE

yo dije	nosotros/as dijimos
tú dijiste	vosotros/as dijisteis
él/ella/usted dijo	ellos/ellas/ustedes dijeron

EMPEZAR *(TO BEGIN)* - PRETERITE

yo empecé	nosotros/as empezamos
tú empezaste	vosotros/as empezasteis
él/ella/usted empezó	ellos/ellas/ustedes empezaron

ESCRIBIR *(TO WRITE)* - PRETERITE

yo escribí	nosotros/as escribimos
tú escribiste	vosotros/as escribisteis
él/ella/usted escribió	ellos/ellas/ustedes escribieron

ESTAR (TO BE) - PRETERITE

yo estuve	nosotros/as estuvimos
tú estuviste	vosotros/as estuvisteis
él/ella/usted estuvo	ellos/ellas/ustedes estuvieron

ESTUDIAR (TO STUDY) - PRETERITE

yo estudié	nosotros/as estudiamos
tú estudiaste	vosotros/as estudiasteis
él/ella/usted estudió	ellos/ellas/ustedes estudiaron

HACER (TO DO, TO MAKE) - PRETERITE

yo hice	nosotros/as hicimos
tú hiciste	vosotros/as hicisteis
él/ella/usted hizo	ellos/ellas/ustedes hicieron

IR (TO GO) - PRETERITE

yo fui	nosotros/as fuimos
tú fuiste	vosotros/as fuisteis
él/ella/usted fue	ellos/ellas/ustedes fueron

LEER (TO READ) - PRETERITE

yo leí	nosotros/as leímos
tú leíste	vosotros/as leísteis
él/ella/usted leyó	ellos/ellas/ustedes leyeron

LLEGAR (TO ARRIVE) - PRETERITE

yo llegué	nosotros/as llegamos
tú llegaste	vosotros/as llegasteis
él/ella/usted llegó	ellos/ellas/ustedes llegaron

OÍR (TO HEAR) - PRETERITE

yo oí	nosotros/as oímos
tú oíste	vosotros/as oísteis
él/ella/usted oyó	ellos/ellas/ustedes oyeron

PODER (TO BE ABLE) - PRETERITE

yo pude	nosotros/as pudimos
tú pudiste	vosotros/as pudisteis
él/ella/usted pudo	ellos/ellas/ustedes pudieron

PONER (TO PUT) - PRETERITE

yo puse	nosotros/as pusimos
tú pusiste	vosotros/as pusisteis
él/ella/usted puso	ellos/ellas/ustedes pusieron

QUERER (TO WANT) - PRETERITE

yo quise	nosotros/as quisimos
tú quisiste	vosotros/as quisisteis
él/ella/usted quiso	ellos/ellas/ustedes quisieron

SABER (TO KNOW) - PRETERITE

yo supe	nosotros/as supimos
tú supiste	vosotros/as supisteis
él/ella/usted supo	ellos/ellas/ustedes supieron

SACAR (TO TAKE OUT) - PRETERITE

yo saqué	nosotros/as sacamos
tú sacaste	vosotros/as sacasteis
él/ella/usted sacó	ellos/ellas/ustedes sacaron

SER *(TO BE)* - PRETERITE

yo fui	nosotros/as fuimos
tú fuiste	vosotros/as fuisteis
él/ella/usted fue	ellos/ellas/ustedes fueron

TENER *(TO HAVE)* - PRETERITE

yo tuve	nosotros/as tuvimos
tú tuviste	vosotros/as tuvisteis
él/ella/usted tuvo	ellos/ellas/ustedes tuvieron

TRAER *(TO BRING)* - PRETERITE

yo traje	nosotros/as trajimos
tú trajiste	vosotros/as trajisteis
él/ella/usted trajo	ellos/ellas/ustedes trajeron

VENIR *(TO COME)* - PRETERITE

yo vine	nosotros/as vinimos
tú viniste	vosotros/as vinisteis
él/ella/usted vino	ellos/ellas/ustedes vinieron

Unit 2 Quiz

A. Rewrite the sentence with the subject in parentheses.

1. Yo traje un racimo de uvas. (Ella) _____

   _____

2. Patricia viajó a las Bahamas el año pasado. (Patricia y Pablo) _____

   _____

3. Ella fue al parque por la noche. (Ustedes) _____

   _____

4. Tú hiciste un viaje muy largo. (Yo) _____

   _____

5. Mateo sacó un libro de la biblioteca. (Tú) _____

   _____

6. Ellos volvieron ayer por la noche. (Usted) _____

   _____

7. Ayer salí a las seis de la tarde. (Nosotros) _____

   _____

8. Hablamos por teléfono y después tomamos un café. (Él) _____

B. Replace the underlined indirect object pronoun with the clue in parentheses.

1. Ella te da el desayuno. (to me) _____

   _____

2. Él me ofrece un regalo. (to you, infml. sg.) _____

   _____

3. El doctor me da la receta. (to you, fml. sg.) _____

   _____

4. Ella le escribe una carta. (to me) _____

   _____

5. Mi amiga me compró un regalo. (to us) _____

   _____

6. Él nos da una copa de vino. (to her) _____

   _____

7. Nosotros te damos las gracias. (to them) _____

   _____

8. Yo te digo la verdad. (to you, infml. pl.) _____

   _____

C. Choose the appropriate vocabulary word.

1. Por la mañana como el desayuno y al mediodía tomo _____ .

   (el almuerzo/la cena)

2. Yo le doy al camarero _____ . (el cuchillo/la propina)

3. Yo compré dos _____ de vino tinto. (botellas/piezas)

4. Nosotros bebimos café y _____ con el desayuno. (jugo/vino)

5. Él _____ un libro interesante. (creyó/leyó)

6. Es bueno _____ la verdad. (decir/traer)

7. La comida de la noche es _____. (la cena/el desayuno)

8. Yo _____ a Chile el año pasado. (fui/oí)

D. Fill in the blanks by conjugating the verb in parentheses in the *preterite*.

1. Ella _____ por la ciudad. (andar)

2. El estudiante _____ completar su tarea a tiempo. (poder)

3. Usted _____ el periódico sobre la mesa. (poner)

4. Yo _____ a tiempo al restaurante. (llegar)

5. Nosotros _____ ir al parque de diversiones. (querer)

6. Los camareros _____ con la comida (venir)

7. Ustedes _____ regalos para las fiesta. (traer)

8. Usted _____ siempre cosas interesantes. (decir)

How Did You Do?

Give yourself a point for every correct answer, then use the following key to determine whether or not you're ready to move on:

0-7 points: It's probably best to go back and study the lessons again to make sure you understood everything completely. Take your time; it's not a race! Make sure you spend time reviewing vocabulary with the flashcards and reading through each grammar note carefully.

8-16 points: If the questions you missed were in sections A or B, you may want to review the vocabulary again; if you missed answers mostly in sections C or D, check the unit essentials to make sure you have your conjugations and other grammar basics down.

17-20 points: Feel free to move on to the next unit! You're doing a great job.

 **points**

Unit 3:
School and Work

In this unit, you'll learn more about expressing the past. You will also learn lots of useful vocabulary related to school and work. By the end of this unit, you should be able to:

☐ Talk confidently about school and work

☐ Know how to use direct and indirect objects in a sentence

☐ Talk about the recent past

☐ Express obligation and necessity

☐ Identify when to use the imperfect or the preterite

☐ Conjugate regular and irregular verbs in the imperfect

Lesson 9: Words

By the end of this lesson, you should be able to:

☐ Talk generally about school and work

☐ Use more irregular verbs in the preterite

☐ Use both indirect and direct object pronouns in one sentence

More Irregular Verbs
in the Preterite

Expressing Past Actions
with **hace** and **acabar de**

Double Object Pronouns

Expressing Obligation
or Necessity

Word Builder 1

▶ 9A Word Builder 1 (CD 8, Track 15)

la materia	*school subject*
la(s) matemática(s)	*mathematics*
la historia	*history*
la literatura	*literature*
la ciencia	*science*
la biología	*biology*
la química	*chemistry*
la geografía	*geography*
la filosofía	*philosophy*
la asignatura	*course*
los estudios	*studies*
la beca	*scholarship*
matricularse	*to register*
la biblioteca	*library*
la sala de conferencias	*lecture hall, conference room*
graduarse	*to graduate*
los derechos de matrícula	*tuition*
la tesis	*dissertation*
la licenciatura	*master's degree (a degree between a bachelor's degree and a master's degree)*
el título académico	*academic degree*

✎ Word Practice 1

Match the Spanish word on the left with its appropriate English translation on
the right.

1. la materia	a. *studies*
2. los estudios	b. *course*
3. la asignatura	c. *library*
4. la tesis	d. *school subject*
5. la biblioteca	e. *scholarship*
6. la beca	f. *dissertation*

ANSWER KEY
1. d; 2. a; 3. b; 4. f; 5. c; 6. e

Grammar Builder 1
MORE IRREGULAR VERBS IN THE PRETERITE

▶ 9B Grammar Builder 1 (CD 8, Track 16)

Here are the irregular preterite forms of **dar** (*to give*), **pedir** (*to ask for*), and **ver**
(*to see*).

DAR *(TO GIVE)* - PRETERITE	
yo di	nosotros/as dimos
tú diste	vosotros/as disteis
él/ella/usted dio	ellos/ellas/ustedes dieron

PEDIR *(TO ASK FOR)* - PRETERITE	
yo pedí	nosotros/as pedimos
tú pediste	vosotros/as pedisteis
él/ella/usted pidió	ellos/ellas/ustedes pidieron

More Irregular Verbs
in the Preterite

Expressing Past Actions
with **hace** and **acabar de**

Double Object Pronouns

Expressing Obligation
or Necessity

VER *(TO SEE)* - PRETERITE	
yo vi	nosotros/as vimos
tú viste	vosotros/as visteis
él/ella/usted vio	ellos/ellas/ustedes vieron

Ella nos dio una noticia muy buena.
She gave us very good news.

Él me pidió mi número de teléfono.
He asked me for my phone number.

Vimos una película romántica.
We saw a romantic movie.

In Spanish, we use the verb **haber** to say *there is/there are.* In the present tense, the form is **hay**, and in the preterite, it is **hubo**.

Hubo mucha gente en la fiesta de anoche.
There were a lot of people at last night's party.

Hubo solamente una película extranjera en el festival de cine.
There was only one foreign movie in the film festival.

⏸

✎ Work Out 1

Fill in the blank with the correct preterite form of **dar**, **pedir**, **ver**, or **haber**.

1. Ella nos _____ disculpas.

2. Tú me _____ un libro muy interesante para leer.

3. _____ una reunión extraordinaria ayer.

4. Ustedes _____ el accidente.

5. _____ cinco personas para la entrevista.

6. Ella le _____ una carta de referencia.

7. Yo no _____ al ladrón.

8. Nosotros te _____ la carta la semana pasada.

ANSWER KEY
1. pidió; 2. diste; 3. Hubo; 4. vieron; 5. Hubo; 6. pidió; 7. vi; 8. dimos

Word Builder 2

▶ 9C Word Builder 2 (CD 8, Track 17)

la cita	*appointment*
la reunión	*meeting*
la sala de conferencias	*conference room, lecture hall*
el contrato	*contract*
el/la empleado/a	*employee*
el sindicato	*union*
el seguro	*insurance*
la entrevista	*interview*
la cualificación	*qualification*
la hoja de vida/la historia de trabajo	*résumé*
las referencias	*references*
el/la jubilado/a	*retired person*

⏸

More Irregular Verbs
in the Preterite

Expressing Past Actions
with **hace** and **acabar de**

Double Object Pronouns

Expressing Obligation
or Necessity

✎ Word Practice 2

Match the Spanish word on the left with its appropriate English translation on the right.

1. el seguro
2. el sindicato
3. la reunión
4. el/la empleado/a
5. la entrevista
6. la cita

a. *employee*
b. *insurance*
c. *union*
d. *meeting*
e. *appointment*
f. *interview*

ANSWER KEY
1. b; 2. c; 3.d ; 4. a; 5. f; 6. e

Grammar Builder 2
DOUBLE OBJECT PRONOUNS

▶ 9D Grammar Builder 2 (CD 8, Track 18)

In Units 1 and 2, you learned about direct and indirect object pronouns. They are basically not much different from one another, except for the third person singular and plural.

INDIRECT OBJECT PRONOUNS	DIRECT OBJECT PRONOUNS
me (a mí)	me
te (a ti)	te
le (a él/ella/usted)	lo/la
nos (a nosotros/as)	nos
os (a vosotros/as)	os
les (a ellos/ellas/ustedes)	los/las

Just as in English, it's possible to have both a direct object pronoun and an indirect object pronoun in the same sentence in Spanish. In that case, the indirect object pronoun comes first. To avoid the awkward repetition of the same sounds, use se instead of le or les preceding lo(s)/la(s). In order to clarify the meaning of se, use a él/a ella/a usted/a ellos/a ellas/a ustedes.

Ellos me dan un libro (a mí).
They give me a book.

Ellos me lo dan (a mí).
They give it to me.

Nosotros le entregamos el informe a ella.
We gave the report to her.

Nosotros se lo entregamos a ella.
We gave it to her.

When the pronouns appear in sentences with more than one verb, they can be placed either before the verbs or attached to the end of the main verb.

Él está entregando su examen al profesor.
He is giving his test to the teacher.

Él se lo está entregando.
He is giving it to him.

Él está entregándoselo.
He is giving it to him.

Vosotros vais a dar una sorpresa a Juan.
You are going to give Juan a surprise.

More Irregular Verbs
in the Preterite

Expressing Past Actions
with **hace** and **acabar de**

Double Object Pronouns

Expressing Obligation
or Necessity

Vosotros se la vais a dar.
You are going to give it to him.

Vosotros vais a dársela.
You are going to give it to him.

✎ Work Out 2

Replace the direct object in these sentences with the corresponding direct object pronoun.

1. Ella nos está vendiendo una radio. _____

_____

2. El estudiante hace el trabajo. _____

_____

3. Yo me compré unos pantalones negros. _____

_____

4. Vosotros os tomáis una medicina. _____

_____

5. Él le va a decir la verdad a Sofía. _____

_____

6. Ellas le trajeron un regalo. _____

_____

7. Él no puede comer carne. _____

_____

8. Ellos le están enviando un correo a su jefe. _____

_____

ANSWER KEY

1. Ella nos la está vendiendo. 2. El estudiante lo hace. 3. Yo me los compré. 4. Vosotros os la tomáis.
5. Él se la va a decir. 6. Ellas se lo trajeron. 7. Él no la puede comer. 8. Ellos se lo están enviando.

Take It Further

Here are a few more false cognates that you should be aware of.

la conferencia	*lecture*
la lectura	*a reading*
la librería	*bookstore*
el colegio	*elementary or secondary school*
la facultad	*department*
el profesorado	*faculty*

✎ Drive It Home

Write the correct *preterite* form of the verb indicated in parentheses.

1. Yo _____ la cuenta. (pedir)

2. Ella _____ la cuenta. (pedir)

3. Nosotros _____ la cuenta. (pedir)

4. Ustedes _____ la cuenta. (pedir)

5. Rogelio _____ una película fantástica. (ver)

More Irregular Verbs
in the Preterite

Expressing Past Actions
with **hace** and **acabar de**

Double Object Pronouns

Expressing Obligation
or Necessity

6. Rogelio y Carmen _____una película fantástica. (ver)

7. Tú _____ una película fantástica. (ver)

8. Tú y yo _____una película fantástica. (ver)

ANSWER KEY

1. pedí; 2. pidió; 3. pedimos; 4. pidieron; 5. vio; 6. vieron; 7. viste; 8. vimos

How Did You Do?

By now, you should be able to:

☐ Talk generally about school and work
(Still unsure? Jump back to pages 132 and 135.)

☐ Use more irregular verbs in the preterite
(Still unsure? Jump back to page 133.)

☐ Use both indirect and direct object pronouns in one sentence
(Still unsure? Jump back to page 136.)

Lesson 10: Phrases

By the end of this lesson, you should be able to:

☐ Talk more specifically about being a student

☐ Talk about the recent past using **hace** and **acabar de**

☐ Converse about applying for a job

☐ Express a strong necessity (*to have to, must, should*)

Phrase Builder 1

▶ 10A Phrase Builder 1 (CD 8, Track 19)

aprobar un curso	*to pass a course*
tomar un examen	*to take a test*
aprobar/suspender un examen	*to pass/fail a test*
escribir un trabajo de investigación	*to write a research paper*
estudiante a tiempo completo	*full-time student*
estudiante a tiempo parcial	*part-time student*
especializarse en ...	*to major in ...*
sacar buenas/malas notas	*to get good/bad grades*
el horario de clases	*class schedule*
me interesa(n) ...	*I'm interested in ...*
No estoy seguro/a todavía.	*I'm not sure yet.*
¿Qué te parece ... ?	*What do you think of ... ?*
Y tú, ¿qué piensas?	*And how about you? What do you think?*

More Irregular Verbs
in the Preterite

Expressing Past Actions
with **hace** and **acabar de**

Double Object Pronouns

Expressing Obligation
or Necessity

✎ Phrase Practice 1

Match the Spanish phrase on the left with its appropriate English translation on
the right.

1. aprobar un curso
2. hacer un examen
3. escribir un trabajo de investigación
4. suspender un examen
5. especializarse en
6. aprobar un examen

a. *to write a research paper*
b. *to pass a course*
c. *to pass a test*
d. *to major in*
e. *to fail a test*
f. *to take a test*

ANSWER KEY
1. b; 2. f; 3. a; 4. e; 5. d; 6. c

Grammar Builder 1
EXPRESSING PAST ACTIONS WITH HACE AND ACABAR DE

▶ 10B Grammar Builder 1 (CD 8, Track 20)

The verb acabar means *to finish* something. But you will hear it often in the
expression acabar de + infinitive, which is equivalent to saying *to have just* in
English. It refers to something that happened recently. Here are a few examples
of how it is used.

Acabo de terminar el informe.
I have just finished the report.

Ella acaba de hacer una llamada a Ecuador.
She has just made a phone call to Ecuador.

Nosotros acabamos de terminar la entrevista.
We've just finished (concluded) the interview.

To express an action that began in the past and continues into the present, use **hace** + time + **que** + present tense. Note that the verb in Spanish is in the present tense, but in English, it's translated as the present perfect progressive (*have/has been doing*).

Hace un año que estudio español.
I've been studying Spanish for a year.

Hace cinco años que ella trabaja aquí.
She's been working here for five years.

¿Cuánto hace que estudia arquitectura?
How long have you been studying architecture?

To express *ago,* use **hace** + time + **que** + preterite. In this case, the verb tense in both languages is the simple past.

Hace un año que estudié español.
I studied Spanish a year ago.

Hace cinco años que ella trabajó aquí.
She worked here five years ago.

¿Cuánto hace que estudió arquitectura?
How long ago did you study architecture?

Ⅱ

More Irregular Verbs
in the Preterite

Expressing Past Actions
with **hace** and **acabar de**

Double Object Pronouns

Expressing Obligation
or Necessity

✎ Work Out 1

Use the English translations to help fill in the blanks.

1. Hace tres semanas que _____ en el informe.

   (She's been working on the report for three weeks.)

2. _____ mi matrícula hace un mes. *(I paid my tuition a month ago.)*

3. Ella _____ aquí hace dos años. *(She worked here two years ago.)*

4. María acaba de _____ un libro. *(María has just read a book.)*

5. Ellos acaban de _____ una nueva computadora.

   (They've just bought a new computer.)

6. Nosotros _____ hace una hora. *(We ate an hour ago.)*

7. Hace tres meses que _____ español.

   (I've been studying Spanish for three months.)

8. Acaban de _____ de vacaciones. *(They've just left on vacation.)*

   ANSWER KEY
   1. trabaja; 2. Pagué; 3. trabajó; 4. leer; 5. comprar; 6. comimos; 7. estudio; 8. partir

Phrase Builder 2

▶ 10C Phrase Builder 2 (CD 8, Track 21)

la solicitud de empleo	*job application*
La jornada es de treinta y siete horas.	*It is a thirty-seven-hour workweek.*
¿Cuándo comienzo?	*When do I start?*
Hay un período de prueba de seis meses.	*There's a probationary period of six months.*
un mes de vacaciones	*a month's vacation*

The Imperfect of
-er and **-ir** Verbs

Using the Preterite and
the Imperfect

¿Hay incentivos?	Are there any incentives?
No tengo referencias.	I don't have references.
contribuciones a la pensión y el seguro	pension and insurance contributions
Domino el francés.	I speak French fluently.
¿Cuántos años de experiencia tiene?	How many years of experience do you have?

✎ Phrase Practice 2

Fill in the blanks in each sentence based on the English translation.

1. _____ es de treinta y siete horas. *It is a thirty-seven-hour workweek.*

2. ¿_____? *When do I start?*

3. ¿Hay _____? *Are there any incentives?*

4. Hay _____ de seis meses. *There's a probationary period of six months.*

5. _____. *I don't have references.*

6. ¿Cuántos _____ tiene? *How many years of experience do you have?*

ANSWER KEY
1. La jornada; 2. Cuándo comienzo; 3. incentivos; 4. un período de prueba; 5. No tengo referencias;
6. años de experiencia

More Irregular Verbs
in the Preterite

Expressing Past Actions
with **hace** and **acabar de**

Double Object Pronouns

Expressing Obligation
or Necessity

Grammar Builder 2
EXPRESSING OBLIGATION OR NECESSITY

▶ 10D Grammar Builder 2 (CD 8, Track 22)

In English, when you want to express obligation or strong necessity, you use *to have to*, *must*, or *should*. In Spanish, use **tener que** + infinitive or **deber** + infinitive, as you learned in Lesson 17 of Intermediate Spanish. You can also use the construction **hay que** + infinitive, which is a bit more impersonal.

Ella tiene que estudiar para el examen.
She has to study for the test.

Debemos hacer una lista de invitados.
We must make a guest list.

Hay que hablar claramente.
It is necessary to speak clearly.

Ⅱ

✎ Work Out 2
Fill in the blanks with the appropriate form of the verb in parentheses.

1. Ellos _____ tener en cuenta la situación. (deber)

2. Yo _____ que vender mi apartamento. (tener)

3. Ella no _____ venir a la oficina hoy. (deber)

4. _____ que consultar a un abogado. (haber)

5. Él _____ que llamar al hospital. (tener)

6. _____ que llamar a Juan inmediatamente. (haber)

7. Nosotros _____ hacer una excepción en este caso. (deber)

8. Ellos _____ que enviar el informe lo antes posible. (tener)

ANSWER KEY
1. deben; 2. tengo; 3. debe; 4. Hay; 5. tiene; 6. Hay; 7. debemos; 8. tienen

---

Take It Further

Take a look at the following words. They are all related to an amount of money, but they are not necessarily synonyms.

el sueldo	*pay*
el salario	*salary*
el jornal/la paga	*wage*
el pago	*payment*
la retribución	*repayment*
los honorarios	*fees*
los ingresos	*earnings*

✎ Drive It Home

Change the sentences below by replacing the subject with the one indicated in each line.

A. Yo acabo de terminar el examen.

1. (Tú) _____

2. (Nosotros) _____

3. (Usted) _____

More Irregular Verbs
in the Preterite

Expressing Past Actions
with **hace** and **acabar de**

Double Object Pronouns

Expressing Obligation
or Necessity

4. (Ellas) _____

B. **Hace un año que tú vives en España.**

1. (yo) _____

2. (vosotros) _____

_____

3. (Marta) _____

_____

4. (Marta y Eloy) _____

_____

ANSWER KEY

A. 1. Tú acabas de terminar el examen. 2. Nosotros acabamos de terminar el examen. 3. Usted acaba de terminar el examen. 4. Ellas acaban de terminar el examen.

B. 1. Hace un año que yo vivo en España. 2. Hace un año que vosotros vivís en España. 3. Hace un año que Marta vive en España. 4. Hace un año que Marta y Eloy viven en España.

How Did You Do?

By now, you should be able to:

☐ Talk more specifically about being a student
(Still unsure? Jump back to page 141.)

☐ Talk about the recent past using hace and acabar de
(Still unsure? Jump back to page 142.)

☐ Converse about applying for a job
(Still unsure? Jump back to page 144.)

☐ Express a strong necessity (*to have to, must, should*)
(Still unsure? Jump back to page 146.)

Lesson 11: Sentences

By the end of this lesson, you should be able to:

☐ Talk about being a student

☐ Use the imperfect when describing actions of the past

☐ Confidently express your job qualifications

Sentence Builder 1

▷ 11A Sentence Builder 1 (CD 8, Track 23)

¿Cuál es tu carrera?	*What is your major?*
¿Cuál es tu especialidad?	*What is your major?*
¿En qué año estás?	*What year are you in?*
Se gradúa el año que viene.	*He/She graduates next year.*
¿Qué clases tomas este semestre?	*What classes are you taking this semester?*
¿Qué notas sacaste?	*What grades did you get?*
¿Qué planes tienes para el futuro?	*What are your plans for the future?*
Pienso ser periodista.	*I'm thinking about being a journalist.*
Acaba de graduarse en medicina.	*He/She just graduated in medicine.*
Tenemos que escribir un trabajo de investigación.	*We have to write a research paper.*

More Irregular Verbs
in the Preterite

Expressing Past Actions
with **hace** and **acabar de**

Double Object Pronouns

Expressing Obligation
or Necessity

✎ Sentence Practice 1

Fill in the blanks in each sentence based on the English translation.

1. ¿Cuál es _____? *What is your major?*

2. ¿_____? *What year are you in?*

3. ¿_____ este semestre? *What classes are you*

   taking this semester?

4. ¿Qué notas _____? *What grades did you get?*

5. ¿_____ para el futuro?

   What are your plans for the future?

   ANSWER KEY
   1. tu carrera/tu especialidad; 2. En qué año estás; 3. Qué clases tomas; 4. sacaste; 5. Qué planes tienes

Grammar Builder 1
THE IMPERFECT OF -AR VERBS

▶ 11B Grammar Builder 1 (CD 8, Track 24)

So far, you've learned how to express actions that happened in the past with the
preterite tense. There is, however, another past tense, called the imperfect, which
is used to describe actions in the past that do not have a clear beginning or end,
or are part of a routine or habit. The imperfect often corresponds to the English
habitual past, with *used to* + verb, or to the past progressive *was/were* + *-ing*.

Durante el verano, me levantaba a las nueve.
During the summer, I used to get up at nine.

Después del desayuno, caminaba por la playa.
After breakfast, I would walk along the beach.

To form the imperfect of -ar verbs, simply take the root of the verb and add the following endings.

REGULAR IMPERFECT ENDINGS FOR -AR VERBS	
yo -aba	nosotros/as -ábamos
tú -abas	vosotros/as -abais
él/ella/usted -aba	ellos/ellas/ustedes -aban

Let's look at how this works with the verb pagar (*to pay*).

PAGAR *(TO PAY)* - IMPERFECT	
yo pagaba	nosotros/as pagábamos
tú pagabas	vosotros/as pagabais
él/ella/usted pagaba	ellos/ellas/ustedes pagaban

Ⅱ

✎ Work Out 1

Complete the following paragraph with the verbs in the imperfect tense.

Cuando tenía nueve años me 1_____ (yo/gustar) jugar con mis amigos en el parque. A veces 2_____ (nosotros/montar) en bicicleta, otras veces 3_____ (nosotros/jugar) al fútbol. El tiempo 4_____ (pasar) muy rápido porque nos divertíamos mucho. Cuando 5_____ (llegar) la noche, 6_____ (nosotros/ jugar) a las escondidas. En el verano, 7_____ (nosotros/acostarse) muy tarde y 8_____ (nosotros/levantarse) muy tarde también.

ANSWER KEY
1. gustaba; 2. montábamos; 3. jugábamos; 4. pasaba; 5. llegaba; 6. jugábamos; 7. nos acostábamos; 8. nos levantábamos

More Irregular Verbs
in the Preterite

Expressing Past Actions
with **hace** and **acabar de**

Double Object Pronouns

Expressing Obligation
or Necessity

Sentence Builder 2

▶ 11C Sentence Builder 2 (CD 8, Track 25)

¿En qué trabaja?	*What do you do for a living?*
Le ofrecemos un contrato por un año.	*We're offering you a one-year contract.*
Hay que trabajar horas extras.	*You have to work overtime.*
Tengo una especialización en farmacia clínica.	*I have a master's degree in clinical pharmacy.*
¿Cuál es su objetivo en solicitar este puesto?	*What is your aim in applying for this job?*
Su oferta es muy interesante.	*Your offer is very interesting.*
¿Cuándo comienzo?	*When do I start?*
¿Qué otras cualificaciones posee?	*What other qualifications do you have?*
Soy bueno/a trabajando en equipo.	*I'm good at working on a team.*
Sé trabajar bajo presión.	*I know how to work under pressure.*

Ⅱ

✎ Sentence Practice 2

Fill in the blanks in each sentence based on the English translation.

1. ¿_____? *What do you do for a living?*

2. ¿_____ en solicitar este puesto?

   What is your aim in applying for this job?

3. _____ es muy interesante. *Your offer is very interesting.*

4. ¿_____ posee?

   What other qualifications do you have?

5. _____ en equipo. *I'm good at working on a team.*

6. Sé trabajar _____. *I know how to work under pressure.*

ANSWER KEY

1. En qué trabaja; 2. Cuál es su objetivo; 3. Su oferta; 4. Qué otras cualificaciones; 5. Soy bueno/a trabajando; 6. bajo presión

Grammar Builder 2
THE IMPERFECT OF -ER AND -IR VERBS

 11D Grammar Builder 2 (CD 8, Track 26)

The same set of endings is used in the imperfect of **-er** and **-ir** verbs.

REGULAR IMPERFECT ENDINGS FOR -ER/-IR VERBS	
yo -ía	nosotros/as -íamos
tú -ías	vosotros/as -íais
él/ella/usted -ía	ellos/ellas/ustedes -ían

VENDER *(TO SELL)* - IMPERFECT	
yo vendía	nosotros/as vendíamos
tú vendías	vosotros/as vendíais
él/ella/usted vendía	ellos/ellas/ustedes vendían

ESCRIBIR *(TO WRITE)* - IMPERFECT	
yo escribía	nosotros/as escribíamos
tú escribías	vosotros/as escribíais
él/ella/usted escribía	ellos/ellas/ustedes escribían

The imperfect doesn't always correspond to habitual or progressive past actions. Sometimes it's translated as the simple past when it describes a number of

More Irregular Verbs
in the Preterite

Expressing Past Actions
with **hace** and **acabar de**

Double Object Pronouns

Expressing Obligation
or Necessity

conditions and qualities, such as physical appearance, age, occupation, traits
or characteristics, mental and emotional states, location, beliefs, opinions, and
wishes. Notice that all of these conditions and qualities are things that you can
think of as "background" information—not some action that happened at a specific
point in time in the past, but rather, characteristics that have lasted over a period.

Ella tenía el pelo rojo y largo.
She had long red hair.

Mi abuelo tenía setenta años, estaba triste, y no quería hablar.
My grandfather was seventy years old, he was sad, and he didn't want to talk.

Su casa estaba lejos de las montañas y estaba en mal estado.
His house was far away from the mountains and in bad shape.

Ⅱ

🖊 Work Out 2

Fill in the blanks with the imperfect form of the verb(s) given.

1. **Ella siempre _____ tarde del trabajo. (salir)**

2. **Mi tío Alfonso _____ una casa cerca al mar. (tener)**

3. **Ella _____ en Brasil. (vivir)**

4. **Ella _____ cincuenta años pero _____ más vieja.**
   (tener/parecer)

5. **Ellos _____ novelas rosa. (escribir)**

6. **Vosotros _____ hasta tarde los fines de semana. (dormir)**

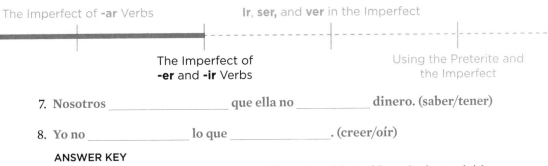

The Imperfect of **-ar** Verbs

Ir, **ser**, and **ver** in the Imperfect

The Imperfect of
-er and **-ir** Verbs

Using the Preterite and
the Imperfect

7. Nosotros _____ que ella no _____ dinero. (saber/tener)

8. Yo no _____ lo que _____. (creer/oír)

ANSWER KEY
1. salía; 2. tenía; 3. vivía; 4. tenía/parecía; 5. escribían; 6. dormíais; 7. sabíamos/tenía; 8. creía/oía

⊕ Culture Note

Some universities in Latin America and Spain are quite different from those in the United States. There may be no on-campus housing, because students generally live at home with their parents or rent and share apartments or houses with other students. Even though students do play a number of different sports, there are often no teams associated with any one university, nor are there scholarships offered to these athletes. Furthermore, there are no fraternities or sororities; students meet more informally at cafés or at home.

✎ Drive It Home

Replace the underlined part of the sentence with the words in parentheses.

1. Durante el verano yo caminaba <u>en la playa</u> con mis amigos. (en el parque)

_____

2. Durante el verano yo caminaba en la playa con <u>mis amigos</u>. (mi familia)

_____

3. Durante <u>el verano</u> yo caminaba en la playa con mis amigos. (la primavera)

_____

4. Durante el verano yo <u>caminaba</u> en la playa con mis amigos. (jugar)

_____

More Irregular Verbs
in the Preterite

Expressing Past Actions
with **hace** and **acabar de**

Double Object Pronouns

Expressing Obligation
or Necessity

5. **Durante el verano <u>yo caminaba</u> en la playa con mis amigos. (ella + caminar)**

_____

6. **Durante el verano <u>yo caminaba</u> en la playa con mis amigos. (tú + caminar)**

_____

7. **Durante el verano <u>yo caminaba</u> en la playa con mis amigos. (ustedes + caminar)**

_____

8. **Durante el verano <u>yo caminaba</u> en la playa con mis amigos. (nosotros + caminar)**

_____

ANSWER KEY
1. Durante el verano yo caminaba en el parque con mis amigos. 2. Durante el verano yo caminaba en la playa con mi familia. 3. Durante la primavera yo caminaba en la playa con mis amigos.
4. Durante el verano yo jugaba en la playa con mis amigos. 5. Durante el verano ella caminaba en la playa con mis amigos. 6. Durante el verano tú caminabas en la playa con mis amigos.
7. Durante el verano ustedes caminaban en la playa con mis amigos. 8. Durante el verano nosotros caminábamos en la playa con mis amigos.

How Did You Do?

By now, you should be able to:

☐ Talk about being a student
(Still unsure? Jump back to page 149.)

☐ Use the imperfect when describing actions of the past
(Still unsure? Jump back to pages 150 and 153.)

☐ Confidently express your job qualifications
(Still unsure? Jump back to page 152.)

Lesson 12: Conversations

By the end of this lesson, you should be able to:

☐ Use **ir**, **ser**, and **ver** in the imperfect

☐ Use the imperfect to express two simultaneous actions in the past

☐ Use the imperfect and the preterite in one sentence

Conversation 1

▶ 12A Conversation 1 (CD 8, Track 27 - Spanish Only; Track 28 - Spanish and English)

Isabel and Olga have been friends since high school, but they haven't seen each other in months. They've just bumped into each other at the university bookstore.

Isabel:	¡Hola, Olga! ¡Qué sorpresa! ¿Cómo estás?
Olga:	¡Lo mismo digo! ¿Cómo te ha ido? ¡No sabía que estudiabas en esta universidad también!
Isabel:	Sí, decidí especializarme en ingeniería mecánica y me gané una beca para estudiar aquí. Y tú, ¿cuál es tu carrera?
Olga:	¡Felicitaciones! Estoy estudiando pediatría.
Isabel:	¿En qué año estás?
Olga:	Me gradúo en dos años. Pero no estoy segura si voy a continuar.
Isabel:	¿Por qué no? Siempre te gustó trabajar con niños.
Olga:	Ya lo sé. Pero estoy pensando especializarme en sicología infantil. Y a ti, ¿cuánto te falta?
Isabel:	Tres semestres más. Ya estoy lista para empezar a trabajar.
Olga:	Sí, te entiendo. Bueno, y ¿qué te parece está universidad?
Isabel:	Me gusta mucho. Estoy muy contenta aquí.

Isabel:	*Hi, Olga! What a surprise! How are you?*

More Irregular Verbs
in the Preterite

Expressing Past Actions
with **hace** and **acabar de**

Double Object Pronouns

Expressing Obligation
or Necessity

Olga:	Same here! How have you been? I didn't know that you studied here as well!
Isabel:	Yes, I decided to major in mechanical engineering and I was awarded a scholarship to study here. And you, what's your major?
Olga:	Congratulations! I'm studying to be a pediatrician.
Isabel:	What year are you in?
Olga:	I'll graduate in two years. But I'm not sure whether I am going to continue.
Isabel:	Why not? You always liked working with kids.
Olga:	I know. But I am thinking about majoring in child psychology. And you, how much more do you have to go?
Isabel:	Three more semesters. I'm ready to start working.
Olga:	Yes, I understand. Well, so, what do you think of the university?
Isabel:	I like it a lot. I'm very happy here.

⊕ Culture Note

More and more women in Latin America and Spain are studying to go into fields that were once associated with men only, such as engineering or physics. Despite this, employment opportunities are not the same, varying from country to country and across social backgrounds.

✎ Conversation Practice 1

Fill in the blanks below with the appropriate word based on the English translations and the dialogue above.

1. ¡No _____ que _____ en esta universidad

también! *I didn't know that you studied here as well!*

2. Sí, _____ especializarme en ingeniería mecánica y _____

una beca para estudiar aquí. *Yes, I decided to major in mechanical engineering*

and I was awarded a scholarship to study here.

3. Y tú, ¿cuál es tu _____? *And you, what's your major?*

4. Siempre _____ trabajar con niños. *You always liked working*

with kids.

5. Pero estoy pensando especializarme en _____.

But I am thinking about majoring in child psychology.

ANSWER KEY
1. sabía/estudiabas; 2. decidí, me/gané; 3. carrera; 4. te gustó; 5. sicología infantil

Grammar Builder 1
IR, SER, AND VER IN THE IMPERFECT

▶ 12B Grammar Builder 1 (CD 9, Track 1)

The good news about the imperfect tense is that there are only three irregular verbs.

IR *(TO GO)* - IMPERFECT	
yo iba	nosotros/as íbamos
tú ibas	vosotros/as ibais
él/ella/usted iba	ellos/ellas/ustedes iban

SER *(TO BE)* - IMPERFECT	
yo era	nosotros/as éramos
tú eras	vosotros/as erais
él/ella/usted era	ellos/ellas/ustedes eran

Móre Irregular Verbs
in the Preterite

Expressing Past Actions
with **hace** and **acabar de**

Double Object Pronouns

Expressing Obligation
or Necessity

VER *(TO SEE)* - IMPERFECT	
yo veía	nosotros/as veíamos
tú veías	vosotros/as veíais
él/ella/usted veía	ellos/ellas/ustedes veían

Here are some examples of these three irregular verbs in sentences. Note that the imperfect in each of the examples below describes a background setting against which the main events of a story take place.

Eran las once de la noche y nevaba.
It was eleven at night and it was snowing.

Era un día de invierno y no se veía a nadie en la calle.
It was a winter day and there was no one to be seen on the street.

Estaba nublado e iba a llover.
It was cloudy and it was going to rain.

Ⓘ

✎ Work Out 1

Change the underlined phrases using the pronoun given in parentheses.

1. Era viernes por la noche y Miguel estaba en una fiesta. (nosotros) _____

   _____

2. Eran las once de la mañana y yo tenía mucho frío. (tú) _____

   _____

The Imperfect of **-ar** Verbs

Ir, ser, and **ver** in the Imperfect

The Imperfect of
-er and **-ir** Verbs

Using the Preterite and
the Imperfect

3. Una vez cuando <u>nadábamos</u> en la piscina … (ellos) _____

_____

4. Era un día muy bonito y <u>ellos querían</u> ir al campo. (nosotros) _____

_____

5. Una noche, cuando <u>caminaba</u> a casa … (vosotros) _____

_____

6. Era tarde y <u>ella caminaba</u> sola. (ellos) _____

_____

ANSWER KEY

1. Era viernes por la noche y nosotros estábamos en una fiesta. 2. Eran las once de la mañana y tú
tenías mucho frío. 3. Una vez cuando nadaban en la piscina … 4. Era un día muy bonito y decidimos
ir al campo. 5. Una noche, cuando caminabais a casa … 6. Era tarde y ellos caminaban solos.

🎙 Conversation 2

▶ 12C Conversation 2 (CD 9, Track 2 - Spanish Only; Track 3 - Spanish and English)

Hernando is applying for a job as a pharmacist and is being interviewed for the
position by the head of pharmacology of a well-known hospital in Buenos Aires.

Doctor:	Su hoja de vida es impresionante. Está muy cualificado. ¿Cuál es su objetivo en solicitar este puesto?
Hernando:	Quiero vincularme con un hospital prestigioso para desarrollarme profesionalmente.
Doctor:	Y, ¿qué es lo que nos ofrece usted a nosotros?
Hernando:	Gran capacidad para el trabajo. Sé manejar situaciones estresantes, y soy bueno trabajando en equipo.
Doctor:	¿Domina el inglés?
Hernando:	Claro que sí. Tengo una especialización en farmacia clínica de la universidad de Brighton en Inglaterra. Además hablo francés e italiano.

More Irregular Verbs
in the Preterite

Expressing Past Actions
with **hace** and **acabar de**

Double Object Pronouns

Expressing Obligation
or Necessity

Doctor:	Bueno, le podemos ofrecer un contrato por un año con jornada de treinta y siete horas y un mes de vacaciones.
Hernando:	Su oferta es muy interesante. ¿Cuándo comienzo?
Doctor:	Nos gustaría que empezara tan pronto como sea posible.
Hernando:	Estoy disponible a partir del quince de este mes, ¿le parece bien?
Doctor:	Perfecto. ¡Bienvenido a bordo!

Doctor:	*Your résumé is impressive. You're very well qualified. What's your aim in applying for this job?*
Hernando:	*I want to join a prestigious hospital in order to advance professionally.*
Doctor:	*And, what do you offer us?*
Hernando:	*Great work capacity. I know how to handle stressful situations, and I'm a good team worker.*
Doctor:	*Do you speak English?*
Hernando:	*Yes, of course. I have a specialized degree in clinical pharmacy from Brighton University in England. Plus, I speak French and Italian.*
Doctor:	*Well, we can offer you a one-year contract with a thirty-seven-hour workweek and a month of vacation.*
Hernando:	*Your offer is very interesting. When do I start?*
Doctor:	*We would like you to start as soon as possible.*
Hernando:	*I'm available as of the fifteenth of this month. How does that sound?*
Doctor:	*Perfect! Welcome!*

Take It Further

There are a number of English words that the Royal Academy of Spanish Language has accepted into the Spanish language. Today these words are so common that Spanish speakers might not even realize that they're borrowed from English. This misimpression is made easier by the spelling of the words, which has often been adapted for the Spanish language.

estresante	stressing
fútbol	soccer
parqueadero	parking lot
computadora	computer

✎ Conversation Practice 2

Fill in the blanks below with the appropriate word based on the English
translations and the dialogue above.

1. Está muy _____. *You're very well qualified.*

2. ¿Cuál es su objetivo en _____? *What's*

   your aim in applying for this job?

3. Y, ¿qué es lo que nos ofrece usted _____? *And, what do you*

   offer us?

4. Sé manejar situaciones _____, y soy bueno trabajando en

   equipo. *I know how to handle stressful situations, and I'm a good team worker.*

5. Bueno, le podemos ofrecer un _____ por un año con _____

   de treinta y siete horas y un mes de vacaciones. *Well, we can offer you a one-year*

   contract with a thirty-seven-hour workweek and a month of vacation.

6. Estoy _____ a partir del quince de este mes, ¿le parece bien?

   I'm available as of the fifteenth of this month. How does that sound?

   ANSWER KEY
   1. cualificado; 2. solicitar este puesto; 3. a nosotros; 4. estresantes; 5. contrato /jornada; 6. disponible

More Irregular Verbs
in the Preterite

Expressing Past Actions
with **hace** and **acabar de**

Double Object Pronouns

Expressing Obligation
or Necessity

Grammar Builder 2
USING THE PRETERITE AND THE IMPERFECT

▶ 12D Grammar Builder 2 (CD 9, Track 4)

You can use the imperfect to express two or more actions that were going on at the same time. Simultaneous actions are often linked with words like mientras (*while*) or mientras tanto (*meanwhile*).

Ella leía el periódico mientras yo cocinaba.
She read the newspaper while I cooked.

Mientras nosotros mirábamos televisión, ellos se vestían.
While we watched television, they got dressed.

To indicate that two or more actions happened sequentially, use the preterite.

Ella desayunó y luego fue a trabajar.
She had breakfast and then went to work.

Yo leí el periódico, tomé mi café y miré la tele.
I read the newspaper, drank my coffee, and watched TV.

In cases where you have an ongoing action that is interrupted by another action, use the imperfect to describe the action that was in progress and the preterite to describe the action that interrupted it.

Yo dormía cuando sonó el teléfono.
I was sleeping when the phone rang.

Empezó a llover cuando jugábamos en el parque.
It began to rain while we were playing in the park.

⏸

✎ Work Out 2

Form sentences using the preterite and/or the imperfect, following the clues given:

1. **Ella/leer/una novela/mientras/yo/jugar/a las cartas.** (*simultaneous actions*)

   _____

2. **Ellos/trabajar/en el jardín/después/ir/de compras.** (*one action happens after the*

   other) _____

   _____

3. **Nosotros/cocinar/cuando/ella/llamar/por teléfono.** (*one action interrupts the*

   other) _____

   _____

4. **Mientras/yo/dormir/vosotros/mirar/la tele.** (*simultaneous actions*) _____

   _____

5. **Vosotros/almorzar/luego/ir de compras.** (*one action happens after the other*)

   _____

6. **Ella/llorar/él/gritar.** (*simultaneous actions*) _____

   _____

7. **Yo/cantar/cuando/ellos/llamar a la puerta.** (*one action interrupts the other*)

   _____

ANSWER KEY
1. Ella leía una novela mientras yo jugaba a las cartas. 2. Ellos trabajaron en el jardín y después fueron de compras. 3. Nosotros cocinábamos cuando ella llamó por teléfono. 4. Mientras yo dormía, vosotros mirabais la tele. 5. Vosotros almorzasteis y luego fuisteis de compras. 6. Ella lloraba y él gritaba. 7. Yo cantaba cuando ellos llamaron a la puerta.

More Irregular Verbs
in the Preterite

Expressing Past Actions
with **hace** and **acabar de**

Double Object Pronouns

Expressing Obligation
or Necessity

Take It Further

Back in Lesson 4 of *Intermediate Spanish,* we touched on accent marks and how they're used in Spanish. Now that you have some more experience under your belt, let's take a closer look. If a word ends in a vowel (a, e, i, o, u) or the letters n or s, and the stress falls on the last syllable, an accent mark is required.

caminó	(he/she) walked
dormí	I slept
canción	song
verás	you will see

If the word ends in a consonant other than n or s and the stress falls on the next-to-last syllable, an accent mark is also required.

lápiz	pencil
difícil	difficult
cárcel	prison
mártir	martyr

Sometimes, accent marks are used only to differentiate between words that would otherwise look identical.

él	he	el	the
qué	what	que	that
más	more	mas	but
tú	you	tu	your
sé	I know	se	himself/herself, etc.
sí	yes	si	if

Remember that question words have an accent when used in a question but the corresponding relative pronouns or connecting words do not.

¿cómo?	how?	como	as, like

¿cuál?	which?	cual	which, as
¿cuándo?	when?	cuando	when
¿dónde?	where?	donde	where
¿qué?	what?	que	which, that
¿quién?	who? whom?	quien	who, whom
¿cuánto?	how much?	cuanto	as much, as many

For example, in the first sentence below, ¿cómo? is a question word, and in the second, como is a relative pronoun, introducing another sentence within the main one.

¿Cómo funciona?
How does it work?

No funciona como yo me imaginaba.
It doesn't work like (lit., how) I thought.

Demonstrative pronouns (éste, ése, aquél) have an accent, while demonstrative adjectives (este, ese, aquel) don't. Of course, if all of this is a bit overwhelming, don't worry. As with everything else, the more you read and write in Spanish, the easier this will become, and you'll get used to seeing certain words with an accent mark.

✎ Drive It Home

In the following sentences an ongoing action is interrupted by another action. Replace the action in progress with the imperfect form of the verb indicated on each line.

A. Yo dormía cuando sonó el teléfono.

1. cocinar _____

More Irregular Verbs
in the Preterite

Expressing Past Actions
with **hace** and **acabar de**

Double Object Pronouns

Expressing Obligation
or Necessity

2. hablar _____

3. leer _____

4. trabajar _____

B. **Ella trabajaba cuando llegó su amigo.**

1. escribir _____

2. bailar _____

3. comer _____

4. bañarse _____

ANSWER KEY

A. 1. Yo cocinaba cuando sonó el teléfono. 2. Yo hablaba cuando sonó el teléfono. 3. Yo leía cuando sonó el teléfono. 4. Yo trabajaba cuando sonó el teléfono.
B. 1. Ella escribía cuando llegó su amigo. 2. Ella bailaba cuando llegó su amigo. 3. Ella comía cuando llegó su amigo. 4. Ella se bañaba cuando llegó su amigo.

How Did You Do?

By now, you should be able to:

☐ Use ir, ser, and ver in the imperfect (Still unsure? Jump back to page 159.)

☐ Use the imperfect to express two simultaneous actions in the past
(Still unsure? Jump back to page 164.)

☐ Use the imperfect and the preterite in one sentence
(Still unsure? Jump back to page 164.)

Don't forget to practice and reinforce what you've learned by visiting **www.livinglanguage.com/ languagelab** for flashcards, games, and quizzes for Unit 3!

Unit 3 Essentials

Vocabulary Essentials

SCHOOL SUBJECTS

	school subject
	mathematics
	history
	literature
	science
	biology
	chemistry
	geography
	philosophy

[Pg. 132]

SCHOOL VERBS AND PHRASES

	to pass a course
	to take a test
	to pass/fail a test
	to write a research paper
	full-time student
	part-time student
	to major in . . .
	to get good/bad grades

	class schedule
	*I'm interested in … *
	I'm not sure yet.
	What do you think of … ?
	And how about you? What do you think?
	What is your major?
	What is your major?
	What year are you in?
	He/She graduates next year.
	What classes are you taking this semester?
	What grades did you get?
	What are your plans for the future?
	I'm thinking about being a journalist.
	He/She just graduated in medicine.
	We have to write a research paper.

[Pgs. 141 and 149]

WORKPLACE VOCABULARY

	appointment
	meeting
	conference room
	contract
	employee
	union
	insurance
	interview

	qualification
	résumé
	references
	retired person

[Pg. 135]

WORKPLACE PHRASES

	job application
	It is a thirty-seven-hour workweek.
	When do I start?
	There's a probationary period of six months.
	a month's vacation
	Are there any incentives?
	I don't have references.
	pension and insurance contributions
	I speak French fluently.
	How many years of experience do you have?
	What do you do for a living?
	We're offering you a one-year contract.
	You have to work overtime.
	I have a master's degree in clinical pharmacy.
	What is your aim in applying for this job?
	Your offer is very interesting.
	When do I start?
	What other qualifications do you have?
	I'm good at working on a team.

	I know how to work under pressure.

[Pgs. 144 and 152]

Grammar Essentials

DOUBLE OBJECT PRONOUNS

When two object pronouns appear in a sentence, the indirect object pronoun comes first. Use se instead of le or les preceding lo(s)/la(s).

In order to clarify the meaning of se, use a él/a ella/a usted/a ellos/a ellas/a ustedes.

When the pronouns appear with more than one verb, they can be placed either before the verbs or attached to the end of the main verb.

EXPRESSING PAST ACTIONS WITH HACE AND ACABAR DE

To express *to have just*, use:

acabar de + infinitive

To express an action that began in the past and continues into the present, use:

hace + time + que + present tense

To express *ago*, use:

hace + time + que + preterite

EXPRESSING OBLIGATION OR NECESSITY

tener que + infinitive

deber + infinitive

hay que + infinitive

THE IMPERFECT

Use the imperfect tense to describe actions in the past that do not have a clear beginning or end, or are part of a routine or habit. To form the imperfect of -ar verbs, simply take the root of the verb and add the following endings.

REGULAR IMPERFECT ENDINGS FOR -AR VERBS	
yo -aba	nosotros/as -ábamos
tú -abas	vosotros/as -abais
él/ella/usted -aba	ellos/ellas/ustedes -aban

REGULAR IMPERFECT ENDINGS FOR -ER/-IR VERBS	
yo -ía	nosotros/as -íamos
tú -ías	vosotros/as -íais
él/ella/usted -ía	ellos/ellas/ustedes -ían

VERBS

DAR *(TO GIVE)* - PRETERITE	
yo di	nosotros/as dimos
tú diste	vosotros/as disteis
él/ella/usted dio	ellos/ellas/ustedes dieron

ESCRIBIR *(TO WRITE)* - IMPERFECT	
yo escribía	nosotros/as escribíamos
tú escribías	vosotros/as escribíais
él/ella/usted escribía	ellos/ellas/ustedes escribían

IR *(TO GO)* - IMPERFECT	
yo iba	nosotros/as íbamos
tú ibas	vosotros/as ibais
él/ella/usted iba	ellos/ellas/nosotros/as iban

PAGAR (TO PAY) - IMPERFECT

yo pagaba	nosotros/as pagábamos
tú pagabas	vosotros/as pagabais
él/ella/usted pagaba	ellos/ellas/ustedes pagaban

PEDIR (TO ASK FOR) - PRETERITE

yo pedí	nosotros/as pedimos
tú pediste	vosotros/as pedisteis
él/ella/usted pidió	ellos/ellas/ustedes pidieron

SER (TO BE) - IMPERFECT

yo era	nosotros/as éramos
tú eras	vosotros/as erais
él/ella/usted era	ellos/ellas/ustedes eran

VENDER (TO SELL) - IMPERFECT

yo vendía	nosotros/as vendíamos
tú vendías	vosotros/as vendíais
él/ella/usted vendía	ellos/ellas/ustedes vendían

VER (TO SEE) - PRETERITE

yo vi	nosotros/as vimos
tú viste	vosotros/as visteis
él/ella/usted vio	ellos/ellas/ustedes vieron

VER (TO SEE) - IMPERFECT

yo veía	nosotros/as veíamos
tú veías	vosotros/as veíais
él/ella/usted veía	ellos/ellas/ustedes veían

Unit 3 Quiz

A. Fill in the blank with the correct form of the verb in the imperfect tense.

1. Yo me _____ mucho en la playa. (divertir)

2. Mi amigo siempre _____ a todas las reuniones. (asistir)

3. Ellos _____ un informe al profesor todas las semanas. (entregar)

4. Usted _____ un trabajo de investigación cuando lo visité. (escribir)

5. Cuando éramos niños nosotros _____ a Disneylandia con toda la familia. (viajar)

6. Ustedes siempre _____ las vacaciones de verano en la playa. (pasar)

7. Ellas _____ en esa universidad también. (estudiar)

8. ¿Tú no _____ seguros de autos en la agencia ? (vender)

B. Decide whether to use the preterite or the imperfect and write the appropriate form in the blank.

1. Yo bailaba mientras ella _____ . (cantar)

2. Ella escuchaba la música cuando José _____ a la casa. (llegar)

3. Nosotros _____ cuando el profesor entró en el aula de clases. (estudiar)

4. Juanita escribía mientras Josefa _____ la novela. (leer)

5. Ustedes asistían a la universidad mientras yo _____alumno. (ser)

6. Primero yo visité la tienda y después yo _____ al supermercado. (ir)

7. Ustedes entraban al cine cuando yo los _____ . (encontrar)

8. Mis padres cocinaban cuando ellos _____ con la comida. (llegar)

C. Select the correct term from the word list below:

la biblioteca, salarios, suspendo, la librería, la ciencia, el título académico, apruebo, la entrevista

1. La biología y la química son materias en el mundo de _____ .

2. En _____ es posible estudiar y sacar libros.

3. Después de graduarse, el estudiante recibe _____ .

4. Durante _____ los candidatos discuten sus cualificaciones.

5. En _____ puedo comprar los libros.

6. Yo _____ el examen porque tengo malas notas.

7. La compañía ofrece beneficios buenos y _____ altos.

8. Yo _____ el curso con notas muy buenas.

D. Unscramble the following sentence fragments. Then give the English translation.

1. dos años/hace/yo/aquí/que/trabajé _____

_____

_____

2. ellas/de/escribir/acaban/un trabajo de investigación _____

_____

_____

3. dos meses/soy/estudiante/que/hace/a tiempo completo _____

4. acabamos/aprobar/el examen/nosotros/de _____

5. que/ella/física/estudia/hace/tres meses _____

6. un correo electrónico/acabo/enviar/yo/de _____

7. acaba/de/una entrevista/ella/tener _____

8. viven/en los Estados Unidos/diez años/hace/que/mis primos _____

How Did You Do?

Give yourself a point for every correct answer, then use the following key to determine whether or not you're ready to move on:

0–7 points: It's probably best to go back and study the lessons again to make sure you understood everything completely. Take your time; it's not a race! Make sure you spend time reviewing vocabulary with the flashcards and reading through each grammar note carefully.

8–16 points: If the questions you missed were in sections A or B, you may want to review the vocabulary again; if you missed answers mostly in sections C or D, check the unit essentials to make sure you have your conjugations and other grammar basics down.

17–20 points: Feel free to move on to the next unit! You're doing a great job.

 **points**

Unit 4:
Sports and Hobbies

In this unit, you'll learn how to express doubt, denial, and emotions in Spanish.
You'll also learn how to talk about the hobbies you have and the sports you enjoy.
By the end of this unit, you should be able to:

☐ Name and talk about different hobbies and sports

☐ Express the probability or possibility that something would happen

☐ Describe what you enjoy doing in your free time

☐ Identify verbs and expressions that require the use of the subjunctive

☐ Form the subjunctive of regular and irregular verbs

☐ Identify the difference in using the subjunctive and the indicative

☐ Use relative pronouns to create clauses

Lesson 13: Words

By the end of this lesson, you should be able to:

☐ Name different types of hobbies and sports

☐ Express the probability or possibility that something would happen

☐ Use se to make general statements

Word Builder 1

▶ 13A Word Builder 1 (CD 9, Track 5)

la afición	hobby
el/la aficionado/a	fan
el pasatiempo	hobby
el tiempo libre	free time
coleccionar	to collect
la artesanía	craft
la fotografía	photography
la música	music
la pintura	painting
el baile	dancing
la filatelia	stamp collecting
las antigüedades	antiques
la cocina	cooking
la costura	sewing
la lectura	reading

(II)

✎ Word Practice 1

Match the Spanish word on the left with its appropriate English translation on the right.

1. la lectura

2. la pintura

3. la afición

4. la artesanía

a. *painting*

b. *craft*

c. *hobby*

d. *sewing*

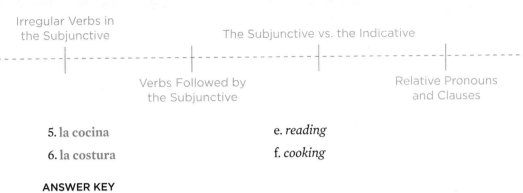

Irregular Verbs in
the Subjunctive

The Subjunctive vs. the Indicative

Verbs Followed by
the Subjunctive

Relative Pronouns
and Clauses

5. la cocina

6. la costura

e. *reading*

f. *cooking*

ANSWER KEY
1. e; 2. a; 3. c; 4. b; 5. f; 6. d

Grammar Builder 1
THE CONDITIONAL

▶ 13B Grammar Builder 1 (CD 9, Track 6)

The present conditional is used to express the probability or possibility that something would happen, depending on specific circumstances. In most cases where *would* is used in English, the conditional is used in Spanish. To form the conditional, simply add the following endings to the infinitive form of any verb.

CONDITIONAL ENDINGS	
yo -ía	nosotros/as -íamos
tú -ías	vosotros/as -íais
él/ella/usted -ía	ellos/ellas/ustedes -ían

Notice that these are the same as the endings that were used for **-er/-ir** verbs in the imperfect, but these are added to the entire infinitive, not the verb root, and are also used for conditional **-ar** verbs. Let's see how this works with the following example verbs: **hablar** (*to talk*), **ser** (*to be*), and **abrir** (*to open*).

HABLAR *(TO TALK)* - CONDITIONAL	
yo hablaría	nosotros/as hablaríamos
tú hablarías	vosotros/as hablaríais
él/ella/usted hablaría	ellos/ellas/ustedes hablarían

SER *(TO BE)* - CONDITIONAL	
yo sería	nosotros/as seríamos
tú serías	vosotros/as seríais
él/ella/usted sería	ellos/ellas/ustedes serían

ABRIR *(TO OPEN)* - CONDITIONAL	
yo abriría	nosotros/as abriríamos
tú abrirías	vosotros/as abriríais
él/ella/usted abriría	ellos/ellas/ustedes abrirían

The following verbs have irregular stems.

saber	sabr-ía	*to know*
tener	tendr-ía	*to have*
salir	saldr-ía	*to go out*
poder	podr-ía	*to be able to*
hacer	har-ía	*to make*
decir	dir-ía	*to say*
haber	habr-ía	*there is/there are*
querer	querr-ía	*to want*
venir	vendr-ía	*to come*

Let's look at some examples of the conditional.

Yo estudiaría ruso, pero no tengo tiempo.
I would study Russian, but I don't have time.

En tu caso, yo no diría nada.
In your case, I wouldn't say anything.

Irregular Verbs in
the Subjunctive

The Subjunctive vs. the Indicative

Verbs Followed by
the Subjunctive

Relative Pronouns
and Clauses

Con más dinero, ella haría maravillas.
With more money, she would perform miracles.

✎ Work Out 1

Form sentences with the verbs in parentheses, using the conditional.

1. Nosotros _____ algo pero no hay nada en la nevera. (comer)

2. Yo _____ medicina pero no me gusta ver sangre. (estudiar)

3. Nadie _____ en esa casa tan vieja. (vivir)

4. Ella _____ la verdad, pero no puede. (decir)

5. Ellos _____ temprano, pero tienen que terminar el informe. (salir)

6. Los chicos _____ su tarea, pero olvidaron sus libros. (hacer)

7. Vosotros _____ al cine, pero ya es muy tarde. (ir)

8. Tú _____ una computadora, pero no tienes el dinero. (comprar)

ANSWER KEY
1. comeríamos; 2. estudiaría; 3. viviría; 4. diría; 5. saldrían; 6. harían; 7. iríais; 8. comprarías

Word Builder 2

▶ 13C Word Builder 2 (CD 9, Track 7)

el deporte	*sport*
el atleta	*athlete*
el deportista	*person who plays sports*
el jugador	*player*
el ciclismo	*biking, cycling*

el fútbol	soccer
el béisbol	baseball
la natación	swimming
el buceo	diving
la equitación	horseback riding
la caza	hunting
el baloncesto	basketball
el ajedrez	chess

✎ Word Practice 2

Match the Spanish word on the left with its appropriate English translation on the right.

1. la caza
2. el jugador
3. la natación
4. el buceo
5. el baloncesto
6. el deporte

a. *swimming*
b. *sport*
c. *diving*
d. *basketball*
e. *hunting*
f. *player*

ANSWER KEY
1. e; 2. f; 3. a; 4. c; 5. d; 6. b

Grammar Builder 2
IMPERSONAL SE

▶ 13D Grammar Builder 2 (CD 9, Track 8)

In English, we can make general statements with words like *you*, *people*, or *one*: *You shouldn't drink in public. In Spain, people eat supper very late. One shouldn't*

Irregular Verbs in
the Subjunctive

The Subjunctive vs. the Indicative

Verbs Followed by
the Subjunctive

Relative Pronouns
and Clauses

swim right after eating. In all of these sentences, words like *you, people,* and *one* are used to mean *people in general,* rather than any particular person. These sentences are impersonal because we don't have anyone specific in mind. In Spanish, the impersonal **se** is used in front of verbs to make general statements like these. Generally, you use **se** with either the third person singular or the third person plural of the verb.

Se dice que va a llover.
They say it's going to rain.

En España, se cena muy tarde.
In Spain, people eat supper very late.

Las oficinas se cierran a las tres.
The offices close at three.

¿Cómo se dice "helado" en francés?
How do you say "ice cream" in French?

No se debe comer a prisa.
One shouldn't eat quickly.

Ⅱ

✎ Work Out 2

Form sentences using the impersonal **se**. Conjugate the verb in the present tense.

1. **En ese lugar no (poder) pagar con tarjetas de crédito.** _____

_____

2. En la universidad no (deber) llegar tarde a una clase. _____

_____

3. En Cuba (conseguir) buenos cigarros. _____

_____

4. Para sacar buenas notas (tener) que estudiar mucho. _____

_____

5. (Pensar) que aprender otro idioma es importante. _____

_____

6. (Decir) que es mala suerte viajar en martes trece. _____

_____

7. ¿Cómo (decir) "buenos días" en ruso? _____

_____

8. ¿Cómo (escribir) esa palabra? _____

_____

ANSWER KEY

1. En ese lugar no se puede pagar con tarjetas de crédito. 2. En la universidad no se debe llegar tarde a una clase. 3. En Cuba se consiguen buenos cigarros. 4. Para sacar buenas notas se tiene que estudiar mucho. 5. Se piensa que aprender otro idioma es importante. 6. Se dice que es mala suerte viajar en martes trece. 7. ¿Cómo se dice "buenos días" en ruso? 8. ¿Cómo se escribe esa palabra?

⚡ Tip!

Reading newspaper and magazine articles in Spanish might turn out to be a frustrating experience at first because of the number of new words and expressions. Some of the tips described in this course will help you decipher the meanings of many words without having to look them up in the dictionary. However, there will be times, especially when a word or expression keeps coming up in the text, that you'll need to look it up. When looking up words in a dictionary, it's important

Irregular Verbs in
the Subjunctive

The Subjunctive vs. the Indicative

Verbs Followed by
the Subjunctive

Relative Pronouns
and Clauses

to remember that verbs are listed in the infinitive form, not the conjugated form. Don't always take the first definition you find listed; many words have multiple meanings and functions. You need to decide which one is the best for the context of the sentence. And a very important rule when dealing with two languages is to be extremely suspicious of word-for-word translations. Idiomatic expressions are often completely different across languages (and sound funny when translated literally!), but even "regular" expressions can be constructed in very different ways with very different words. So, don't abuse your dictionary; it is a tool that can provide you with a wealth of information, but it can lead you astray if you use it in the wrong way.

✎ Drive It Home

Silvina always plays the lottery. What would she do if she won the top prize? Make conditional sentences with the clues in parentheses.

1. Silvina (ser más generosa) _____

_____

2. Silvina (viajar mucho) _____

_____

3. Silvina (tener tiempo libre) _____

_____

4. Silvina (comprar un apartamento en la playa) _____

_____

5. Silvina (dar mucho dinero a su familia) _____

_____

6. Silvina (comer en muchos restaurantes) _____

_____

7. Silvina (estudiar otros idiomas) _____

_____

8. Silvina (coleccionar antigüedades) _____

_____

ANSWER KEY

1. Silvina sería más generosa. 2. Silvina viajaría mucho. 3. Silvina tendría tiempo libre. 4. Silvina compraría un apartamento en la playa. 5. Silvina daría mucho dinero a su familia. 6. Silvina comería en muchos restaurantes. 7. Silvina estudiaría otros idiomas. 8. Silvina coleccionaría antigüedades.

How Did You Do?

By now, you should be able to:

☐ Name different types of hobbies and sports
(Still unsure? Jump back to pages 180 and 183.)

☐ Express the probability or possibility that something would happen
(Still unsure? Jump back to page 181.)

☐ Use se to make general statements
(Still unsure? Jump back to page 184.)

Lesson 14: Phrases

By the end of this lesson, you should be able to:

☐ Describe what you enjoy doing in your free time

☐ Identify the subjunctive and when to use it

☐ Talk about a game like soccer

☐ Use the subjunctive to express things or events

Irregular Verbs in
the Subjunctive

The Subjunctive vs. the Indicative

Verbs Followed by
the Subjunctive

Relative Pronouns
and Clauses

Phrase Builder 1

▶ 14A Phrase Builder 1 (CD 9, Track 9)

The following phrases will help you describe what you enjoy doing in your free time.

coleccionar objetos de arte	*to collect pieces of art*
visitar tiendas de antigüedades	*to visit antique shops*
asistir a una subasta	*to attend an auction*
descansar	*to rest*
tener un pasatiempo costoso	*to have an expensive hobby*
pasar el día en la piscina	*to spend the day at the swimming pool*
ser perezoso	*to be lazy*
escuchar música	*to listen to music*
practicar un deporte	*to play sports*
hacer ejercicio	*to exercise*
llevar un diario	*to keep a diary*

⏸

✎ Phrase Practice 1

Match the Spanish phrase on the left with its appropriate English translation on the right.

1. practicar un deporte

2. hacer ejercicio

3. llevar un diario

4. descansar

5. ser perezoso

6. escuchar música

a. *to be lazy*

b. *to listen to music*

c. *to rest*

d. *to keep a diary*

e. *to exercise*

f. *to play sports*

ANSWER KEY
1. f; 2. e; 3. d; 4. c; 5. a; 6. b

Grammar Builder 1
THE SUBJUNCTIVE

▶ 14B Grammar Builder 1 (CD 9, Track 10)

Up to this point, you've been studying ways to express facts related to time (present, past, and future) in what is known as the *indicative mood*. All this means is that you have been learning how to present information in a factual and objective way; you're *indicating* how things are (or how you think they are). However, there are ways of expressing things that aren't necessarily part of the world as it is. These may include things like emotions, persuasion, doubt, denial, and uncertainty. In the next few lessons, we'll be looking at the *subjunctive mood*, a way to express things or events that are not factual or concrete, but rather, hypothetical or subjective. In Spanish, the subjunctive is usually introduced by que. Take a look at these examples.

Espero que mi equipo gane el partido.
I hope my team wins the match.

Ojalá que no llueva hoy.
I hope it doesn't rain today.

Both examples express a hope for something that may or may not turn out to be true or to happen, so the subjunctive is used instead of the indicative. To form the present subjunctive of regular verbs, take the conjugation of the verb in the first person singular (yo) of the present tense, drop the final -o, and add the following endings. Note the use of opposite vowels: -ar verbs use -e endings, and -er and -ir verbs use -a endings.

SUBJUNCTIVE ENDINGS OF REGULAR -AR VERBS	
yo -e	nosotros/as -emos
tú -es	vosotros/as -éis
él/ella/usted -e	ellos/ellas/ustedes -en

Irregular Verbs in
the Subjunctive

The Subjunctive vs. the Indicative

Verbs Followed by
the Subjunctive

Relative Pronouns
and Clauses

SUBJUNCTIVE ENDINGS OF REGULAR -ER/-IR VERBS	
yo -a	nosotros/as -amos
tú -as	vosotros/as -áis
él/ella/usted -a	ellos/ellas/ustedes -an

Let's see how that looks with some example verbs: comprar (*to buy*), comer (*to eat*), and escribir (*to write*).

COMPRAR *(TO BUY)* - SUBJUNCTIVE	
yo compre	nosotros/as compremos
tú compres	vosotros/as compréis
él/ella/usted compre	ellos/ellas/ustedes compren

COMER *(TO EAT)* - SUBJUNCTIVE	
yo coma	nosotros/as comamos
tú comas	vosotros/as comáis
él/ella/usted coma	ellos/ellas/ustedes coman

ESCRIBIR *(TO WRITE)* - SUBJUNCTIVE	
yo escriba	nosotros/as escribamos
tú escribas	vosotros/as escribáis
él/ella/usted escriba	ellos/ellas/ustedes escriban

Verbs with an irregular stem in the yo form keep that stem in all forms of the present subjunctive, such as the following verbs.

tener (yo tengo)	teng-a	*to have*
hacer (yo hago)	hag-a	*to make*
venir (yo vengo)	veng-a	*to come*

salir (yo salgo)	salg-a	*to go out*
poner (yo pongo)	pong-a	*to put*
decir (yo digo)	dig-a	*to say*
traer (yo traigo)	traig-a	*to bring*
conocer (yo conozco)	conozc-a	*to know*

Verbs with a stem change in the present indicative have the same kind of stem change in the present subjunctive. In -ar and -er verbs, the stem change occurs in all persons except nosotros(as) and vosotros(as). On the other hand, -ir verbs undergo the stem change in all persons. Here are three examples.

PENSAR *(TO THINK)* - SUBJUNCTIVE	
yo piense	nosotros/as pensemos
tú pienses	vosotros/as penséis
él/ella/usted piense	ellos/ellas/ustedes piensen

PODER *(TO BE ABLE TO)* - SUBJUNCTIVE	
yo pueda	nosotros/as podamos
tú puedas	vosotros/as podáis
él/ella/usted pueda	ellos/ellas/ustedes puedan

SERVIR *(TO SERVE)* - SUBJUNCTIVE	
yo sirva	nosotros/as sirvamos
tú sirvas	vosotros/as sirváis
él/ella/usted sirva	ellos/ellas/ustedes sirvan

✎ Work Out 1

Give the corresponding subjunctive form of the following verbs.

1. que tú (querer) _____

2. que él (oír) _____

3. que yo (venir) _____

4. que nosotros (salir) _____

5. que ellas (traer) _____

6. que vosotras (comer) _____

7. que ustedes (pedir) _____

8. que él (hablar) _____

9. que usted (partir) _____

10. que ella (sentir) _____

ANSWER KEY
1. que tú quieras; 2. que él oiga; 3. que yo venga; 4. que nosotros salgamos; 5. que ellas traigan;
6. que vosotras comáis; 7. que ustedes pidan; 8. que él hable; 9. que usted parta; 10. que ella sienta

Phrase Builder 2

▶ 14C Phrase Builder 2 (CD 9, Track 11)

The following phrases will help you when talking about a game such as soccer.

ganar un partido	to win a game
perder un partido	to lose a game
llenar un estadio	to fill up a stadium
el número de espectadores	the number of spectators
marcar/hacer/anotar un gol	to score a goal

intercambiar camisetas	to exchange T-shirts
comprar boletos en la taquilla	to buy tickets at the gate
quedar empatados	to be tied
hacer una cola/fila	to stand in line
el medio tiempo	halftime
vitorear a un equipo	to cheer for a team
el campeonato mundial de fútbol	the world soccer championship

✎ Phrase Practice 2

Fill in the blanks in each phrase based on the English translation.

1. _____ un partido *to win a game*

2. _____ un partido *to lose a game*

3. _____ un estadio *to fill up a stadium*

4. _____ camisetas *to exchange T-shirts*

5. _____ una cola/fila *to stand in line*

6. _____ a un equipo *to cheer for a team*

ANSWER KEY

1. ganar; 2. perder; 3. llenar; 4. intercambiar; 5. hacer; 6. vitorear

Irregular Verbs in
the Subjunctive

The Subjunctive vs. the Indicative

Verbs Followed by
the Subjunctive

Relative Pronouns
and Clauses

Grammar Builder 2
USING THE SUBJUNCTIVE

▶ 14D Grammar Builder 2 (CD 9, Track 12)

So, how do you use the subjunctive? Whenever you want to express a request, a
desire, or a demand, or give advice, you will be using the subjunctive mood. Usually,
when the verb in the main clause of the sentence expresses any of these, the verb
that comes after (in the dependent **que** clause) must be in the subjunctive. The
following verbs and phrases are usually followed by another verb in the subjunctive.

aconsejar que ...	*to advise that/to ...*
querer que ...	*to want that/to ...*
desear que ...	*to wish that ...*
pedir que ...	*to request that ...*
insistir que ...	*to insist that ...*
recomendar que ...	*to recommend that ...*
sugerir que ...	*to suggest that ...*
preferir que ...	*to prefer that ...*
prohibir que ...	*to forbid that/to ...*
Es preferible que ...	*It's preferable that ...*
Es mejor que ...	*It's better that ...*
Es necesario que ...	*It's necessary that ...*

Here are a few examples to illustrate how the subjunctive is used.

Quiero que se vaya inmediatamente.
I want him to leave right now.

Te prohíbo que hables con ellos.
I forbid you to talk to them.

Es preferible que nos llame mañana.
It is preferable that you call us tomorrow.

Ella desea que tú vuelvas pronto.
She wishes that you come back soon.

Ustedes sugieren que se cambie la fecha.
You suggest that the date be changed.

Notice that where Spanish uses the subjunctive, English often uses infinitives, such as *I want him to leave now* or *I want you to talk to them*. But English also has a subjunctive, as shown in the last three examples: *that you call us*, *that you come back*, and *that the date be changed* are all examples of the English subjunctive. It may sound stuffy and formal in English, because the subjunctive is dying out in English. But in Spanish, it's alive and well, and it doesn't sound overly formal.

⑪

✎ Work Out 2

Fill in the blanks with the correct form of the verb in the subjunctive mood.

1. **Es mejor que tú** _____ **(venir) más temprano.**

2. **Le recomiendo a usted que** _____ **(traer) los documentos necesarios.**

3. **Yo insisto en que los niños** _____ **(comer) todas sus verduras.**

4. **Nosotros preferimos que ellos** _____ **(salir) de viaje el lunes.**

5. **Te aconsejo que no** _____ **(mirar) tanta televisión.**

6. **Les sugerimos que** _____ **(llamar) antes de venir.**

7. **Te prohíbo que** _____ **(fumar).**

Irregular Verbs in
the Subjunctive

The Subjunctive vs. the Indicative

Verbs Followed by
the Subjunctive

Relative Pronouns
and Clauses

8. **Les pedimos que** _____ **(escribir) una carta.**

ANSWER KEY

1. Es mejor que tú vengas más temprano. 2. Le recomiendo a usted que traiga los documentos necesarios. 3. Yo insisto en que los niños coman todas sus verduras. 4. Nosotros preferimos que ellos salgan de viaje el lunes. 5. Te aconsejo que no mires tanta televisión. 6. Les sugerimos que llamen antes de venir. 7. Te prohíbo que fumes. 8. Les pedimos que escriban una carta.

🔅 Tip!

A good way of learning the subjunctive is to remember that it is always introduced by the word que. When you ask a Spanish speaker how to conjugate a verb in this mood, they will always respond by using que plus the verb. It simply sounds correct and it is an easier way to remember how to conjugate the verbs.

✎ Drive It Home

Use the subjunctive form to tell a friend that you're hoping that these actions happen. Use **Espero que** … (*I hope that* …) to introduce the phrase followed by the **tú** form of the subjunctive.

1. **ganar el partido de fútbol** _____

_____

2. **comprar un coche nuevo** _____

_____

3. **cocinar una cena fantástica** _____

_____

4. **hablar español bien** _____

_____

5. vivir en una casa más grande _____

_____

6. salir a tiempo _____

_____

7. tener vacaciones pronto _____

_____

8. venir a mi casa _____

_____

ANSWER KEY

1. Espero que ganes el partido de fútbol. 2. Espero que compres un coche nuevo. 3. Espero que cocines una cena fantástica. 4. Espero que hables español bien. 5. Espero que vivas en una casa más grande. 6. Espero que salgas a tiempo. 7. Espero que tengas vacaciones pronto. 8. Espero que vengas a mi casa.

How Did You Do?

By now, you should be able to:

☐ Describe what you enjoy doing in your free time
(Still unsure? Jump back to page 189.)

☐ Identify the subjunctive and when to use it
(Still unsure? Jump back to page 190.)

☐ Talk about a game like soccer
(Still unsure? Jump back to page 193.)

☐ Use the subjunctive to express things or events
(Still unsure? Jump back to page 195.)

Irregular Verbs in
the Subjunctive

The Subjunctive vs. the Indicative

Verbs Followed by
the Subjunctive

Relative Pronouns
and Clauses

Lesson 15: Sentences

By the end of this lesson, you should be able to:

☐ Confidently converse about hobbies and sports

☐ Form the subjunctive of some irregular verbs

☐ Identify verbs and expressions that require the use of the subjunctive.

Sentence Builder 1

▶ 15A Sentence Builder 1 (CD 9, Track 13)

Los discos de vinilo tienen su encanto.	*LPs have a certain charm.*
¿Eres un aficionado al fútbol?	*Are you a soccer fan?*
Me gusta el sonido que hace la aguja.	*I like the sound the needle makes.*
Tengo una colección enorme.	*I have a huge collection.*
Lo cual quiere decir que no te gusta mi música.	*Which means you don't like my music.*
Prefiero la música clásica.	*I prefer classical music.*
Tenemos gustos muy diferentes.	*We have very different tastes.*
Es el deporte que menos me gusta.	*It's the sport that I like the least.*
La tecnología nos permite escuchar la música de forma tan clara.	*Technology allows us to listen to music in such a clear way.*

⏸

✎ Sentence Practice 1

Fill in the blanks in each sentence based on the English translation.

1. ¿Eres _____ al fútbol? *Are you a soccer fan?*

2. _____ que hace la aguja. *I like the sound the needle makes.*

3. Lo cual quiere decir que _____.

   Which means you don't like my music.

4. _____ la música clásica. *I prefer classical music.*

5. _____ muy diferentes. *We have very different tastes.*

6. Es el deporte _____. *It's the sport I like the least.*

   ANSWER KEY
   1. un aficionado; 2. Me gusta el sonido; 3. no te gusta mi música; 4. Prefiero; 5. Tenemos gustos;
   6. que menos me gusta

Grammar Builder 1
IRREGULAR VERBS IN THE SUBJUNCTIVE

▶ 15B Grammar Builder 1 (CD 9, Track 14)

A few verbs have an irregular present subjunctive form.

ESTAR *(TO BE)* - SUBJUNCTIVE	
yo esté	nosotros/as estemos
tú estés	vosotros/as estéis
él/ella/usted esté	ellos/ellas/ustedes estén

Irregular Verbs in
the Subjunctive

The Subjunctive vs. the Indicative

Verbs Followed by
the Subjunctive

Relative Pronouns
and Clauses

SER _(TO BE)_ - SUBJUNCTIVE

yo sea	nosotros/as seamos
tú seas	vosotros/as seáis
él/ella/usted sea	ellos/ellas/ustedes sean

SABER _(TO KNOW)_ - SUBJUNCTIVE

yo sepa	nosotros/as sepamos
tú sepas	vosotros/as sepáis
él/ella/usted sepa	ellos/ellas/ustedes sepan

DAR _(TO GIVE)_ - SUBJUNCTIVE

yo dé	nosotros/as demos
tú des	vosotros/as deis
él/ella/usted dé	ellos/ellas/ustedes den

IR _(TO GO)_ - SUBJUNCTIVE

yo vaya	nosotros/as vayamos
tú vayas	vosotros/as vayáis
él/ella/usted vaya	ellos/ellas/ustedes vayan

Es mejor que todos sepan los resultados del examen.
It is better that everyone know the results of the test.

Ella prefiere que estemos en su casa a las ocho.
She prefers us to be at her house at eight. (She wants us to be at her house at eight.)

Te sugiero que seas más puntual.
I suggest you be more punctual.

The present subjunctive of the verb **haber** (*there is/there are*) is **haya**.

Es mejor que haya suficiente comida.
It is better that there be enough food.

Sugiero que haya más invitados.
I suggest there be more guests.

Verbs ending in -**car**, -**gar**, and -**zar** undergo small spelling changes in all persons of the present subjunctive.

BUSCAR *(TO LOOK FOR)* - SUBJUNCTIVE	
yo busque	nosotros/as busquemos
tú busques	vosotros/as busquéis
él/ella/usted busque	ellos/ellas/ustedes busquen

PAGAR *(TO PAY)* - SUBJUNCTIVE	
yo pague	nosotros/as paguemos
tú pagues	vosotros/as paguéis
él/ella/usted pague	ellos/ellas/ustedes paguen

COMENZAR *(TO BEGIN)* - SUBJUNCTIVE	
yo comience	nosotros/as comencemos
tú comiences	vosotros/as comencéis
él/ella/usted comience	ellos/ellas/ustedes comiencen

Irregular Verbs in
the Subjunctive

The Subjunctive vs. the Indicative

Verbs Followed by
the Subjunctive

Relative Pronouns
and Clauses

Te recomiendo que busques tu pasaporte.
I recommend that you look for your passport.

Es mejor que pagues esa cajetilla de cigarrillos.
It is better that you pay for that pack of cigarettes.

Nos sugieren que comencemos de inmediato.
They suggest that we begin immediately.

Ⓘ

🖉 Work Out 1

Fill in the blanks with the correct form of the present subjunctive of the verbs in parentheses.

A mí me gusta coleccionar violines, pero mi esposa me prohíbe que los 1
_____ (poner) en la sala de nuestra casa. Ella prefiere que
2 _____ (ellos/estar) en el sótano. Ella me prohíbe que
3 _____ (yo/comprar) más violines. Insiste en
que 4 _____ (yo/buscar) otra afición. Ella me sugiere que
5 _____ (yo/coleccionar) algo más pequeño y
fácil de guardar. Deseo que nosotros 6 _____ (ganar) la lotería
para comprar una casa muy grande donde pueda poner mis violines. Pero es
mejor que yo 7 _____ (ser) más realista y 8 _____
(comenzar) a buscar otra afición. Voy a sugerirle que 9 _____
(nosotros/ir) al Museo de Historia Natural. Tal vez ella prefiera que 10 _____
_____ (yo/saber) más de fósiles y los empiece a coleccionar.

ANSWER KEY
1. ponga; 2. estén; 3. compre; 4. busque; 5. coleccione; 6. ganemos; 7. sea; 8. comience; 9. vayamos;
10. yo sepa

Sentence Builder 2

▶ 15C Sentence Builder 2 (CD 9, Track 15)

¡Ni lo sueñes!	*Don't even dream about it!*
No nos lo podemos perder.	*We can't miss it.*
¿Quieres ir al partido el sábado?	*Would you like to go to Saturday's game?*
Es mejor que pase por tu apartamento más tarde.	*It is better that I drop by your apartment later on.*
Te apuesto a que el Boca gana.	*I bet you Boca will win.*
El marcador va a ser dos a cero.	*The score will be two to zero.*
¿Quieres que te recoja en tu casa?	*Would you like me to pick you up at your place?*
Tengo unos boletos para el partido.	*I have a few tickets for the game.*
Soy un hincha de ese equipo.	*I'm a fan of that team.*

⏸

✎ Sentence Practice 2

Fill in the blanks in each sentence based on the English translation.

1. ¡_____! *Don't even dream about it!*

2. _____ perder. *We can't miss it.*

3. _____ el Boca gana. *I bet you Boca will win.*

4. _____ va a ser dos a cero. *The score will be two to zero.*

5. Tengo _____ para el partido. *I have a few tickets for the game.*

6. _____ de ese equipo. *I'm a fan of that team.*

ANSWER KEY

1. Ni lo sueñes; 2. No nos lo podemos; 3. Te apuesto a que; 4. El marcador; 5. unos boletos; 6. Soy un hincha

Irregular Verbs in
the Subjunctive

The Subjunctive vs. the Indicative

Verbs Followed by
the Subjunctive

Relative Pronouns
and Clauses

Grammar Builder 2
VERBS FOLLOWED BY THE SUBJUNCTIVE

▶ 15D Grammar Builder 2 (CD 9, Track 16)

The subjunctive mood is also used to express feelings, emotions, and personal perceptions. Here are a few verbs and expressions that require the use of the subjunctive. They're all followed by the word que + the verb in the subjunctive mood (notice that some verbs are reflexive).

sentir que ...	*to regret that ...*
esperar que ...	*to hope that ...*
tener miedo de que ...	*to be afraid that ...*
gustar que ...	*to like (it) that ...*
enfadarse que ...	*to be angry that ...*
alegrarse de que ...	*to be glad that ...*
preocuparse de que ...	*to worry that ...*
sorprenderse que ...	*to be surprised that ...*
molestarse que ...	*to be bothered that ...*
Es una lástima que ...	*It's a pity that ...*
Es triste que ...	*It's sad that ...*
Es bueno que ...	*It's good that ...*

Let's take a look at some examples, and again, notice the different ways that the subjunctive can be translated into English.

Nos enfada que (ellas) lleguen tarde.
We're angry that they arrive late.

Me preocupa que (él) viaje de noche.
It worries me that he travels at night.

Le gusta que lo despierten temprano.
He likes to be woken up early.

Tengo miedo de que (ella) sepa la verdad.
I'm afraid of her learning the truth.

Es una lástima que (ustedes) no estén aquí.
It's a pity that you aren't here.

Notice in the above examples, that subject pronouns (for both the indicative and the subjunctive verbs) are usually omitted. Because most sentences occur in a context, it's easy to know who the subject of each verb is. The subject pronoun is specified only when it's necessary to make the meaning clear.

Ⓘ

✎ Work Out 2
Answer the following questions using the words provided.

1. ¿De qué te alegras? Yo/alegrarse/tú/estar aquí. _____

   _____

2. ¿Qué le preocupa a Martín? Él/preocuparse/no haber/boletos para el cine.

   _____

3. ¿Qué espera usted que ella haga? Yo/esperar/ella/llegar temprano. _____

   _____

4. ¿Qué le sorprende a ella de él? Ella/sorprenderse/él/coleccionar rocas.

   _____

Irregular Verbs in
the Subjunctive

The Subjunctive vs. the Indicative

Verbs Followed by
the Subjunctive

Relative Pronouns
and Clauses

5. ¿Qué temen ellos? Ellos/temer/su equipo/perder/el partido. _____

_____

6. ¿Qué alegra a tus padres? Ellos/alegrarse/yo/llamarlos por teléfono.

_____

7. ¿Qué os molesta de Enrique? Nosotros/molestarse/él/fumar. _____

_____

8. ¿Qué te enfada? Yo/enfadarse/la gente/decir/mentiras. _____

ANSWER KEY

1. Me alegro de que estés aquí. 2. Le preocupa que no haya boletos para el cine. 3. Espero que ella llegue temprano. 4. A ella le sorprende que él coleccione rocas. 5. Ellos temen que su equipo pierda el partido. 6. Les alegra que yo los llame por teléfono. 7. Nos molesta que él fume. 8. Me enfada que la gente diga mentiras.

Tip!

Explore the internet to find more examples of the subjunctive at work. In a search engine, type the phrases que él sea or que ella vaya or any other examples of the subjunctive. Collect three or four sentences and see if you can figure out why the subjunctive is used. What is the speaker conveying? Is it emotion, doubt, uncertainty, desire, etc.? The more examples of the subjunctive you see, the easier it will be for you to master it.

Drive It Home

You have a lot of suggestions for your friend. Use the subjunctive form of the verb to give your recommendation. Start each sentence with Te sugiero que ... (*I suggest that you ...*) followed by the tú form in the subjunctive.

1. ser honesto _____

_____

2. estar a tiempo _____

_____

3. saber otro idioma _____

_____

4. dar tu abrigo _____

_____

5. ir al cine _____

_____

6. pagar con tarjeta de crédito _____

_____

7. comenzar inmediatamente _____

_____

8. buscar los resultados _____

_____

ANSWER KEY

1. Te sugiero que seas honesto. 2. Te sugiero que estés a tiempo. 3. Te sugiero que sepas otro idioma.
4. Te sugiero que des tu abrigo. 5. Te sugiero que vayas al cine. 6. Te sugiero que pagues con tarjeta
de crédito. 7. Te sugiero que comiences inmediatamente. 8. Te sugiero que busques los resultados.

Irregular Verbs in
the Subjunctive

The Subjunctive vs. the Indicative

Verbs Followed by
the Subjunctive

Relative Pronouns
and Clauses

How Did You Do?

By now, you should be able to:

☐ Confidently converse about hobbies and sports
(Still unsure? Jump back to pages 199 and 204.)

☐ Form the subjunctive of some irregular verbs
(Still unsure? Jump back to page 200.)

☐ Identify verbs and expressions that require the use of the subjunctive.
(Still unsure? Jump back to page 205.)

Lesson 16: Conversations

By the end of this lesson, you should be able to:

☐ Identify the difference in using the subjunctive and the indicative

☐ Use relative pronouns to create clauses

Conversation 1

16A Conversation 1 (CD 9, Track 17 - Spanish Only; Track 18 - Spanish and English)

Clarisa is on a date with Manuel. They are getting to know each other and are
talking about each other's interests.

Clarisa: Tengo una colección enorme de discos de vinilo.

Manuel: Es un poco extraño hoy en día en que la tecnología nos permite
             escuchar la música de una forma más clara con los discos
             compactos.

Clarisa:	Para mí, los discos de vinilo tienen su encanto. Me encanta escuchar el sonido que hace la aguja cuando se termina el disco. No sé … me parece que hoy todo tiene que ser tan perfecto, que las cosas pierden su gracia.
Manuel:	¿Y coleccionas toda clase de música?
Clarisa:	No, no toda. Me gusta mucho la música clásica y me encanta el jazz. También tengo discos de los años cicuenta y sesenta.
Manuel:	Lo cual quiere decir que no te gusta la música más moderna.
Clarisa:	No, no mucho … Y a ti, ¿qué música te gusta?
Manuel:	Bueno, pues yo tengo una colección de guitarras eléctricas.
Clarisa:	Así que te gusta el "heavy metal".
Manuel:	Sí, así es. Tenemos gustos muy diferentes en cuanto a música.
Clarisa:	No me dirás que también eres un aficionado al fútbol, porque es el deporte que menos me gusta.
Manuel:	Mmm … ¿Te gustaría otro martini?

Clarisa:	*I have an enormous collection of LPs.*
Manuel:	*That's a bit strange nowadays when technology allows us to listen to music in such a clear way with CDs.*
Clarisa:	*LPs have a certain charm for me. I love to hear the sound the needle makes once the record is over. I don't know … I think that today, everything has to be so perfect that things lose their appeal.*
Manuel:	*Do you collect all kinds of music?*
Clarisa:	*No, not all. I like classical music very much and I love jazz. I also have records from the fifties and sixties.*
Manuel:	*So, that means you don't like more modern music.*
Clarisa:	*No, not really … And you, what kind of music do you like?*
Manuel:	*I have a collection of electric guitars.*
Clarisa:	*So you like heavy metal.*
Manuel:	*Yes, that's right. We have very different tastes regarding music.*

Irregular Verbs in
the Subjunctive

The Subjunctive vs. the Indicative

Verbs Followed by
the Subjunctive

Relative Pronouns
and Clauses

Clarisa: *Don't tell me that you're a soccer fan, because it's the sport I like the least.*

Manuel: *Mmm ... Would you like another martini?*

🌐 Culture Note

Soccer, or fútbol in Spanish, is a multibillion-dollar business in Latin America, Spain and throughout the world, and it moves millions of fans to follow their teams wherever they go. Brazil, Argentina, and Uruguay are the Latin American countries with the longest soccer traditions. Regardless of the political instability of some countries and the deep economic and social differences that exist, soccer has the power to bring people closer together like no other sport or event.

When you talk about fútbol, you are talking about some of the greatest athletes in the world. Players such as Pelé (Edson Arantes do Nascimento), also known as the King of Soccer in Brazil, the country's top goal scorer; Diego Armando Maradona, Argentina's greatest soccer player and perhaps one of the most controversial; Brazilians Ronaldo, Ronaldinho, and Kaká; young Spanish stars from the 2010 World Cup winning squad such as David Villa, Xabi Alonso, and Cesc Fàbregas; and others such as the Colombian goalkeeper Huiguita and el Pibe Valderrama are every kid's role model and every adult's hero. Soccer is played on neighborhood streets, parks, and beaches all over Latin America. It's a sport that knows no social class, race, or age. It can bring people together in a way that no other sport can, filling stadiums the size of the Estadio Maracana in Rio de Janeiro, which, in the 1950 World Championship, held 199,548 fans to see the final between Uruguay and Brazil. To learn more about fútbol, and to practice your Spanish, check out *es.fifa.com*.

✎ Conversation Practice 1

Fill in the blanks below with the appropriate word based on the English translations and the dialogue above.

1. Para mí, los discos de vinilo_____.

   LPs have a certain charm for me.

2. No sé ... me parece que hoy todo _____tan perfecto,

   que las cosas pierden su gracia. *I don't know ... I think that today, everything has*

   to be so perfect that things lose their appeal.

3. Lo cual _____ que no te gusta la música más moderna.

   So, that means you don't like more modern music.

4. Tenemos _____ muy diferentes en cuanto a música.

   We have very different tastes regarding music.

5. No me dirás que también eres _____al fútbol, porque es el

   deporte que menos me gusta. *Don't tell me that you're a soccer fan, because it's*

   the sport I like the least.

   ANSWER KEY
   1. tienen su encanto; 2. tiene que ser; 3. quiere decir; 4. gustos; 5. un aficionado

Grammar Builder 1
THE SUBJUNCTIVE VS. THE INDICATIVE

▶ 16B Grammar Builder 1 (CD 9, Track 19)

The subjunctive is also used to express disbelief, doubt, denial, and uncertainty.

Irregular Verbs in
the Subjunctive

The Subjunctive vs. the Indicative

Verbs Followed by
the Subjunctive

Relative Pronouns
and Clauses

Dudo que nuestro equipo gane.
I doubt our team will win.

Es posible que me trasladen a Nueva York.
It's possible that I'll be transferred to New York.

However, if the verb in the main clause expresses certainty, belief, or affirmation, the indicative is used.

Creo que nuestro equipo va a ganar.
I believe our team will win.

Es verdad que me han trasladado a Nueva York.
It's true that I've been transferred to New York.

The following verbs and phrases are commonly used to express disbelief, doubt, denial, and uncertainty.

no creer que …	*not to believe that …*
no pensar que …	*not to think that …*
Es posible que …	*It is possible that …*
dudar que …	*to doubt that …*
No es verdad que …	*It is not true that …*
No es cierto que …	*It is not true that …*
Es imposible que …	*It is impossible that …*
No hay nada que …	*There's nothing that …*
No hay nadie que …	*There's no one who…*
No hay ningún/ninguna … que …	*There's no (thing) that…/There's no (person) who…*
negar que …	*to deny that …*

Ⅱ

✎ Work Out 1

Change the following sentences using the clues given.

Example: Creo que van a comprar un apartamento en Lima. (yo no creer que)
No creo que vayan a comprar un apartamento en Lima.

1. Es cierto que Ana está embarazada. (No es cierto que) _____

   _____

2. Vamos a sacar una buena nota en el examen. (Es posible que) _____

   _____

3. Es seguro que el equipo está retrasado. (Es posible que) _____

   _____

4. Es verdad que en esa compañía pagan un sueldo muy alto. (No es verdad que)

   _____

5. Ellos están buscando trabajo. (yo dudar) _____

   _____

6. Estoy seguro de que va a llover. (yo no creer) _____

   _____

7. Hay otro deporte más exigente que el fútbol. (nosotros dudar) _____

   _____

8. Todo en esta vida es difícil. (yo negar) _____

   _____

ANSWER KEY

1. No es cierto que Ana esté embarazada. 2. Es posible que saquemos una buena nota en el examen. 3. Es posible que el equipo esté retrasado. 4. No es verdad que en esa compañía paguen un sueldo muy

Irregular Verbs in
the Subjunctive

The Subjunctive vs. the Indicative

Verbs Followed by
the Subjunctive

Relative Pronouns
and Clauses

alto. 5. Dudo que ellos estén buscando trabajo. 6. No creo que vaya a llover. 7. Nosotros dudamos que haya otro deporte más exigente que el fútbol. 8. Niego que todo en esta vida sea difícil.

 Conversation 2

16C Conversation 2 (CD 9, Track 20 - Spanish Only; Track 21 - Spanish and English)

Carlos and Manuel are making plans for the weekend and are talking about their favorite sport.

Carlos: Oye, Manuel, ¿quieres ir al partido del sábado?

Manuel: ¡Me encantaría! ¿Tienes boletos?

Carlos: Sí, precisamente tengo dos boletos para el partido entre Boca Juniors y el Atlético River Plate.

Manuel: Bueno, pues es un partido que no nos lo podemos perder. Tú sabes que yo soy un hincha del Boca. ¿A qué hora juegan?

Carlos: El partido empieza a las siete de la noche. ¿Quieres que te recoja en tu casa a eso de las cinco y media?

Manuel: No, creo que estaré en la oficina trabajando. Es mejor que me pase por tu apartamento cuando termine.

Carlos: Está bien. Y ... ¿cómo van a ser nuestras apuestas esta vez?

Manuel: Te apuesto a que el Boca gana uno a cero en los primeros treinta minutos de juego.

Carlos: ¡Ni lo sueñes! El River Plate está jugando muy bien y creo que va a ganar. Te apuesto a que el marcador va a ser dos a cero. Además, tu equipo tiene un portero pésimo.

Manuel: Bueno, ya veremos. Nosotros vamos a llegar a la Copa Libertadores. Hasta el sábado.

Carlos: *Hey, Manuel, would you like to go to the soccer game on Saturday?*

Manuel: *I'd love to! Do you have tickets?*

Carlos: *Yes, I have two tickets for the game between Boca Juniors and Atlético River Plate.*

Manuel:	Well, it's a game we can't miss. You know I'm a big fan of Boca. What time do they play?
Carlos:	The game starts at seven in the evening. Do you want me to pick you up at your place at around five thirty?
Manuel:	No, I think I'll be at work. I'll drop by your apartment when I'm done.
Carlos:	Okay. So what are our bets going to be this time?
Manuel:	I bet you Boca will win one to nothing in the first thirty minutes of the game.
Carlos:	In your dreams! River Plate is playing very well and I think they'll win. I bet you the score will be two to zero. Plus, your team has a terrible goalkeeper.
Manuel:	We'll see. We'll make it to the Copa Libertadores. See you Saturday.

⊕ Culture Note

The soccer club Atlético Boca Juniors is one of the most popular and successful in Argentina. It's located in La Boca, a neighborhood in Buenos Aires. This club, along with its rival, Atlético River Plate, can fill up entire stadiums in Argentina. The Boca Juniors have won several soccer cups, including the Intercontinental Cup in 1978, 2000, and 2003; and the Copa Libertadores in 1977, 1978, 2000, 2001, 2003, and 2007. To read more about both clubs, check out **www. bocajuniors.com.ar** and **www.cariverplate.com.ar**.

✎ Conversation Practice 2

Fill in the blanks below with the appropriate word based on the English translations and the dialogue above.

1. Bueno, pues es un partido que no _____ perder.

   Well, it's a game we can't miss.

Irregular Verbs in
the Subjunctive

The Subjunctive vs. the Indicative

Verbs Followed by
the Subjunctive

Relative Pronouns
and Clauses

2. El partido _____ a las siete de la noche.

The game starts at seven in the evening.

3. ¿Quieres que te _____ en tu casa a eso de las cinco y media?

Do you want me to pick you up at your place at around five thirty?

4. Te apuesto a que el Boca _____ en los primeros

treinta minutos de juego. *I bet you Boca will win one to nothing in the first thirty*

minutes of the game.

5. Además, tu equipo tiene _____ pésimo.

Plus, your team has a terrible goalkeeper.

ANSWER KEY
1. nos lo podemos; 2. empieza; 3. recoja; 4. gana uno a cero; 5. un portero

Grammar Builder 2
RELATIVE PRONOUNS AND CLAUSES

▶ 16D Grammar Builder 2 (CD 9, Track 22)

Relative pronouns, such as *that*, *which*, and *who(m)*, are used to refer back to a previous noun in a sentence. They introduce relative clauses, which are mini-sentences that give more information about that previous noun: *The book that I read is very interesting. The team that I like the most just won.* In many cases in English, we can even omit relative pronouns like *who* and *that*. In Spanish, however, relative pronouns cannot be left out, and there is a wider variety to choose from.

The two most common relative pronouns are **que** and **quien**. **Que** is used to refer to both people and things. **Quien** (plural form **quienes**) is used only to refer to people, and it's preceded by the prepositions **a**, **con**, **para**, or **de**.

El equipo que acaba de ganar es mi favorito.
The team that has just won is my favorite.

El jugador con quien hablaste es muy famoso.
The player you talked to is very famous.

El hombre que está afuera es su esposo.
The man who's outside is her husband.

Las mujeres a quienes entrevistaste son atletas profesionales.
The women you interviewed are professional athletes.

When the relative pronoun must specify one among several previously mentioned nouns, a compound form using the definite article (el, la, los, las) + que or cual(es) is used. They are generally used after prepositions, such as en, sin, por, and para. Notice that the definite article agrees in number and gender with the noun it refers to.

No es el auto en el que viajé la semana pasada.
It's not the car that I traveled in last week. (… in which I traveled last week.)

Es la calle por la que caminamos ayer.
It's the street we walked along yesterday. (… along which we walked yesterday.)

Son los sueños en los cuales siempre piensas.
They are the dreams that you always think of. (… in which you always think.)

Es la mujer de la cual está enamorado.
She's the woman he's in love with. (… with whom he's in love.)

Cuyo (cuya, cuyos, cuyas) is also a relative pronoun but looks more like an adjective, because it agrees in gender and number with the person or thing possessed, not with the person or thing it refers to.

Irregular Verbs in
the Subjunctive

The Subjunctive vs. the Indicative

Verbs Followed by
the Subjunctive

Relative Pronouns
and Clauses

El autor, cuyo nombre no recuerdo, vivió en esta ciudad.
The author, whose name I don't remember, lived in this city.

Los niños, cuyas manos están sucias, no quieren lavarse.
The children, whose hands are dirty, don't want to wash up.

⏸

✎ Work Out 2

Choose the relative pronoun that best completes the sentence.

1. Los pasajes _____ compré son solamente de ida. (los cuales, que, los que)

2. La cantante, _____ fama es mundial, viene a finales de septiembre.
   (que, quien, cuya)

3. El apartamento en _____ quiero vivir está en el último piso de ese
   edificio. (la cual, el cual, los cuales)

4. Las mujeres _____ nos visitaron eran espías. (quienes, que, cuyas)

5. Los chicos, _____ nombres desconozco, son los hijos de nuestra vecina.
   (cuyos, que, quienes)

6. Esos son los documentos con _____ te debes presentar ante
   el juez. (quienes, los cuales, cuyos)

7. El hombre con _____ nos encontramos era el esposo de Maura.
   (los cuales, quienes, quien)

8. Las estampillas _____ compré son para mi colección. (la cual, quien, que)

ANSWER KEY
1. que; 2. cuya; 3. el cual; 4. que; 5. cuyos; 6. los cuales; 7. quien; 8. que

🌐 Culture Note

One of the most prestigious soccer trophies is without doubt **La Copa Libertadores de América**. It's an international cup organized by **CONMEBOL** (**Confederación Sudaméricana de Fútbol**) and is played for by the leading clubs in South America. Teams from Argentina have been the most successful in the competition, earning a total of twenty-two trophies over the course of the **Copa**'s history. A Brazilian team has won the trophy fourteen times. For more information, visit www.conmebol.com.

The **Copa América** is another important national competition in South America. It's played every two years. Twelve countries participate: Argentina, Brazil, Bolivia, Chile, Colombia, Ecuador, Paraguay, Peru, Uruguay, and Venezuela, along with two additional guests from other soccer confederations.

✎ Drive It Home

Change each sentence from the indicative to the subjunctive. Start each sentence by saying **Yo no creo que él ...** (*I don't think that he ...*)

1. **Creo que él compra un apartamento nuevo.** _____

   _____

2. **Creo que él vive en Miami.** _____

   _____

3. **Creo que él habla inglés.** _____

   _____

4. **Creo que él estudia otros idiomas.** _____

   _____

Irregular Verbs in
the Subjunctive

The Subjunctive vs. the Indicative

Verbs Followed by
the Subjunctive

Relative Pronouns
and Clauses

5. Creo que él va a Nueva York. _____

_____

6. Creo que él dice la verdad. _____

_____

7. Creo que él saca buenas notas en los exámenes. _____

_____

8. Creo que él viene a visitarnos. _____

_____

ANSWER KEY

1. Yo no creo que él compre un apartamento nuevo. 2. Yo no creo que él viva en Miami. 3. Yo no creo que él hable inglés. 4. Yo no creo que él estudie otros idiomas. 5. Yo no creo que él vaya a Nueva York. 6. Yo no creo que él diga la verdad. 7. Yo no creo que él saque buenas notas en los exámenes. 8. Yo no creo que él venga a visitarnos.

How Did You Do?

By now, you should be able to:

☐ Identify the difference in using the subjunctive and the indicative.
(Still unsure? Jump back to page 212.)

☐ Use relative pronouns to create clauses
(Still unsure? Jump back to page 217.)

Don't forget to practice and reinforce what you've learned by visiting **www.livinglanguage.com/ languagelab** for flashcards, games, and quizzes for Unit 4!

Unit 4 Essentials

Vocabulary Essentials

LEISURE VOCABULARY

	hobby
	fan
	hobby
	free time
	to collect
	craft
	photography
	music
	painting
	dancing
	stamp collecting
	antiques
	cooking
	sewing
	reading

[Pg. 180]

LEISURE VERBS

	to collect pieces of art
	to visit antique shops

	to attend an auction
	to rest
	to have an expensive hobby
	to spend the day at the swimming pool
	to be lazy
	to listen to music
	to play sports
	to do exercise
	to keep a diary

[Pg. 189]

LEISURE EXPRESSIONS

	LPs have a certain charm.
	Are you a soccer fan?
	I like the sound the needle makes.
	I have a huge collection.
	Which means you don't like my music.
	I prefer classical music.
	We have very different tastes.
	It's the sport I like the least.
	Technology allows us to listen to music in such a clear way.

[Pg. 199]

SPORTS VOCABULARY

	sport
	athlete
	person who plays sports
	player
	biking, cycling
	soccer
	baseball
	swimming
	diving
	horseback riding
	hunting
	basketball
	chess

[Pg. 183]

SPORTS VERBS

	to win a game
	to lose a game
	to fill up a stadium
	to score a goal
	to exchange T-shirts
	to buy tickets at the gate
	to be tied
	to stand in line
	to cheer for a team

[Pg. 193]

SPORTS EXPRESSIONS

	Don't even dream about it!
	We can't miss it.
	Would you like to go to Saturday's game?
	It is better that I drop by your apartment later on.
	I bet you Boca will win.
	The score will be two to zero.
	Would you like me to pick you up at your place?
	I have a few tickets for the game.
	I'm a fan of that team.

[Pg. 204]

Grammar Essentials

IMPERSONAL SE

The impersonal se is used in front of verbs to make general statements referring to *people in general* or *one*.

Use se with either the third person singular or the third person plural of the verb.

RELATIVE PRONOUNS

Relative pronouns are used to refer back to a previous noun in a sentence. They introduce relative clauses, which are mini-sentences that give more information about that previous noun. In Spanish, relative pronouns cannot be omitted.

que *(that, which, who, whom)*	Refers to people and things
quien/quienes *(that, which, who, whom)*	Refers to people, usually preceded by the prepositions a, con, para, or de

cuyo/cuya/cuyos/cuyas (whose)	agrees in gender and number with the person or thing possessed, not with the person or thing it refers to

When the relative pronoun must specify one among several previously mentioned nouns, a compound form using the definite article (el, la, los, las) + que or cual(es) is used, generally after prepositions, such as en, sin, por, and para.

THE CONDITIONAL

The present conditional is used to express the probability or possibility that something would happen, depending on specific circumstances. To form the conditional, simply add the following endings to the infinitive form of any verb.

CONDITIONAL ENDINGS	
yo -ía	nosotros/as -íamos
tú -ías	vosotros/as -íais
él/ella/usted -ía	ellos/ellas/ustedes -ían

IRREGULAR CONDITIONAL VERB STEMS

saber	sabr-ía	to know
tener	tendr-ía	to have
salir	saldr-ía	to go out
poder	podr-ía	to be able to
hacer	har-ía	to make
decir	dir-ía	to say
haber	habr-ía	there is/there are
querer	querr-ía	to want
venir	vendr-ía	to come

THE SUBJUNCTIVE

The subjunctive mood expresses things or events that are not factual or concrete, but rather, hypothetical or subjective.

The subjunctive is usually introduced by que.

To form the present subjunctive of regular verbs, take the conjugation of the verb in the first person singular (yo) of the present tense, drop the final -o, and add the following endings.

SUBJUNCTIVE ENDINGS OF REGULAR -AR VERBS	
yo -e	nosotros/as -emos
tú -es	vosotros/as -éis
él/ella/usted -e	ellos/ellas/ustedes -en

SUBJUNCTIVE ENDINGS OF REGULAR -ER/-IR VERBS	
yo -a	nosotros/as -amos
tú -as	vosotros/as -áis
él/ella/usted -a	ellos/ellas/ustedes -an

EXPRESSIONS THAT REQUIRE THE SUBJUNCTIVE

Es preferible que …	It's preferable that …
Es mejor que …	It's better that …
Es necesario que …	It's necessary that …
Es posible que …	It is possible that …
No es verdad que …	It is not true that …
No es cierto que …	It is not true that …
Es imposible que …	It is impossible that …
No hay nada que …	There's nothing that …
No hay nadie que …	There's no one who that …
No hay ningún/ninguna … que …	There's no … that/who …

Es una lástima que ...	It's a pity that ...
Es triste que ...	It's sad that ...
Es bueno que ...	It's good that ...

VERBS THAT REQUIRE THE SUBJUNCTIVE

aconsejar que ...	to advise that/to ...
alegrarse de que ...	to be glad that ...
desear que ...	to wish that ...
dudar que ...	to doubt that ...
enfadarse que ...	to be angry that ...
esperar que ...	to hope that ...
gustar que ...	to like (it) that ...
insistir en que ...	to insist that ...
molestarse que ...	to be bothered that ...
negar que ...	to deny that ...
no creer que ...	not to believe that ...
no pensar que ...	not to think that ...
pedir que ...	to request that ...
preferir que ...	to prefer that ...
preocuparse de que ...	to worry that ...
prohibir que ...	to forbid that/to ...
querer que ...	to want that/to ...
recomendar que ...	to recommend that ...
sentir que ...	to regret that ...
sorprenderse de que ...	to be surprised that ...
sugerir que ...	to suggest that ...
tener miedo de que ...	to be afraid that ...

VERBS

ABRIR *(TO OPEN)* - CONDITIONAL

yo abriría	nosotros/as abriríamos
tú abrirías	vosotros/as abriríais
él/ella/usted abriría	ellos/ellas/ustedes abrirían

BUSCAR *(TO LOOK FOR)* - SUBJUNCTIVE

yo busque	nosotros/as busquemos
tú busques	vosotros/as busquéis
él/ella/usted busque	ellos/ellas/ustedes busquen

COMENZAR *(TO BEGIN)* - SUBJUNCTIVE

yo comience	nosotros/as comencemos
tú comiences	vosotros/as comencéis
él/ella/usted comience	ellos/ellas/ustedes comiencen

COMER *(TO EAT)* - SUBJUNCTIVE

yo coma	nosotros/as comamos
tú comas	vosotros/as comáis
él/ella/usted coma	ellos/ellas/ustedes coman

COMPRAR *(TO BUY)* - SUBJUNCTIVE

yo compre	nosotros/as compremos
tú compres	vosotros/as compréis
él/ella/usted compre	ellos/ellas/ustedes compren

DAR *(TO GIVE)* - SUBJUNCTIVE

yo dé	nosotros/as demos
tú des	vosotros/as deis
él/ella/usted dé	ellos/ellas/ustedes den

ESTAR *(TO BE)* - SUBJUNCTIVE

yo esté	nosotros/as estemos
tú estés	vosotros/as estéis
él/ella/usted esté	ellos/ellas/ustedes estén

HABLAR *(TO TALK)* - CONDITIONAL

yo hablaría	nosotros/as hablaríamos
tú hablarías	vosotros/as hablaríais
él/ella/usted hablaría	ellos/ellas/ustedes hablarían

IR *(TO GO)* - SUBJUNCTIVE

yo vaya	nosotros/as vayamos
tú vayas	vosotros/as vayáis
él/ella/usted vaya	ellos/ellas/ustedes vayan

PAGAR *(TO PAY)* - SUBJUNCTIVE

yo pague	nosotros/as paguemos
tú pagues	vosotros/as paguéis
él/ella/usted pague	ellos/ellas/ustedes paguen

PENSAR *(TO THINK)* - SUBJUNCTIVE

yo piense	nosotros/as pensemos
tú pienses	vosotros/as penséis
él/ella/usted piense	ellos/ellas/ustedes piensen

PODER *(TO BE ABLE TO)* - SUBJUNCTIVE

yo pueda	nosotros/as podamos
tú puedas	vosotros/as podáis
él/ella/usted pueda	ellos/ellas/ustedes puedan

Advanced Spanish

SABER *(TO KNOW)* - SUBJUNCTIVE

yo sepa	nosotros/as sepamos
tú sepas	vosotros/as sepáis
él/ella/usted sepa	ellos/ellas/ustedes sepan

SER *(TO BE)* - CONDITIONAL

yo sería	nosotros/as seríamos
tú serías	vosotros/as seríais
él/ella/usted sería	ellos/ellas/ustedes serían

SER *(TO BE)* - SUBJUNCTIVE

yo sea	nosotros/as seamos
tú seas	vosotros/as seáis
él/ella/usted sea	ellos/ellas/ustedes sean

SERVIR *(TO SERVE)* - SUBJUNCTIVE

yo sirva	nosotros/as sirvamos
tú sirvas	vosotros/as sirváis
él/ella/usted sirva	ellos/ellas/ustedes sirvan

Unit 4 Quiz

A. Give the corresponding subjunctive form of the verb in parentheses.

1. Te recomiendo que (tú buscar) tu pasaporte pronto. _____

   _____

2. Es posible que (ellos pasar) mucho tiempo buscándolo. _____

   _____

3. Me sorprende que (ella no encontrar) las llaves. _____

   _____

4. Te aconsejo que (tú hacer) fila. _____

   _____

5. Me molesta que (ellos fumar). _____

   _____

6. Espero que (ustedes ir) al aeropuerto. _____

   _____

7. Es mejor que (ellos tener) más cuidado con sus bicicletas. _____

   _____

8. Es preferible que (nosotros visitar) a la familia mañana. _____

   _____

B. Match the column on the left with the English word on the right.

1. perder un partido		a. *swimming*	
2. quedar empatados		b. *to be tied*	
3. descansar		c. *chess*	
4. la natación		d. *to rest*	
5. la caza		e. *hobby*	
6. el ajedrez		f. *to lose a game*	
7. el pasatiempo		g. *reading*	
8. la lectura		h. *hunting*	

C. Determine whether each verb should be in the indicative or subjunctive form. Then conjugate each verb in the blanks below.

1. Yo no _____ (creer) que tú _____ (llegar) a tiempo.

2. Es posible que él te _____ su plato favorito. (servir)

3. Nosotros _____ (esperar) que ella _____ (asistir) a la subasta.

4. Ojalá que ellos _____ a tiempo. (llegar)

5. Él me _____ (aconsejar) que yo _____ (ir) al estadio temprano.

6. Ella _____ (desear) que usted _____ (comer) toda la comida.

7. Ellos _____ (sugerir) que nosotros _____ (pagar) con tarjeta de crédito.

8. Es posible que ellos _____ el campeonato mundial. (perder)

D. Select the correct term from each pair:

1. Paquito es _____ a los deportes. (afición/aficionado)

2. La música, la pintura y _____ son mis formas de arte favoritas.

   (el baile/la cocina)

3. Cuando tengo _____ voy a comprar antigüedades.

   (la costura/tiempo libre)

4. Yo _____ una computadora nueva pero no tengo dinero.

   (compraría/compro)

5. Me gusta mucho el agua, por eso prefiero _____ y la natación.

   (el buceo/la equitación)

6. Mi _____ favorito es el fútbol. (deporte/deportista)

7. El equipo ganó el partido porque _____ un gol más.

   (intercambió/marcó)

8. Voy ahora a comprar los boletos en _____ .

   (la camiseta/la taquilla)

How Did You Do?

Give yourself a point for every correct answer, then use the following key to determine whether or not you're ready to move on:

0–7 points: It's probably best to go back and study the lessons again to make sure you understood everything completely. Take your time; it's not a race! Make sure you spend time reviewing vocabulary with the flashcards and reading through each grammar note carefully.

8–16 points: If the questions you missed were in sections A or B, you may want to review the vocabulary again; if you missed answers mostly in sections C or D, check the unit essentials to make sure you have your conjugations and other grammar basics down.

17–20 points: Great! Your Spanish has come a long way! Even though you've reached the end of this course, there's no reason to stop learning.

 **points**

Consider some of these activities to keep your Spanish fresh, and to continue learning.

- ☐ Watch Spanish language movies.
- ☐ Download (legally!) a few Spanish songs and pay attention to the lyrics or look up the lyrics online to read along.
- ☐ Bookmark an online Spanish language newspaper or magazine. Read a little bit every day.
- ☐ Buy a book in Spanish and try to read it every day.
- ☐ Check out chatrooms or other online communities in Spanish.
- ☐ Remember to visit **www.livinglanguage.com/languagelab** for further practice, and return to this book to review any time you want.
- ☐ Use your imagination! You can tailor your Spanish exposure to your interests— food, music, theater, music, sports: the path is up to you. Enjoy, and buena suerte!

Pronunciation Guide

If you've ever had trouble with English spelling, or if you've ever come across an unfamiliar word and had no idea how to pronounce it, you'll be happy to know that neither of these things is likely to be an issue in Spanish. Spanish spelling is phonetic, meaning that things are pronounced the way they're written. The rules for stress—which SYL-la-ble gets the EM-pha-sis—are very regular in Spanish, and any irregularities are marked in spelling with an accent mark. We'll cover all of that little by little, but let's get started with an overview of Spanish pronunciation.

1. VOWELS

Each vowel in Spanish is pronounced clearly and distinctly, and each vowel has one and only one pronunciation. A vowel may be written with an accent, as in sí or América, but this never changes the pronunciation of that vowel. It may mark stress, as in América, or it may only serve to distinguish between two words, as in sí (*yes*) and si (*if*). Let's look at each vowel, starting with simple vowels.

a	like *a* in *father*	a, amigo, la, las, pan, habla, Santiago
e	like *ay* in *day*, but cut off before the *ee*	él, de, en, padre, tren, este, Mercedes
i	like *i* in *police*	mí, amiga, hiciste, cinco, Chile, Sevilla
o	like *o* in *no*, but cut off before the *oo*	no, dos, hombre, costar, ocho, teléfono, Colombia
u	like *u* in *rule*	uno, tú, mucho, azúcar, Honduras, puro

Vowels can also appear in pairs, which are called diphthongs. A diphthong is usually a combination of a weaker vowel (i or u) and a more prominent one.

| ai, ay | like *i* in *bide* | aire, hay, traigo, ¡ay! |

au	like *ou* in *house*	restaurante, autobús, automóvil, Mauricio
ei, ey	like *ay* in *day*	seis, ley, treinta, rey
ia, ya	like *ya* in *yard*	gracias, comercial, estudiar, ya
ie, ye	like *ye* in *yet*	pie, quiero, tiene, yerba, abyecto
io, yo	like *yo* in *yoga*	yo, acción, despacio, estudio
iu, yu	like *u* in *united*	ciudad, yuca, yugo, yunta
oi, oy	like *oy* in *toy*	estoy, hoy, oiga, voy
ua	like *wa* in *want*	cuatro, Juan, ¿cuál?, ¿cuánto?
ue	like *we* in *west*	nueve, fuego, puerta, cuesta, bueno
uo	like *wo* in *woe*	continuo, antiguo, mutuo, superfluo
ui, uy	like *we* in *week*	muy, ruido, cuidado, huir

2. CONSONANTS

b	like *b* in *boy* at the beginning of a word	bueno, brazo, bajo, barca, bocadillo
b	between vowels for some speakers, as above, but the lips don't touch	Cuba, haber, beber, cobayo, deber, ubicar
c	like *k* in *kite* before consonants, a, o, and u	Cristóbal, cosa, casa, cuánto, cuál, truco

c	like *s* in *sea* before e and i	cerca, servicio, cierto, fácil, posición
ch	like *ch* in *choose*	charlar, chico, muchacho, ocho, mucho
d	at the beginning of a word or after n, like *d* in *day*, but with the tongue touching the back of the upper teeth	día, despegar, durante, cuándo, donde, mando
d	between vowels, like *th* in *thin*	media, nada, todo, poder, freiduría, prometido
f	like *f* in *father*	familia, Francisco, Federico, formulario
g	like *g* in *go* before consonants, a, o, and u	grande, Gloria, gustar, gusano, goloso, ganar, vengo
g	like the strong *h* in *hope* before e or i	general, Gibraltar, girar, rígido, urgente
gü	like *gw* in *Gwen*	vergüenza, lengüeta, cigüeña
h	silent	hablo, hay, hubo, ahora, hombre, deshonroso
j	like the strong *h* in *hope*	julio, jabón, mejor, José, tarjeta, jefe, trujar
ll	like *y* in *yes*	llamo, pollo, llama, llover, allí, llaves, trulla
m	like *m* in *met*	mismo, Marco, mano, Manuel, pluma, mandar

n	like *n* in *not*	nunca, no, Nicaragua, Argentina, nombre
ñ	like *ni* in *onion*	español, mañana, muñeca, ñame, gañir
p	like *p* in *pear*	para, pueblo, postre, Panamá, Perú
qu	like *k* in *kite*	que, querer, paquete, saquen, quemar, quizás
r	at the beginning of a word, a trilled sound made with the tongue against the ridge behind the upper teeth	rico, rubio, Ramón, Rosa, rincón, red, risa
r	otherwise like the tapped *d* in *ladder*	América, pero, quisiera, aire, libre, brazo, caro
rr	like word-initial r, a trilled sound made with the tongue against the ridge behind the upper teeth	perro, carro, tierra, horror, irritar, terrible
s	like *s* in *see* (never like *z* in *zone*)	casa, sucio, San Salvador, soltero, vasto, rosa
t	like *t* in *take*, but with the tongue touching the back of the upper teeth	tocar, fruta, tú, teclado, traje, tener
v	like *b* in *boy* at the beginning of a word	vaso, veinte, vivir, vivo, veramente
y	like *y* in *yes*; on its own, like *ee* in *teen*	ayer, ayudo, Bayamo, poyo

z	like *s* in *see*	zona, diez, luz, marzo, azul, azúcar

3. STRESS

There are three simple rules to keep in mind when it comes to stress. First, if a word ends in any consonant other than -n or -s, the last syllable receives the stress.

cuidad, capaz, notabilidad, navegar, familiar, refrigerador

Second, if a word ends in a vowel or in -n or -s, the penultimate (second-to-last) syllable receives the stress.

amigo, hablan, derechos, cubierto, portorriqueño, examen, libros

Note that diphthongs with the weak vowels i or u count as one syllable, so the stress will regularly fall before them.

academia, continuo, manubrio, sanitario, justicia

Combinations with two strong vowels count as two syllables.

tarea, menudeo, banqueteo, barbacoa

Any time stress doesn't follow these rules, an accent is used.

inglés, teléfono, tomó, práctico, drogaría, todavía, título, farmacéutico, petróleo, revés, apagón

4. REGIONAL SPANISH PRONUNCIATION

The Spanish pronunciation that you'll learn in this course is standard Latin American Spanish. There are certainly some local differences in pronunciation that you will probably come across, the most commonly known being the difference between Latin American and European Spanish. The major difference in pronunciation is that the sound *th*, as in *thin*, is much more common in Spain. In Latin America, this sound is typically only found in *d* when it comes between vowels.

media, nada, todo, poder, puedo

These words are pronounced with a *th* in Spain, too. But in Spain, c before i or e and z is also pronounced like *th* in *thin*.

cerca, servicio, cierto, fácil, docena, diez, voz, luz, marzo, azul, razón

There are some noticeable differences in local varieties of Spanish found in Latin America and Spain, as well. You don't need to worry about imitating these differences; the standard pronunciation you'll learn in this course will serve you perfectly well. But you may notice, for example, that in some countries or regions the combination ll is pronounced like the *lli* in *million*, the *j* in *juice*, the *sh* in *show*, or the *s* in *pleasure*. The semivowel y may have a similar range of pronunciation. In some countries, particularly in the Caribbean, final s may be dropped altogether, if not the entire last syllable! You may even hear r pronounced as something similar to l. There's certainly nothing wrong with any of these variations, although as a student, you'll probably find it useful to concentrate on the standard pronunciation offered in this course first.

Grammar Summary

Keep in mind that there are always at least some exceptions to every grammar rule.

1. ARTICLES

	DEFINITE		INDEFINITE	
	Singular	Plural	Singular	Plural
Masculine	el	los	un	unos
Feminine	la	las	una	unas

Note: **El** is used before a feminine noun beginning with stressed **a** (or **ha**). The article **lo** is used before parts of speech other than nouns when they are used as nouns. **Unos** (**unas**) is often used to mean *some* or *a few*.

2. CONTRACTIONS

de + el = del (*from/of the*)
a + el = al (*to the*)

3. PLURALS

a. Nouns ending in an unstressed vowel or diphthong add -s.
b. Nouns ending in a stressed vowel or diphthong add -es.
c. Nouns ending in a consonant add -es.
d. Nouns ending in -z change the z to c and then add -es.

4. POSSESSION

Possession is shown by the preposition **de**: **el libro de Juan** (*Juan's book*).

5. ADJECTIVES

Adjectives agree with the nouns they modify in both gender and number.

a. If the masculine singular ending is -o, the feminine singular is -a, the masculine plural is -os, and the feminine plural is -as.

b. If the masculine singular ending is not -o, there is no change in the feminine singular, and both genders are -es in the plural.

6. COMPARISON

The regular comparative is formed with más (*more*) or menos (*less*), and the regular superlative is formed with the definite article + más (*the most*) or menos (*the least*).

7. PRONOUNS

	SUBJECT	DIRECT OBJECT	INDIRECT OBJECT	PREPOSITIONAL	REFLEXIVE
1st sg.	yo	me	me	mí	me
2nd sg.	tú	te	te	ti	te
3rd m. sg.	él	lo	le	él	se
3rd f. sg.	ella	la	le	ella	se
2nd sg., fml.	usted	lo/la	le	usted	se
1st pl.	nosotros/ nosotras	nos	nos	nosotros	nos
2nd pl.	vosotros/ vosotras	os	os	vosotros	os
3rd m. pl.	ellos	los	les	ellos	se

	SUBJECT	DIRECT OBJECT	INDIRECT OBJECT	PREPOSITIONAL	REFLEXIVE
3rd f. pl.	ellas	las	les	ellas	se
2nd pl., fml.	ustedes	los/las	les	ustedes	se

8. QUESTION WORDS

¿Qué?	What?	¿Cuál? ¿Cuáles?	What?/ Which one?
¿Por qué?	Why?	¿Quién? ¿Quiénes?	Who?
¿Cómo?	How?	¿Dónde?	Where?
¿Cuánto? ¿Cuánta? ¿Cuántos? ¿Cuántas?	How much?/How many?	¿Cuándo?	When?

9. ADVERBS

Spanish -mente corresponds to -ly in English. It is added to the feminine form of the adjective.

10. DEMONSTRATIVES

ADJECTIVES		PRONOUNS			
Masculine	Feminine	Masculine	Feminine	Neuter	
este	esta	éste	ésta	esto	*this*
ese	esa	ése	ésa	eso	*that*
aquel	aquella	aquél	aquélla	aquello	*that (farther removed)*
estos	estas	éstos	éstas	estos	*these*
esos	esas	ésos	ésas	esos	*those*
aquellos	aquellas	aquéllos	aquéllas	aquellos	*those (farther removed)*

11. *IF* SENTENCES

IF THE MAIN CLAUSE HAS A VERB IN THE:	THE SI *(IF)* CLAUSE HAS A VERB IN THE:
Present	*Present/Future*
Future	*Present*
Imperfect	*Imperfect*
Preterite	*Preterite*
Conditional	*Imperfect Subjunctive* (-ra *or* -se)
Past Conditional	*Past Perfect Subjunctive* (hubiera *or* hubiese)

If the subject of the main clause and the subject of the *if* clause are the same, it's possible to replace a verb in the subjunctive with an infinitive. In this case si is replaced by de.

12. SUBJUNCTIVE

The subjunctive is used:

a. with verbs of desire, request, suggestion, permission, approval and disapproval, judgment, opinion, uncertainty, emotion, surprise, fear, denial, and so on. It is often used in a dependent clause introduced by **que** (*that*).

b. in affirmative or negative commands in the polite form, in negative commands in the familiar form, in *let's* suggestions, and in indirect or third person commands with *let (him/her/them)*.

c. in **si** (*if*) conditional clauses that are unreal or contrary to fact.

d. after impersonal verbs that do not express certainty.

e. after certain conjunctions that never introduce statements of accomplished fact (**antes de que, aunque, como si**, etc.). Other conjunctions may or may not introduce a statement of accomplished fact. When they do, they take the indicative; otherwise they take the subjunctive (**a menos que, a pesar de que**, etc.).

f. to refer to indefinites like **ningún** (*no*) or **alguien** (*someone*) when there's a doubt about that person's existence.

g. after compounds with **-quiera** (*-ever*): **quienquiera** (*whoever*), **dondequiera** (*wherever*), **cualquier** (*whatever, whichever*).

comer
to eat

yo	nosotros/as
tú	vosotros/as
él/ella/usted	ellos/ellas/ustedes

Present

como	comemos
comes	coméis
come	comen

Present Progressive

estoy comiendo	estamos comiendo
estás comiendo	estáis comiendo
está comiendo	están comiendo

Preterite

comí	comimos
comiste	comisteis
comió	comieron

Imperfect

comía	comíamos
comías	comíais
comía	comían

Future

comeré	comeremos
comerás	comeréis
comerá	comerán

Conditional

comería	comeríamos
comerías	comeríais
comería	comerían

Imperative

come	comed
coma	

Subjunctive

coma	comamos
comas	comáis
coma	coman

conducir
to drive

yo	nosotros/as
tú	vosotros/as
él/ella/usted	ellos/ellas/ustedes

Present

conduzco	conducimos
conduces	conducís
conduce	conducen

Present Progressive

estoy conduciendo	estamos conduciendo
estás conduciendo	estáis conduciendo
está conduciendo	están conduciendo

Preterite

conduje	condujimos
condujiste	condujisteis
condujo	condujeron

Imperfect

conducía	conducíamos
conducías	conducíais
conducía	conducían

Future

conduciré	conduciremos
conducirás	conduciréis
conducirá	conducirán

Conditional

conduciría	conduciríamos
conducirías	conduciríais
conduciría	conducirían

Imperative

conduce	conducid
conduzca	

Subjunctive

conduzca	conduzcamos
conduzcas	conduzcáis
conduzca	conduzcan

conocer
to know

yo	nosotros/as
tú	vosotros/as
él/ella/usted	ellos/ellas/ustedes

Present

conozco	conocemos
conoces	conocéis
conoce	conocen

Present Progressive

estoy conociendo	estamos conociendo
estás conociendo	estáis conociendo
está conociendo	están conociendo

Preterite

conocí	conocimos
conociste	conocisteis
conoció	conocieron

Imperfect

conocía	conocíamos
conocías	conocíais
conocía	conocían

Future

conoceré	conoceremos
conocerás	conoceréis
conocerá	conocerán

Conditional

conocería	conoceríamos
conocerías	conoceríais
conocería	conocerían

Imperative

conoce	conoced
conozca	

Subjunctive

conozca	conozcamos
conozcas	conozcáis
conozca	conozcan

dar
to give

yo	nosotros/as
tú	vosotros/as
él/ella/usted	ellos/ellas/ustedes

Present

doy	damos
das	dais
da	dan

Present Progressive

estoy dando	estamos dando
estás dando	estáis dando
está dando	están dando

Preterite

di	dimos
diste	disteis
dio	dieron

Imperfect

daba	dábamos
dabas	dabais
daba	daban

Future

daré	daremos
darás	daréis
dará	darán

Conditional

daría	daríamos
darías	daríais
daría	darían

Imperative

da	dad
dé	

Subjunctive

dé	demos
des	deis
dé	den

deber
to have to, must

yo	nosotros/as
tú	vosotros/as
él/ella/usted	ellos/ellas/ustedes

Present		Present Progressive	
debo	debemos	estoy debiendo	estamos debiendo
debes	debéis	estás debiendo	estáis debiendo
debe	deben	está debiendo	están debiendo

Preterite		Imperfect	
debí	debimos	debía	debíamos
debiste	debisteis	debías	debíais
debió	debieron	debía	debían

Future		Conditional	
deberé	deberemos	debería	deberíamos
deberás	deberéis	deberías	deberíais
deberá	deberán	debería	deberían

Imperative		Subjunctive	
		deba	debamos
debe	debed	debas	debáis
deba		deba	deban

escoger
to choose

yo	nosotros/as
tú	vosotros/as
él/ella/usted	ellos/ellas/ustedes

Present

escojo	escogemos
escoges	escogéis
escoge	escogen

Present Progressive

estoy escogiendo	estamos escogiendo
estás escogiendo	estáis escogiendo
está escogiendo	están escogiendo

Preterite

escogí	escogimos
escogiste	escogisteis
escogió	escogieron

Imperfect

escogía	escogíamos
escogías	escogíais
escogía	escogían

Future

escogeré	escogeremos
escogerás	escogeréis
escogerá	escogerán

Conditional

escogería	escogeríamos
escogerías	escogeríais
escogería	escogerían

Imperative

escoge	escoged
escoja	

Subjunctive

escoja	escojamos
escojas	escojáis
escoja	escojan

estar
to be

yo	nosotros/as
tú	vosotros/as
él/ella/usted	ellos/ellas/ustedes

Present		Present Progressive	
estoy	estamos	estoy estando	estamos estando
estás	estáis	estás estando	estáis estando
está	están	está estando	están estando

Preterite		Imperfect	
estuve	estuvimos	estaba	estábamos
estuviste	estuvisteis	estabas	estábais
estuvo	estuvieron	estaba	estaban

Future		Conditional	
estaré	estaremos	estaría	estaríamos
estarás	estaréis	estarías	estaríais
estará	estarán	estaría	estarían

Imperative		Subjunctive	
		esté	estemos
está	estad	estés	estéis
esté		esté	estén

hablar
to speak, to talk

yo	nosotros/as
tú	vosotros/as
él/ella/usted	ellos/ellas/ustedes

Present		Present Progressive	
hablo	hablamos	estoy hablando	estamos hablando
hablas	habláis	estás hablando	estáis hablando
habla	hablan	está hablando	están hablando

Preterite		Imperfect	
hablé	hablamos	hablaba	hablábamos
hablaste	hablasteis	hablabas	hablabais
habló	hablaron	hablaba	hablaban

Future		Conditional	
hablaré	hablaremos	hablaría	hablaríamos
hablarás	hablaréis	hablarías	hablaríais
hablará	hablarán	hablaría	hablarían

Imperative		Subjunctive	
		hable	hablemos
habla	hablad	hables	habléis
hable		hable	hablen

hacer
to do, to make

yo	nosotros/as
tú	vosotros/as
él/ella/usted	ellos/ellas/ustedes

Present		Present Progressive	
hago	hacemos	estoy haciendo	estamos haciendo
haces	hacéis	estás haciendo	estáis haciendo
hace	hacen	está haciendo	están haciendo

Preterite		Imperfect	
hice	hicimos	hacía	hacíamos
hiciste	hicisteis	hacías	hacíais
hizo	hicieron	hacía	hacían

Future		Conditional	
haré	haremos	haría	haríamos
harás	haréis	harías	haríais
hará	harán	haría	harían

Imperative		Subjunctive	
		haga	hagamos
haz	haced	hagas	hagáis
haga		haga	hagan

ir
to go

yo	nosotros/as
tú	vosotros/as
él/ella/usted	ellos/ellas/ustedes

Present		Present Progressive	
voy	vamos	estoy yendo	estamos yendo
vas	vais	estás yendo	estáis yendo
va	van	está yendo	están yendo

Preterite		Imperfect	
fui	fuimos	iba	íbamos
fuiste	fuisteis	ibas	ibais
fue	fueron	iba	iban

Future		Conditional	
iré	iremos	iría	iríamos
irás	iréis	irías	iríais
irá	irán	iría	irían

Imperative		Subjunctive	
		vaya	vayamos
ve	id	vayas	vayáis
vaya		vaya	vayan

pedir
to ask for

yo	nosotros/as
tú	vosotros/as
él/ella/usted	ellos/ellas/ustedes

Present		Present Progressive	
pido	pedimos	estoy pidiendo	estamos pidiendo
pides	pedís	estás pidiendo	estáis pidiendo
pide	piden	está pidiendo	están pidiendo

Preterite		Imperfect	
pedí	pedimos	pedía	pedíamos
pediste	pedisteis	pedías	pedíais
pidió	pidieron	pedía	pedían

Future		Conditional	
pediré	pediremos	pediría	pediríamos
pedirás	pediréis	pedirías	pediríais
pedirá	pedirán	pediría	pedirían

Imperative		Subjunctive	
		pida	pidamos
pide	pedid	pidas	pidáis
pida		pida	pidan

pensar
to think

yo	nosotros/as
tú	vosotros/as
él/ella/usted	ellos/ellas/ustedes

Present		Present Progressive	
pienso	pensamos	estoy pensando	estamos pensando
piensas	pensáis	estás pensando	estáis pensando
piensa	piensan	está pensando	están pensando

Preterite		Imperfect	
pensé	pensamos	pensaba	pensábamos
pensaste	pensasteis	pensabas	pensabais
pensó	pensaron	pensaba	pensaban

Future		Conditional	
pensaré	pensaremos	pensaría	pensaríamos
pensarás	pensaréis	pensarías	pensaríais
pensará	pensarán	pensaría	pensarían

Imperative		Subjunctive	
		piense	pensemos
piensa	pensad	pienses	penséis
piense		piense	piensen

poder
to be able to, can

yo	nosotros/as
tú	vosotros/as
él/ella/usted	ellos/ellas/ustedes

Present

puedo	podemos
puedes	podéis
puede	pueden

Present Progressive

estoy pudiendo	estamos pudiendo
estás pudiendo	estáis pudiendo
está pudiendo	están pudiendo

Preterite

pude	pudimos
pudiste	pudisteis
pudo	pudieron

Imperfect

podía	podíamos
podías	podíais
podía	podían

Future

podré	podremos
podrás	podréis
podrá	podrán

Conditional

podría	podríamos
podrías	podríais
podría	podrían

Imperative

puede	poded
pueda	

Subjunctive

pueda	podamos
puedas	podáis
pueda	puedan

poner
to put

yo	nosotros/as
tú	vosotros/as
él/ella/usted	ellos/ellas/ustedes

Present		Present Progressive	
pongo	ponemos	estoy poniendo	estamos poniendo
pones	ponéis	estás poniendo	estáis poniendo
pone	ponen	está poniendo	están poniendo

Preterite		Imperfect	
puse	pusimos	ponía	poníamos
pusiste	pusisteis	ponías	poníais
puso	pusieron	ponía	ponían

Future		Conditional	
pondré	pondremos	pondría	pondríamos
pondrás	pondréis	pondrías	pondríais
pondrá	pondrían	pondría	pondrían

Imperative		Subjunctive	
		ponga	pongamos
pon	poned	pongas	pongáis
ponga		ponga	pongan

querer
to want

yo	nosotros/as
tú	vosotros/as
él/ella/usted	ellos/ellas/ustedes

Present

quiero	queremos
quieres	queréis
quiere	quieren

Present Progressive

estoy queriendo	estamos queriendo
estás queriendo	estáis queriendo
está queriendo	están queriendo

Preterite

quise	quisimos
quisiste	quisisteis
quiso	quisieron

Imperfect

quería	queríamos
querías	queríais
quería	querían

Future

querré	querremos
querrás	querréis
querrá	querrán

Conditional

querría	querríamos
querrías	querríais
querría	querrían

Imperative

quiere	quered
quiera	

Subjunctive

quiera	queramos
quieras	queráis
quiera	quieran

saber
to know

yo	nosotros/as
tú	vosotros/as
él/ella/usted	ellos/ellas/ustedes

Present

sé	sabemos
sabes	sabéis
sabe	saben

Present Progressive

estoy sabiendo	estamos sabiendo
estás sabiendo	estáis sabiendo
está sabiendo	están sabiendo

Preterite

supe	supimos
supiste	supisteis
supo	supieron

Imperfect

sabía	sabíamos
sabías	sabíais
sabía	sabían

Future

sabré	sabremos
sabrás	sabréis
sabrá	sabrán

Conditional

sabría	sabríamos
sabrías	sabríais
sabría	sabrían

Imperative

sabe	sabed
sepa	

Subjunctive

sepa	sepamos
sepas	sepáis
sepa	sepan

salir
to go out

yo	nosotros/as
tú	vosotros/as
él/ella/usted	ellos/ellas/ustedes

Present

salgo	salimos
sales	salís
sale	salen

Present Progressive

estoy saliendo	estamos saliendo
estás saliendo	estáis saliendo
está saliendo	están saliendo

Preterite

salí	salimos
saliste	salisteis
salió	salieron

Imperfect

salía	salíamos
salías	salíais
salía	salían

Future

saldré	saldremos
saldrás	saldréis
saldrá	saldrán

Conditional

saldría	saldríamos
saldrías	saldríais
saldría	saldrían

Imperative

sal	salid
salga	

Subjunctive

salga	salgamos
salgas	salgáis
salga	salgan

ser
to be

yo	nosotros/as
tú	vosotros/as
él/ella/usted	ellos/ellas/ustedes

Present

soy	somos
eres	sois
es	son

Present Progressive

estoy siendo	estamos siendo
estás siendo	estáis siendo
está siendo	están siendo

Preterite

fui	fuimos
fuiste	fuisteis
fue	fueron

Imperfect

era	éramos
eras	erais
era	eran

Future

seré	seremos
serás	seréis
será	serán

Conditional

sería	seríamos
serías	seríais
sería	serían

Imperative

sé	sed
sea	

Subjunctive

sea	seamos
seas	seáis
sea	sean

tener
to have

yo	nosotros/as
tú	vosotros/as
él/ella/usted	ellos/ellas/ustedes

Present		Present Progressive	
tengo	tenemos	estoy teniendo	estamos teniendo
tienes	tenéis	estás teniendo	estáis teniendo
tiene	tienen	está teniendo	están teniendo

Preterite		Imperfect	
tuve	tuvimos	tenía	teníamos
tuviste	tuvisteis	tenías	teníais
tuvo	tuvieron	tenía	tenían

Future		Conditional	
tendré	tendremos	tendría	tendríamos
tendrás	tendréis	tendrías	tendríais
tendrá	tendrán	tendría	tendrían

Imperative		Subjunctive	
		tenga	tengamos
ten	tened	tengas	tengáis
tenga		tenga	tengan

traer
to bring

yo	nosotros/as
tú	vosotros/as
él/ella/usted	ellos/ellas/ustedes

Present

traigo	traemos
traes	traéis
trae	traen

Present Progressive

estoy trayendo	estamos trayendo
estás trayendo	estáis trayendo
está trayendo	están trayendo

Preterite

traje	trajimos
trajiste	trajisteis
trajo	trajeron

Imperfect

traía	traíamos
traías	traíais
traía	traían

Future

traeré	traeremos
traerás	traeréis
traerá	traerán

Conditional

traería	traeríamos
traerías	traeríais
traería	traerían

Imperative

trae	traed
traiga	

Subjunctive

traiga	traigamos
traigas	traigáis
traiga	traigan

venir
to come

yo	nosotros/as
tú	vosotros/as
él/ella/usted	ellos/ellas/ustedes

Present

vengo	venimos
vienes	venís
viene	vienen

Present Progressive

estoy viniendo	estamos viniendo
estás viniendo	estáis viniendo
está viniendo	están viniendo

Preterite

vine	vinimos
viniste	vinisteis
vino	vinieron

Imperfect

venía	veníamos
venías	veníais
venía	venían

Future

vendré	vendremos
vendrás	vendréis
vendrá	vendrán

Conditional

vendría	vendríamos
vendrías	vendríais
vendría	vendrían

Imperative

ven	venid
venga	

Subjunctive

venga	vengamos
vengas	vengáis
venga	vengan

ver
to see

yo	nosotros/as
tú	vosotros/as
él/ella/usted	ellos/ellas/ustedes

Present		Present Progressive	
veo	vemos	estoy viendo	estamos viendo
ves	veis	estás viendo	estáis viendo
ve	ven	está viendo	están viendo

Preterite		Imperfect	
vi	vimos	veía	veíamos
viste	visteis	veías	veíais
vio	vieron	veía	veían

Future		Conditional	
veré	veremos	vería	veríamos
verás	veréis	verías	veríais
verá	verán	vería	verían

Imperative		Subjunctive	
		vea	veamos
ve	ved	veas	veáis
vea		vea	vean

vivir
to live

yo	nosotros/as
tú	vosotros/as
él/ella/usted	ellos/ellas/ustedes

Present		Present Progressive	
vivo	vivimos	estoy viviendo	estamos viviendo
vives	vivís	estás viviendo	estáis viviendo
vive	viven	está viviendo	están viviendo

Preterite		Imperfect	
viví	vivimos	vivía	vivíamos
viviste	vivisteis	vivías	vivíais
vivió	vivieron	vivía	vivían

Future		Conditional	
viviré	viviremos	viviría	viviríamos
vivirás	viviréis	vivirías	viviríais
vivirá	vivirán	viviría	vivirían

Imperative		Subjunctive	
		viva	vivamos
vive	vivid	vivas	viváis
viva		viva	vivan

Glossary

Note that the following abbreviations will be used in this glossary: (m.) = masculine, (f.) = feminine, (sg.) = singular, (pl.) = plural, (fml.) = formal/polite, (infml.) = informal/familiar. If a word has two grammatical genders, (m./f.) or (f./m.) is used.

Spanish-English

A

a *to, at*
  a las cinco *at five (o'clock)*
  ¿A qué hora es? *At what time is it?*
  A ver ... *Let's see ...*
  de ... a ... *from ... through ...*
abdomen (m.) *abdomen*
abogado/abogada (m./f.) *lawyer*
abonado/abonada (m./f.) *subscriber*
  línea (f.) de abonado digital (DSL) *DSL*
abrigo (m.) *overcoat*
abril (m.) *April*
abrir *to open*
  abrir la puerta *to open the door*
abrochar *to fasten*
  abrocharse el cinturón de seguridad *to buckle up*
absolutamente *absolutely*
absoluto/absoluta (m./f.) *absolute*
  en absoluto *absolutely not*
absurdo/absurda (m./f.) *absurd*
abuela (f.) *grandmother*
abuelo (m.) *grandfather*
  abuelos (pl.) *grandfathers, grandparents*
aburrido/aburrida (m./f.) *bored, boring*
aburrir *to bore*
aburrirse *to be bored, to get bored*
  Me aburre/aburren ... (sg./pl.) *I'm bored by ...*
acabar *to finish*
  acabar de ... *to have just ... (done something)*
academia (f.) *school, academy*
académico/académica (m./f.) *academic*
accidente (m.) *accident*
aceite (m.) *oil*

aceptar *to accept*
acera (f.) *sidewalk*
aconsejar *to advise*
  aconsejar que ... *to advise that/to ...*
acostarse *to go to bed*
actor (m.) *actor*
actriz (f.) *actress*
actualmente *at the present time*
acuerdo (m.) *agreement*
  De acuerdo. *All right.*
acupuntura (f.) *acupuncture*
además *moreover*
Adiós. *Good-bye.*
adjuntar *to attach*
  adjuntar un documento *to attach a file*
adjunto/adjunta (m./f.) *enclosed*
  documento (m.) adjunto *attachment*
adolescente (m.) *adolescent, teenager*
adulto/adulta (m./f.) *adult*
aerolínea (f.) *airline*
aeropuerto (m.) *airport*
afeitar *to shave*
  navaja (f.) de afeitar *razor*
afeitarse *to shave (oneself)*
afición (f.) *hobby*
aficionado/aficionada (m./f.) *fan*
afuera *outside*
afueras (f. pl.) *outskirts*
agencia (f.) *agency*
agente (m./f.) *agent*
agitado/agitada (m./f.) *agitated, rough*
agosto (m.) *August*
agradable (m./f.) *pleasant*
agradecer *to be thankful*
  Le agradezco su ayuda. *Thank you for your help.*
agrio/agria (m./f.) *sour*
agua (f.) *water*

agua mineral *mineral water*
el agua *the water*
las aguas *the waters*
aguacate (m.) *avocado*
aguja (f.) *needle*
ahí *there*
ahora *now*
  ahora mismo *right now*
ahorrar *to save*
ahumado/ahumada (m./f.) *smoked*
ajedrez (m.) *chess*
ajustado/ajustada (m./f.) *tight*
al (a + el) *to the* (m.)/*at the* (m.)
albornoz (m.) *robe*
alcalde (m.) *mayor*
alcaldía (f.) *municipal building*
alcoba (f.) *bedroom, room*
aldea (f.) *village*
alegrarse *to be glad*
  alegrarse de que … *to be glad that …*
alegre (m./f.) *happy*
alemán (m.) *German (language)*
alemán/alemana (m./f.) *German*
alergia (f.) *allergy*
alérgico/alérgica (m./f.) *allergic*
alfombra (f.) *carpet*
álgebra (f.) *algebra*
algo *something, somewhat*
  ¿Algo más? *Anything else?*
algodón (m.) *cotton*
alguien *somebody, someone*
  alguien más *somebody else*
algún/alguno/alguna (before m. sg. nouns/
  m. sg./f. sg.) *some, something*
algunos/algunas (m. pl./f. pl.) *some, something*
allí *there*
almorzar *to have lunch*
almuerzo (m.) *lunch*
¿Aló? *Hello? (on the phone)*
alquilar *to rent*
alto (m.) *stop, height*
  ¡Alto! *Stop!*
alto/alta (m./f.) *tall, high*
  tener la tensión alta *to have high blood*
    pressure
alumno/alumna (m./f.) *student*
amanecer (m.) *dawn*
  al amanecer *at dawn*

amar *to love*
amargo/amarga (m./f.) *bitter, sour*
amarillo/amarilla (m./f.) *yellow*
  páginas (f. pl.) amarillas *yellow pages*
americana (f.) *jacket*
americano/americana (m./f.) *American*
amigo/amiga (m./f.) *friend*
amueblado/amueblada (m./f.) *furnished*
anaranjado/anaranjada (m./f.) *orange (color)*
ancho/ancha (m./f.) *wide, baggy*
andar *to walk*
andén (m.) *sidewalk, platform*
  por el andén *on the sidewalk*
anexo (m.) *attachment*
  anexo al correo electrónico *e-mail*
    attachment
angosto/angosta (m./f.) *narrow*
anillo (m.) *ring*
año (m.) *year*
  año pasado *last year*
  año que viene *next year*
  año entrante *next year*
  ¿Cuántos años tiene? *How old are you*
    (sg. fml.)/is he/is she?
  este año *this year*
  los años cincuenta *the fifties*
  segundo año *second year*
  tercer año *third year*
  tener … años *to be … years old*
anoche *last night*
anotar *to record, to write down*
  anotar un gol *to score a goal*
antes *before*
  antes de … *before …*
  lo antes posible *as soon as possible*
antigüedad (f.) *antique*
  tienda (f.) de antigüedades *antique store*
antigüedades (f. pl.) *antiques*
antiguo/antigua (m./f.) *old*
antipático/antipática (m./f.) *unfriendly*
apagar *to turn off*
  apagar las luces *to turn off the lights*
aparador (m.) *cupboard*
apartamento (m.) *apartment*
apetito (m.) *appetite*
apostar *to bet*
  apuesto a que … *to bet that …*
aprender *to learn*

aprender a ... *to learn how to ...*
Estoy aprendiendo español. *I'm learning Spanish.*
aprobar *to pass*
  aprobar un curso *to pass a course*
  aprobar un examen *to pass a test*
apuesta (f.) *bet*
apuro (m.) *difficult situation*
aquel/aquella (m. sg./f. sg.) *that (far from the speaker and the listener)*
aquél/aquélla (m. sg./f. sg.) *that (one) over there (far from the speaker and the listener)*
aquello (neuter) *that (one, thing) over there (far from the speaker and the listener)*
aquellos/aquellas (m. pl./f. pl.) *those (far from the speaker and the listener)*
aquéllos/aquéllas (m. pl./f. pl.) *those (ones) over there (far from the speaker and the listener)*
aquí *here*
  Aquí está ... *Here is ...*
  Aquí tiene. *Here you are.*
árbol (m.) *tree*
archivo (m.) *file*
área (m.) *area*
arena (f.) *sand*
Argentina (f.) *Argentina*
argentino/argentina (m./f.) *Argentinian*
armario (m.) *closet, filing cabinet*
arquitecto/arquitecta (m./f.) *architect*
arquitectura (f.) *architecture*
arroz (m.) *rice*
arte (m.) *art*
artesanía (f.) *craft*
artista (m./f.) *artist*
asar *to grill*
  bien asada *well-done*
así *so*
  Así es. *That's right.*
  Así que ... *So ...*
  por así decir *so to speak*
asignatura (f.) *subject, course*
asistente (m./f.) *assistant*
asistir *to attend, to be present*
astronauta (m./f.) *astronaut*
atardecer (m.) *dusk*
  al atardecer *at dusk*
atención (f.) *attention*
atender *to attend to, to serve, to take care of*

atentamente *carefully*
atleta (m./f.) *athlete*
atlético/atlética (m./f.) *athletic*
atracción (f.) *attraction*
atractivo/atractiva (m./f.) *attractive*
atrás *behind, back*
atún (m.) *tuna*
audífonos (m. pl.) *headphones*
aula (m.) *classroom*
auto (m.) *car*
autobús (m.) *bus*
  recorrido (m.) por autobús *tour bus*
automático/automática (m./f.) *automatic*
  contestador (m.) automático *answering machine*
automóvil (m.) *car*
autopista (f.) *highway, freeway*
autor/autora (m./f. less common) *author*
autovía (f.) *highway, freeway*
avenida (f.) *avenue*
aventura (f.) *adventure*
  películas (pl.) de aventuras *adventure films*
avión (m.) *airplane*
ayer *yesterday*
ayuda (f.) *help*
  Le agradezco su ayuda. *Thank you for your help.*
ayudar *to help*
  ¿Puede ayudarme? *Can you help me?*
ayuntamiento (m.) *city hall*
azúcar (m.) *sugar*
azul (m.) claro *the color light blue*
azul (m./f.) *blue*
  azul claro *light blue*
  azul marino *navy blue*
  azul oscuro *dark blue*
  ser de sangre azul *to have blue blood (lit., to be of blue blood)*

B

bailar *to dance*
baile (m.) *dancing*
bajar *to lower, to download*
bajo *under, below*
bajo/baja (m./f.) *short*
  tener la tensión baja *to have low blood pressure*
balcón (m.) *balcony*

balón (m.) *ball*
baloncesto (m.) *basketball*
bañador (m.) *bathing trunks*
banana (f.) *banana*
bañarse *to take a bath, to bathe*
banco (m.) *bank*
banda (f.) *band*
bañera (f.) *bathtub*
baño (m.) *bathroom*
   traje (m.) de baño *bathing suit*
banquero/banquera (m./f.) *banker*
bar (m.) *bar*
barato/barata (m./f.) *cheap*
barbería (f.) *barbershop*
barbilla (f.) *chin*
barrio (m.) *neighborhood*
base (f.) *base*
bastante *quite, enough, quite a lot*
bata (f.) *robe*
batidora (f.) *blender*
bebé (m./f.) *baby*
beber *to drink*
bebida (f.) *drink*
bebito/bebita (m./f.) *little baby*
beca (f.) *scholarship*
béisbol (m.) *baseball*
   partido (m.) de béisbol *baseball game*
beneficio (m.) *benefit*
besar *to kiss*
biblioteca (f.) *library*
bicicleta (f.) *bicycle*
bien *well*
   Estoy bien. *I'm fine.*
   Que esté bien. *May you be well.*
   Que estés bien. *Take care.*
   ¡Qué bien! *How nice!*
Bienvenido./Bienvenida. (m./f.) *Welcome.* (to a
   man/to a woman)
billar (m.) *pool, billiards*
billete (m.) *ticket*
biología (f.) *biology*
blanco/blanca (m./f.) *white*
   ir de punta en blanco *to be dressed to the*
     nines (lit., *to go from the tip in white*)
   vino (m.) blanco *white wine*
bloquear *to block*
blusa (f.) *blouse*
bobo/boba (m./f.) *fool, idiot*

boca (f.) *mouth*
boleto (m.) *ticket*
bolígrafo (m.) *pen*
Bolivia (f.) *Bolivia*
boliviano/boliviana (m./f.) *Bolivian*
bolsa (f.) *bag, sack*
bolso (m.) *handbag*
bombachas (f. pl.) *women's underwear*
bonito/bonita (m./f.) *nice, pretty*
bordo (m.) *board*
   a bordo *on board*
   Bienvenidos a bordo. *Welcome aboard.*
borracho/borracha (m./f.) *drunk*
borrar *to erase*
bosque (m.) *forest*
bote (m.) *carton*
botella (f.) *bottle*
botiquín (m.) *medicine cabinet*
bragas (f. pl.) *women's underwear*
Brasil (m.) *Brazil*
brasileño/brasileña (m./f.) *Brazilian* (noun)
brasilero/brasilera (m./f.) *Brazilian* (adjective)
brazo (m.) *arm*
brote (m.) *rash*
buceo (m.) *diving*
buen/bueno/buena (before m. sg. nouns/
   m./f.) *good*
   Buenas noches. *Good evening./Good night.*
   Buenas tardes. *Good afternoon.*
   Buenos días. *Good morning.*
   ¡Buen provecho! *Enjoy the meal!*
   ¡Buen trabajo! *Good job!*
   El tiempo es bueno. *The weather is good.*
   Es bueno que … *It's good that …*
   Hace muy buen tiempo. *It's beautiful.*
   Nochebuena (f.) *Christmas Eve*
bufanda (f.) *scarf*
buscar *to look for, to pick up*
buzón (m.) *mailbox*
   buzón de voz *voice mail*

C

caballero (m.) *gentleman*
caballo (m.) *horse*
cabecera (f.) *head*
   pediatra (m./f.) de cabecera *regular*
     pediatrician
cabeza (f.) *head*

pararse de cabeza *to go crazy, to go out of one's mind*
perder la cabeza *to lose one's head*
tener dolor de cabeza *to have a headache*
tener la cabeza fría *to keep a cool head*
cabina (f.) *booth, cabin*
  cabina telefónica *telephone booth*
cable (m.) *cable*
cada (m./f.) *each, every*
cadera (f.) *hip*
caer *to fall*
café (m.) *coffee*
café (m./f.) *coffee-colored*
cafetera (f.) *coffeemaker*
cafetería (f.) *café, coffee shop, cafeteria, diner*
caja (f.) *cash register, box*
cajetilla (f.) *packet*
  cajetilla de cigarrillos *pack of cigarettes*
cajón (m.) *drawer*
calcetines (m. pl.) *socks*
caliente (m./f.) *hot*
calificaciones (f. pl.) *grades*
calle (f.) *street*
  luz (f.) de la calle *streetlight*
callejón (m.) *alley*
calor (m.) *heat*
  Hace calor. *It's hot.*
  tener calor *to be hot, to be warm*
calvo/calva (m./f.) *bald*
calzar *to wear (shoes)*
  ¿Qué número calza? *What shoe size do you wear?*
calzoncillos (m. pl.) *men's underpants*
calzoncitos (m. pl.) *women's underwear*
calzones (m. pl.) *men's undergarments*
cama (f.) *bed*
cámara (f.) *camera*
camarera (f.) *waitress*
camarero (m.) *waiter*
camarón (m.) *shrimp*
cambiar *to change, to exchange*
cambio (m.) *change*
caminar *to walk*
camino (m.) *way, path*
camisa (f.) *shirt*
camiseta (f.) *T-shirt, undershirt*
camisilla (f.) *undershirt*
campeón/campeona (m./f.) *champion*

campeonato (m.) *championship*
camping (m.) *camping*
  ir de camping *to go camping*
campo (m.) *field, camp*
Canadá (m.) *Canada*
canadiense (m./f.) *Canadian*
canal (m.) *channel*
cancelar *to cancel*
canción (f.) *song*
candidato/candidata (m./f.) *candidate*
cansado/cansada (m./f.) *tired*
cansancio (m.) *fatigue*
  tener cansancio *to be tired*
cantante (m./f.) *singer*
cantar *to sing*
capacidad (f.) *capacity*
cara (f.) *face*
  dar la cara *to face the circumstances*
  ser caradura *to be shameless*
carbón (m.) *coal*
cárcel (f.) *prison*
carnaval (m.) *carnival*
carne (f.) *meat, beef*
  carne de cerdo (f.) *pork*
carnicería (f.) *butcher shop*
caro/cara (m./f.) *expensive*
carpeta (f.) *file*
carpintero/carpintera (m./f.) *carpenter*
carpio (m.) *carpus*
  síndrome (m.) del túnel del carpio *carpal tunnel syndrome*
carrera (f.) *major, university course*
carretera (f.) *highway, freeway*
carril (m.) *lane*
  Siga por el carril de la derecha. *Stay in the right lane.*
carro (m.) *car*
carta (f.) *menu, letter*
  cartas (f. pl.) *playing cards*
cartelera (f.) *billboard, list of plays*
  cartelera de cine *movie listing*
cartera (f.) *wallet, handbag*
cartón (m.) *carton, cardboard*
casa (f.) *house*
casado/casada (m./f.) *married*
casarse *to get married*
  casarse con *to marry (someone)*
casi *almost*

casi nunca *seldom, almost never*
caso (m.) *case*
casualidad (f.) *chance, coincidence*
  por casualidad *by chance*
catedral (f.) *cathedral*
catorce *fourteen*
caza (f.) *hunting*
CD (m.) *CD*
  CD rom (m.) *CD-ROM*
  lector (m.) de CD *CD player*
  lector (m.) de CD rom *CD-ROM drive*
cebolla (f.) *onion*
ceja (f.) *eyebrow*
celeste (m./f.) *sky blue*
celoso/celosa (m./f.) *jealous*
celular (m.) *cell phone*
cena (f.) *dinner*
cenar *to eat dinner*
centralita (f.) *switchboard*
centro (m.) *center*
  centro comercial *shopping mall*
  centro de información *information center*
cerca *close, near*
  cerca de ... *close to/near ...*
cerdo (m.) *pork*
  carne (f.) de cerdo *pork*
cerdo/cerda (m./f.) *pig*
  carne (f.) de cerdo *pork*
cerebro (m.) *brain*
cero *zero*
cerrar *to close*
cerro (m.) *hill*
cerveza (f.) *beer*
cesar *to stop*
  cesar de ... *to stop ... (doing something)*
césped (m.) *lawn, grass*
champaña (m.) *champagne*
champú (m.) *shampoo*
chanchito/chanchita (m./f.) *piglet*
Chao. *Bye.*
chaqueta (f.) *jacket*
charcutería (f.) *delicatessen*
charla (f.) *chat*
  espacio (m.) para charla *chat room*
chat (m.) *chat room*
che *hey (filler word, Argentina)*
cheque (m.) *check*
chica (f.) *girl*

chico (m.) *boy*
Chile (m.) *Chile*
chileno/chilena (m./f.) *Chilean*
chinelas (f. pl.) *slippers*
chino (m.) *Chinese (language)*
chiste (m.) *joke*
  contar un chiste verde *to tell an obscene joke*
    (lit., to tell a green joke)
chocolate (m.) *chocolate*
chuleta (f.) *chop*
  chuleta de cordero *lamb chop*
ciclismo (m.) *biking, cycling*
cielo (m.) *sky*
cien/ciento (before a noun/before a number except
  mil) *one hundred*
  cien personas *one hundred people*
  cien por ciento *one hundred percent*
  ciento tres dólares *one hundred and three*
    dollars
  por ciento *percent*
ciencia (f.) *science*
cierto/cierta (m./f.) *true*
  No es cierto que ... *It is not true that ...*
cigarrillo (m.) *cigarette*
  cajetilla (f.) de cigarrillos *pack of cigarettes*
cinco *five*
  a las cinco *at five (o'clock)*
  cuarenta y cinco *forty-five*
cincuenta *fifty*
cine (m.) *movie*
cinturón (m.) *belt*
  abrocharse el cinturón de seguridad *to*
    buckle up
circo (m.) *circus*
cita (f.) *appointment*
ciudad (f.) *city, town*
claramente *clearly*
claro *clearly*
  ¡Claro que sí! *Of course!*
  Sí, claro. *Yes, of course.*
claro/clara (m./f.) *light*
  azul (m./f.) claro *light blue*
clase (f.) *class, kind*
  toda clase *all kinds*
clásico/clásica (m./f.) *classic*
  música (f.) clásica *classical music*
cliente (m./f.) *customer*
clínica (f.) *clinic*

farmacia (f.) clínica *clinical pharmacy*
club (m.) *club*
coca (f.) *coca*
coche (m.) *car*
cocina (f.) *kitchen, stove, cooking*
cocinar *to cook*
código (m.) *code*
codo (m.) *elbow*
coger *to catch, to pick up, to take*
  coger fuerzas (f. pl.) *to regain strength*
  coger un examen *to take a test*
coincidencia (f.) *coincidence*
  ¡Qué coincidencia! *What a coincidence!*
cola (f.) *tail, line*
  hacer una cola *to stand in line*
colección (f.) *collection*
coleccionar *to collect*
colega/colega (m./f.) *colleague*
colegio (m.) *elementary/secondary school*
colgar *to hang*
  colgar el teléfono *to hang up the phone*
colina (f.) *hill*
collar (m.) *necklace*
Colombia (f.) *Colombia*
colombiano/colombiana (m./f.) *Colombian*
colonia (f.) *cologne*
color (m.) *color*
  ¿De qué color es … ? *What color is … ?*
  ver todo color de rosa *to be an optimist, to wear rose colored glasses*
colorado/colorada (m./f.) *red*
  ponerse colorado *to be embarrassed (lit., to turn red)*
columna (f.) *column*
  columna vertebral *backbone, spinal column*
coma (f.) *comma*
combinar *to combine, to match*
  combinar con … *to go with …*
comedia (f.) *comedy*
comedor (m.) *dining room*
comenzar *to start, to begin*
  comenzar a … *to start … (doing something)*
comer *to eat*
comercial (m./f.) *commercial*
  centro (m.) comercial *shopping mall*
comida (f.) *food, dinner*
como *as, like*
  como ya sabes *as you already know*

cómo *how* (question)
  ¿Cómo? *What?/Pardon me?*
  ¿Cómo estás (tú)? *How are you?* (infml.)
  ¿Cómo estás de tiempo? *Do you have time?/ How are you doing for time?*
  ¿Cómo está usted? *How are you?* (fml.)
  ¿Cómo se llama usted? *What's your name?* (fml.)
  ¿Cómo te llamas? *What's your name?* (infml.)
  ¿Cómo te trata la vida? *How's life treating you?*
  ¿Cómo va todo? *How is everything going?*
  ¿Sabe cómo … ? *Do you know how to … ?*
cómodo/cómoda (m./f.) *comfortable*
compañía (f.) *company*
completamente *completely*
completar *to complete*
completo/completa (m./f.) *full*
  a tiempo completo *full-time*
compra (f.) *purchase*
  ir de compras *to go shopping*
comprar *to buy, to shop*
  comprar en rebaja *to buy on sale*
comprender *to understand*
computadora (f.) *computer*
comunicar *to communicate*
  Está comunicando. *The line is busy.*
con *with, to*
concierto (m.) *concert*
condimentado/condimentada (m./f.) *spicy*
conducir *to drive*
conectar *to connect*
conexión (f.) *connection*
conferencia (f.) *conference, meeting, lecture*
  sala (f.) de conferencias *meeting room*
conjunto (m.) *band (music)*
conocer *to know (people, places), to meet*
  conocer de vista *to know by sight*
  conocer palmo a palmo *to know like the back of one's hand*
  dar a conocer *to make known*
  Gusto en conocerlo/la. *Pleased to meet you.* (to a man/to a woman)
consultar *to look up, to consult*
consultorio (m.) *office*
  consultorio del médico *doctor's office*
contable (m./f.) *accountant*
contar *to count, to tell*

contar un chiste verde *to tell an obscene joke*
   (lit., to tell a green joke)
contento/contenta (m./f.) *happy*
contestador (m.) (automático) *answering*
   machine
contestar *to reply to, to answer*
   contestar el teléfono *to answer the phone*
contigo *with you*
continuar *to continue*
   Continúa recto. *Continue straight.*
contra *against*
contrato (m.) *contract*
contribución (f.) *contribution*
copa (f.) *wineglass*
   copa de vino *glass of wine*
copia (f.) *copy*
copiar *to copy*
corazón (m.) *heart*
corbata (f.) *tie*
cordero/cordera (m./f.) *lamb*
   chuleta (f.) de cordero *lamb chop*
coro (m.) *choir*
correo (m.) *post office*
   correo electrónico (correo-e) *e-mail*
   dirección (f.) de correo electrónico *e-mail*
      address
correr *to run*
cortado/cortada (m./f.) *sour*
cortina (f.) *curtain*
corto/corta (m./f.) *short*
cosa (f.) *thing*
   ¿Cómo van las cosas? *How are things?*
cosquilleo (m.) *tingling feeling*
costar *to cost*
   ¿Cuánto cuesta? *How much does it cost?*
costoso/costosa (m./f.) *expensive*
costura (f.) *sewing*
crédito (m.) *loan, credit*
   tarjeta (f.) de crédito *credit card*
creer *to believe, to think*
   Creo que sí. *I think so.*
   no creer que … *not to believe that …*
   ¿No crees? *Don't you think?*
crema (f.) *creme*
   crema de afeitar *shaving cream*
crío/cría (m./f.) *kid*
cruce (m.) *intersection*
cruzar *to cross*

cuaderno (m.) *notebook*
cuadra (f.) *block*
   Está a dos cuadras de aquí. *It's two blocks*
      from here.
cuadro (m.) *painting, picture, square*
   a cuadros *plaid*
cual/cuales (sg./pl.) *which* (relative pronoun), *as*
cuál/cuáles (sg./pl.) *which, what* (question)
cualificación (f.) *qualification, skill*
cualificado/cualificada (m./f.) *qualified*
cualquier *any*
cuando *when* (relative adverb)
cuándo *when* (question)
cuanto/cuanta/cuantos/cuantas (m. sg./f. sg./
   m. pl./f. pl.) *as much, as many*
   en cuanto a … *regarding …*
cuánto/cuánta/cuántos/cuántas (m. sg./f. sg./
   m. pl./f. pl.) *how much, how many*
   ¿Cuántos años tiene? *How old are you* (sg.
      fml.)/*is he/is she?*
   ¿Cuánto cuesta? *How much does it cost?*
   ¿Cuánto es? *How much is it?*
cuarenta *forty*
   cuarenta y cinco *forty-five*
cuarto (m.) *quarter, room, bedroom*
   a las seis menos cuarto *at a quarter to six*
   a las seis y cuarto *at a quarter past six*
   término (m.) tres cuartos *medium (cooked*
      meat)
cuatro *four*
cuatrocientos/cuatrocientas (m./f.) *four*
   hundred
cuchara (f.) *spoon*
cuchillo (m.) *knife*
cuello (m.) *neck*
cuenco (m.) *bowl*
cuenta (f.) *bill, check, account*
   tener en cuenta *to take into account*
   pagar la cuenta *to check out*
cuero (m.) *leather*
cuerpo (m.) *body*
   cuerpo humano *human body*
cuestionario (m.) *questionnaire*
cuñada (f.) *sister-in-law*
cuñado (m.) *brother-in-law*
currículum (m.) *curriculum*
   currículum vítae *résumé, CV*
curso (m.) *course*

cuyo/cuya/cuyos/cuyas (m. sg./f. sg./m. pl./f. pl.) *whose, of which* (relative pronoun)

D

dar *to give, to show*
  dar a conocer *to make known*
  dar a luz *to give birth*
  dar con *to find (something)*
  dar de narices *to fall flat on one's face*
  dar la cara *to face the circumstances*
  dar la hora *to tell time*
  dar la mano *to shake hands*
  dar la vuelta *to turn around*
  dar (las) gracias *to give thanks*
de *of, from, about*
  de … a … *from … through …*
  ¿De dónde eres? *Where are you from?*
  de la madrugada *in the early morning (before daybreak)*
  de la mañana *in the morning*
  de la noche *in the evening, at night*
  de la tarde *in the afternoon*
  De nada. *You're welcome.*
  ¿De qué color es … ? *What color is … ?*
debajo *underneath*
  debajo de … *underneath …*
deber *must, to owe*
débil (m./f.) *weak*
década (f.) *decade*
decidir *to decide*
decir *to tell, to say*
  ¿Cómo se dice " … " en … ? *How do you say " … " in … ?*
  ¿Díga(me)? *Hello? (on the phone)*
  No me digas. *Really?*
  por así decir *so to speak*
  ¿Qué quiere decir eso? *What does that mean?*
decisión (f.) *decision*
dedicar *to dedicate*
dedo (m.) *finger*
  dedo del pie *toe*
dejar *to leave*
  dejar un mensaje después de oír la señal *to leave a message after the tone*
del (de + el) *of the* (m.)*, from the* (m.)*, about the* (m.)
delante *in front*
  delante de … *in front of …*
delgado/delgada (m./f.) *thin*

delicioso/deliciosa (m./f.) *delicious*
delito (m.) *crime*
demasiado/demasiada (m./f.) *too much, too many*
dentista (m./f.) *dentist*
dentro *inside*
  dentro de … *inside of …*
departamento (m.) *department*
  tienda (f.) por departamentos *department store*
depender *to depend*
  depender de … *to depend on …*
dependiente/dependienta (m./f.) *store clerk*
deporte (m.) *sport*
deportista (m./f.) *person who plays sports*
deportivo/deportiva (m./f.) *athletic*
  zapatillas (f. pl.) deportivas *sneakers, tennis shoes*
derecha (f.) *right side*
  a la derecha *on the right*
  Gira a la derecha. *Turn right.*
derecho *straight*
  Siga derecho. *Go straight.*
derecho (m.) *law, right, duty*
  derechos (pl.) de matrícula *tuition*
derecho/derecha (m./f.) *right-side*
  a mano derecha *on the right-hand side*
desafortunadamente *unfortunately*
desagradable (m./f.) *unpleasant*
desarrollar *to develop*
desastre (m.) *disaster*
desayuno (m.) *breakfast*
descansar *to rest*
desconocer *not to know*
descremado/descremada (m./f.) *skimmed*
  leche (f.) descremada *skim milk*
describir *to describe*
descripción (f.) *description*
descuento (m.) *discount*
  hacer un descuento *to give a discount*
  treinta por ciento de descuento *thirty percent off*
desde *since, from*
desear *to want, to wish*
  desear que … *to wish that …*
  ¿Qué desea? *What would you like?*
desgracia (f.) *misfortune*
  por desgracia *unfortunately*

deshabillé (m.) *robe*
desierto (m.) *desert*
desodorante (m.) *deodorant*
despacho (m.) *office*
despacio *slowly*
  Hable más despacio, por favor. *Speak more slowly, please.*
despedirse *to say good-bye*
despertarse *to wake up, to get up*
después *afterwards*
  después de … *after …*
detalle (m.) *detail*
detergente (m.) *detergent*
  detergente de ropa *laundry detergent*
  detergente de vajilla *dishwashing detergent*
detestar *to detest*
detrás *behind*
  detrás de … *behind …*
día (m.) *day*
  Buenos días. *Good morning.*
  día festivo *holiday*
  dos días a la semana *twice a week*
  este día *this day*
  hoy en día *nowadays*
  Que tenga un buen día. *Have a nice day.*
  todo el día *all day*
  todos los días *every day*
diario (m.) *diary*
  llevar un diario *to keep a diary*
diario/diaria (m./f.) *daily*
diarrea (f.) *diarrhea*
diciembre (m.) *December*
diecinueve *nineteen*
dieciocho *eighteen*
dieciséis *sixteen*
diecisiete *seventeen*
diente (m.) *tooth*
diez *ten*
  a las ocho y diez *at eight ten (8:10)*
  diez mil *ten thousand*
  diez y seis *sixteen*
  diez y siete *seventeen*
  diez y ocho *eighteen*
  diez y nueve *nineteen*
diferencia (f.) *difference*
diferente (m./f.) *different*
difícil (m./f.) *difficult*
digital (m./f.) *digital*

línea (f.) de suscriptor/abonado digital (DSL) *DSL*
diligentemente *diligently*
dinero (m.) *money*
Dios (m.) *God*
  ¡Por Dios! *For God's sake!*
diploma (m.) *diploma*
dirección (f.) *address, direction*
  dirección de correo electrónico *e-mail address*
dirigir *to direct*
disco (m.) *disk, record*
  disco de vinilo *vinyl record, LP*
disculpa (f.) *excuse, apology*
disculpar *to excuse*
  Disculpa./Disculpe. *Excuse me.* (infml./fml.)
discutir *to discuss*
diseño (m.) *design*
Disneylandia *Disneyland*
disponible (m./f.) *available*
diversión (f.) *amusement*
  parque (m.) de diversiones *amusement park*
divertido/divertida (m./f.) *fun*
divertirse *to have fun*
divorciado/divorciada (m./f.) *divorced*
divorciarse *to get a divorce*
  divorciarse de … *to divorce (someone)*
doblar *to turn*
doce *twelve*
doctor/doctora (m./f.) *doctor*
documental (m.) *documentary*
documento (m.) *document, file*
  documento adjunto *attachment*
dólar (m.) *dollar*
dolor (m.) *pain*
  tener dolor de cabeza *to have a headache*
  tener dolor de garganta *to have a sore throat*
dominar *to dominate, to master*
  Domino el francés. *I speak French fluently.*
domingo (m.) *Sunday*
don (m.) *Mr.*
doña (f.) *Mrs.*
donde *where* (relative adverb)
dónde *where* (question)
  ¿De dónde eres? *Where are you from?*
dorado/dorada (m./f.) *gold (color)*
dormir *to sleep*
dormitorio (m.) *bedroom*

dos *two*
  dos días a la semana *twice a week*
doscientos/doscientas (m./f.) *two hundred*
dotado/dotada (m./f.) *talented*
drama (m.) *drama*
dramático/dramática (m./f.) *dramatic*
  obra (f.) dramática *drama*
ducha (f.) *shower*
ducharse *to take a shower/bath*
dudar *to doubt*
  dudar que … *to doubt that …*
dulce (m.) *sweet, pastry*
dulce (m./f.) *sweet*
durante *during*
duro/dura (m./f.) *hard*
  ser caradura *to be shameless*
DVD (m.) *DVD*
  lector (m.) de DVD *DVD player*

E

economía (f.) *economics*
económico/económica (m./f.) *economical, low-cost*
  precio (m.) económico *reasonable price*
Ecuador (m.) *Ecuador*
ecuatoriano/ecuatoriana (m./f.) *Ecuadorian*
edad (f.) *age*
edificio (m.) *building*
efectivamente *actually*
efectivo (m.) *cash*
  pagar en efectivo *to pay cash*
eficientemente *efficiently*
ejercicio (m.) *exercise*
el *the* (m. sg.)
  el de ella *hers*
  el de ellas *theirs* (f. pl.)
  el de ellos *theirs* (m. pl./mixed group)
  el de él *his*
  el de usted *yours* (sg. fml.)
  el de ustedes *yours* (pl.)
él *he*
  el de él (m. sg.) *his*
  la de él (f. sg.) *his*
eléctrico/eléctrica (m./f.) *electric, electrical*
electricista/electricista (m./f.) *electrician*
electrodoméstico (m.) *electrical appliance*
  tienda (f.) de electrodomésticos *electronics store*

electrónico/electrónica (m./f.) *electronic*
  correo (m.) electrónico *e-mail*
  dirección (f.) de correo electrónico *e-mail address*
elefante (m.) *elephant*
elegante (m./f.) *elegant*
elegir *to choose*
eliminar *to delete, to eliminate*
ella *she*
  el de ella (m. sg.) *hers*
  la de ella (f. sg.) *hers*
ellas *they* (f. pl.)
  el de ellas (m. sg.) *theirs* (f. pl.)
  la de ellas (f. sg.) *theirs* (f. pl.)
ellos *they* (m. pl./mixed group)
  el de ellos (m. sg.) *theirs* (m. pl./mixed group)
  la de ellos (m. sg.) *theirs* (m. pl./mixed group)
embarazada (f.) *pregnant*
embotellamiento (m.) *traffic jam*
emocionante (m./f.) *exciting*
empatado/empatada (m./f.) *tied*
  quedar empatados *to be tied*
empatar *to draw, to tie*
empezar *to begin*
empleado/empleada (m./f.) *employee*
empleo (m.) *job, employment*
en *in, at, by (means), on*
enamorado/enamorada (m./f.) *in love*
encantar *to enchant*
  Encantado./Encantada. *Pleased to meet you.*
  (said by a man/said by a woman)
  Me encanta/encantan … (sg./pl.) *I really like …*
  ¡Me encantaría! *I'd love to!*
encanto (m.) *charm*
encima *above*
  encima de … *above …*
  y encima … *and on top of that …*
encontrar *to meet up with, to find*
  encontrarse con … *to meet … (somebody)*
enero (m.) *January*
enfadarse *to get angry*
  enfadarse de que … *to be angry that …*
enfermedad (f.) *illness, disease*
enfermo/enferma (m./f.) *sick*
enfrente *opposite*
  enfrente de … *across from … , in front of …*
enhorabuena (f.) *congratulations*

enorme (m./f.) *huge*

ensalada (f.) *salad*

entender *to understand*

enterizo/enteriza (m./f.) *one-piece*

entero/entera (m./f.) *whole*

  leche (f.) entera *whole milk*

entonces *then*

  Hasta entonces. *Until then.*

entrada (f.) *entrance, ticket, appetizer*

entrante (m./f.) *coming*

  mes (m.) entrante *next month*

entrar *to enter*

entre *between*

  entre … y … *between … and …*

entregar *to submit*

entrenador/entrenadora (m./f.) *coach*

entretenimiento (m.) *entertainment*

entrevista (f.) *interview*

  programa (m.) de entrevistas *talk show*

entrevistar *to interview*

enviar *to send*

equipo (m.) *team*

equitación (f.) *horseback riding*

equivocado/equivocada (m./f.) *wrong*

  número (m.) equivocado *wrong number*

escaleras (f. pl.) *stairs*

escaparate (m.) *display window*

  ir de escaparates *to go window-shopping*

escoba (f.) *broom*

escoger *to choose*

escondidas (f. pl.) *hide-and-seek*

escotado/escotada (m./f.) *low-cut*

escribir *to write*

escritor/escritora (m./f.) *writer*

escritorio (m.) *desk, study*

escuchar *to listen to*

escuela (f.) *school*

escultura (f.) *sculpture*

ese/esa (m. sg./f. sg.) *that (near the listener)*

ése/ésa (m. sg./f. sg.) *that (one) (near the listener)*

eso (neuter) *that (one, thing) (near the listener)*

  a eso de *about, around*

  a eso de las nueve *at about nine o'clock*

  por eso *for this reason*

esos/esas (m. pl./f. pl.) *those (near the listener)*

ésos/ésas (m. pl./f. pl.) *those (ones) (near the listener)*

espacio (m.) *space*

espacio para charla *chat room*

espalda (f.) *back*

España (f.) *Spain*

español (m.) *Spanish (language)*

  Estoy aprendiendo español. *I'm learning Spanish.*

  Hablo un poco de español. *I speak a little Spanish.*

español/española (m./f.) *Spanish*

espantoso/espantosa (m./f.) *scary*

especialidad (f.) *specialty, major*

especialización (f.) *specialization, master's degree*

especializarse *to specialize*

  especializarse en … *to major in …*

espectador/espectadora (m./f.) *spectator*

espejo (m.) *mirror*

espera (f.) *wait*

  poner en espera *to put on hold*

esperar *to hope, to wait*

  esperar que … *to hope that …*

  Espere, por favor. *Hold on, please.*

  ¡Yo espero que sí! *I hope so!*

espeso/espesa (m./f.) *thick*

espía (m./f.) *spy*

esposa (f.) *wife*

esposo (m.) *husband*

esquiar *to ski*

esquina (f.) *corner*

  a la vuelta de la esquina *around the corner*

estación (f.) *station*

  estación de ferrocarril *train station*

  estación de tren *train station*

estación (f.) *season*

estadio (m.) *stadium*

estado (m.) *state*

  los Estados Unidos *the United States*

estadounidense (m./f.) *American*

estampado/estampada (m./f.) *with a pattern, patterned*

estampilla (f.) *postage stamp*

estanque (m.) *pond*

estante (m.) *shelf, bookshelf*

estar *to be*

  Aquí está … *Here is …*

  ¿Cómo estás (tú)? *How are you?* (infml.)

  ¿Cómo estás de tiempo? *Do you have time?/ How are you doing for time?*

¿Cómo está usted? *How are you?* (fml.)
Está granizando. *It's hailing.*
Está lloviendo. *It's raining.*
Está nevando. *It's snowing.*
Está nublado. *It's cloudy.*
estar en buenas manos *to be in good hands*
estar mal *to be not doing well*
Estoy aprendiendo español. *I'm learning Spanish.*
Estoy bien. *I'm fine.*
No está mal. *It's not bad.*
Que esté bien. *May you be well.*
Que estés bien. *Take care.*
este (m.) *east*
este/esta (m. sg./f. sg.) *this (near the speaker)*
  esta noche (f.) *this evening, tonight*
éste/ésta (m. sg./f. sg.) *this (one) (near the speaker)*
estilo (m.) *style*
esto (neuter) *this (one, thing) (near the speaker)*
estómago (m.) *stomach*
  tener mal de estómago *to have an upset stomach*
estos/estas (m. pl./f. pl.) *these (near the speaker)*
éstos/éstas (m. pl./f. pl.) *these (ones) (near the speaker)*
estrecho/estrecha (m./f.) *narrow*
estrella (f.) *star*
estrenar *to use for the first time*
estresante (m./f.) *stressing, stressful*
estudiante/estudiante (m./f.) *student*
estudiar *to study*
estudio (m.) *study, office*
  estudios (pl.) *studies*
estupendo/estupenda (m./f.) *fine, wonderful, marvelous*
  ¡Estupendo! *Great!*
etiqueta (f.) *tag, label*
  etiqueta con el precio *price tag*
ex *ex-*
exacto/exacta (m./f.) *exact*
  Exacto. *Exactly.*
examen (m.) *test*
  aprobar un examen *to pass a test*
  hacer un examen, presentarse a un examen *to take a test*
  hacerse un examen de sangre *to take a blood test*

suspender un examen *to fail a test*
exceder *to exceed*
excelente (m./f.) *excellent*
excepción (f.) *exception*
excursionismo (m.) *hiking*
  hacer excursionismo *to go hiking*
exigente (m./f.) *demanding*
exigir *to demand*
éxito (m.) *success*
experiencia (f.) *experience*
explicación (f.) *explanation*
exterior (m.) *outside*
extra (m./f.) *extra*
  horas (f. pl.) extras *extra hours, overtime*
extranjero/extranjera (m./f.) *foreign, foreigner*
extraño/extraña (m./f.) *strange*
  persona (f.) extraña *strange person*
extraordinario/extraordinaria (m./f.) *extraordinary*
extrovertido/extrovertida (m./f.) *extroverted*

F

fábrica (f.) *factory*
fácil (m./f.) *easy*
fácilmente *easily*
facultad (f.) *department (at college/university)*
falda (f.) *skirt*
faltar *to miss, to be lacking, to be necessary*
fama (f.) *fame*
familia (f.) *family*
familiar (m./f.) *(of) family, familiar*
famoso/famosa (m./f.) *famous*
fantástico/fantástica (m./f.) *fantastic*
farmacéutico/farmacéutico (m./f.) *pharmacist*
farmacia (f.) *drugstore, pharmacy*
  farmacia clínica *clinical pharmacy*
farola (f.) *lamppost*
favor (m.) *favor*
  Hágame el favor de … *Do me the favor of …*
  Por favor. *Please.*
favorito/favorita (m./f.) *favorite*
fax (m.) *fax machine*
febrero (m.) *February*
fecha (f.) *date*
felicitar *to congratulate*
  ¡Felicitaciones! *Congratulations!*
feliz (m./f.) *happy*
felizmente *happily*

feo/fea (m./f.) *ugly*

ferrocarril (m.) *railroad, train*
  estación (f.) de ferrocarril *train station*

festivo/festiva (m./f.) *festive*
  día (m.) festivo *holiday*

fiebre (f.) *fever*
  tener fiebre *to have a fever*

fiesta (f.) *party, holiday*

fijo/fija (m./f.) *fixed, permanent*
  trabajo (m.) fijo *steady job*

fila (f.) *line*
  hacer una fila *to stand in line*

filatelia (f.) *stamp collecting*

filosofía (f.) *philosophy*

fin (m.) *end*
  fin de semana *weekend*
  por fin *finally, at last*

final (m.) *end*

finanzas (f. pl.) *finance*

firma (f.) *signature*

física (f.) *physics*

flor (f.) *flower*

folleto (m.) *brochure*

fontanero/fontanera (m./f.) *plumber*

forma (f.) *way, manner*

fósil (m.) *fossil*

foto (f.) *picture, photograph*
  hacer una foto *to take a picture*

fotografía (f.) *photography*

francés (m.) *French (language)*

francés/francesa (m./f.) *French*

frasco (m.) *jar, bottle*

frase (f.) *phrase*

frecuencia (f.) *frequency*
  con frecuencia *frequently, often*

frecuente (m./f.) *frequent*

frecuentemente *frequently*

fregadero (m.) *(kitchen) sink*

freno (m.) *brake (automobile)*
  poner el pie en el freno *to hit the brakes*

frente (f.) *forehead*

fríjol (m.) *bean*

frío (m.) *cold temperature/sensation*
  Hace frío. *It's cold.*
  tener frío *to be cold*

frío/fría (m./f.) *cold*
  tener la cabeza fría *to keep a cool head*

frito/frita (m./f.) *fried*

fruta (f.) *fruit*

fuera *outside*
  fuera de … *outside of…*

fuerte (m./f.) *strong*

fuerza (f.) *strength*
  coger fuerzas (f. pl.) *to regain strength*

fumar *to smoke*

funcionar *to work, to function*

fútbol (m.) *soccer*
  fútbol americano *football*

futuro (m.) *future*

G

gabardina (f.) *raincoat*

gafas (f. pl.) *eyeglasses*
  gafas de sol *sunglasses*

galería (f.) *gallery*

galleta (f.) *cookie*

gamba (f.) *shrimp*

gamuza (f.) *suede*

gana (f.) *wish, desire*
  tener ganas de … *to feel like …*

ganar *to earn, to win*
  ¡Ojalá que ganen! *I hope they win!*

ganga (f.) *bargain*

garaje (m.) *garage*

garganta (f.) *throat*
  tener dolor de garganta *to have a sore throat*

gasolinera (f.) *gas station*

gasto (m.) *expense*

gato (m.) *cat*

gel (m.) *gel*

generalmente *generally*

generoso/generosa (m./f.) *generous*

gente (f.) *people*

geografía (f.) *geography*

gerente (m.) *manager*

gimnasia (f.) *gymnastics*

gimnasio (m.) *gymnasium*

girar *to turn*
  Gira a la derecha. *Turn right.*
  Gira a la izquierda. *Turn left.*

gol (m.) *goal*
  anotar/hacer/marcar un gol *to score a goal*

gordo/gorda (m./f.) *fat, big*

gracia (f.) *grace, appeal*
  dar (las) gracias *to give thanks*
  gracias (pl.) *thanks*

Gracias. *Thank you.*

Muchas gracias. *Thanks a lot.*

gracioso/graciosa (m./f.) *funny*

grado (m.) *degree*

graduarse *to graduate*

gráfico/gráfica (m./f.) *graphic*

gramo (m.) *gram*

gran/grande (before sg. nouns/all other cases) *big, large, great*

granizar *to hail*

Está granizando. *It's hailing.*

granjero/granjera (m./f.) *farmer*

gratis *free*

grave (m./f.) *serious*

gris (m.) *the color gray*

gris (m./f.) *gray*

gritar *to shout, to scream*

grito (m.) *cry, scream*

último grito *the very latest*

guantes (m. pl.) *gloves*

guardar *to save, to keep*

guayaba (f.) *guava*

guía (f.) *(guide) book*

guía telefónica *phone book*

guitarra (f.) *guitar*

tocar la guitarra *to play the guitar*

gustar *to please*

gustar que ... *to like (it) that ...*

Me gusta/gustan ... (sg./pl.) *I like ...*

Me gustaría ... *I'd like ...*

gusto (m.) *pleasure, taste*

Gusto en conocerlo/la. *Pleased to meet you.* (to a man/to a woman)

Mucho gusto. *It's a pleasure.*

H

haber *to have*

¿Cómo te ha ido? *How have you been?*

Hay ... *There is ... /There are ...*

Hay que ... *It is necessary to ...*

No hay nada que ... *There's nothing that ...*

No hay nadie que ... *There's no one who/ that ...*

No hay ningún ... que ... *There's no ... that/ who ...*

¿Qué hay? *What's up?/What's going on?*

habitación (f.) *room, bedroom*

hablar *to speak, to talk*

hablar con .... *to speak to ...*

¿Hablas inglés? *Do you speak English?* (infml.)

¿Habla usted inglés? *Do you speak English?* (fml.)

Hable más despacio, por favor. *Speak more slowly, please.*

Hablo un poco de español. *I speak a little Spanish.*

hacer *to do, to make*

Hace calor. *It's hot.*

Hace frío. *It's cold.*

Hace muy buen tiempo. *It's beautiful.*

hacer a la medida *to custom sew*

hacer deporte *to play sports*

hacer una cola/fila *to stand in line*

hacer un descuento *to give a discount*

hacer excursionismo *to go hiking*

hacer senderismo *to go hiking*

hacer una foto *to take a picture*

hacer una llamada internacional/local/ nacional *to make an international/local/ national call*

hacerse un examen de sangre *to take a blood test*

Hace sol. *It's sunny.*

Hace viento. *It's windy.*

Hágame el favor de ... *Do me the favor of ...*

Se me hace tarde. *I'm late.*

hacha (f.) *axe*

hacia *toward*

hambre (f.) *hunger*

tener hambre *to be hungry*

hasta *until, even*

Hasta entonces. *Till then.*

Hasta luego. *I'll see you later.*

Hasta mañana. *Until tomorrow./See you tomorrow.*

Hasta más tarde. *Until later.*

Hasta pronto. *See you soon.*

hecho/hecha (m./f.) *made, done*

heladería (f.) *ice cream parlor*

helado (m.) *ice cream*

heredar *to inherit*

hermana (f.) *sister*

hermano (m.) *brother*

hermanos (pl.) *brothers, brothers and sisters, siblings*

hielo (m.) *ice*

hierba (f.) *herb*
higiénico/higiénica (m./f.) *hygienic*
  papel (m.) higiénico *toilet paper*
hija (f.) *daughter*
hijastra (f.) *stepdaughter*
hijastro (m.) *stepson*
hijo (m.) *son*
  hijos (pl.) *sons, children (sons and daughters)*
hincha (m./f.) *fan, supporter*
hincharse *to swell*
historia (f.) *history*
historial (m.) *background, record*
  historial de trabajo *résumé*
hockey (m.) *hockey*
hoja (f.) *sheet (of paper)*
  hoja de vida *résumé*
Hola. *Hello.*
hombre (m.) *man*
  hombre de negocios *businessman*
hombro (m.) *shoulder*
homeopatía (f.) *homeopathy*
honesto/honesta (m./f.) *honest*
honorarios (m. pl.) *fees*
hora (f.) *time, hour*
  ¿A qué hora es? *At what time is it?*
  dar la hora *to tell time*
  horas (f. pl.) extras *extra hours, overtime*
  ¿Qué hora es? *What time is it?*
  ¿Qué horas son? *What time is it?*
  ¿Qué hora tiene? *What time do you have?*
horario (m.) *schedule*
horno (m.) *oven*
horror (m.) *horror*
hospital (m.) *hospital*
hostal (m.) *youth hostel*
hotel (m.) *hotel*
hoy *today*
  hoy en día *nowadays*
hueso (m.) *bone*
huevo (m.) *egg*
humano/humana (m./f.) *human*
  cuerpo (m.) humano *human body*
huracán (m.) *hurricane*

I

ida (f.) *outbound journey*
idea (f.) *idea*
ideal (m./f.) *ideal*

idioma (m.) *language*
iglesia (f.) *church*
igual (m./f.) *equal*
  … es igual a … *… equals (=) …*
igualmente *also, likewise*
  Igualmente. *The same to you.*
imaginar *to imagine*
impedir *to prevent*
importante (m./f.) *important*
importar *to matter*
  No importa. *It doesn't matter.*
imposible (m./f.) *impossible*
  Es imposible que … *It is impossible that …*
impresionante (m./f.) *impressive*
impresora (f.) *printer*
impuesto (m.) *tax*
  planilla (f.) de impuestos *tax return*
incentivo (m.) *incentive*
incluir *to include*
  ¿Está incluido el servicio? *Is service included?*
incómodo/incómoda (m./f.) *uncomfortable*
infantil (m./f.) *children's*
  sicología (f.) infantil *child psychology*
información (f.) *information*
  centro (m.) de información *information center*
informal (m./f.) *casual*
informe (m.) *report*
ingeniería (f.) *engineering*
  ingeniería mecánica *mechanical engineering*
ingeniero/ingeniera (m./f.) *engineer*
Inglaterra (f.) *England*
inglés (m.) *English (language)*
  ¿Hablas inglés? *Do you speak English?* (infml.)
  ¿Habla usted inglés? *Do you speak English?* (fml.)
inglés/inglesa (m./f.) *English*
ingrediente (m.) *ingredient*
ingreso (m.) *earnings*
inmediatamente *immediately*
inmediato/inmediata (m./f.) *immediate*
  de inmediato *immediately*
inodoro (m.) *toilet*
insistir *to insist*
  insistir en que … *to insist that …*
instantáneo/instantánea (m./f.) *instantaneous*
  mensaje (m.) instantáneo *instant message*

inteligente (m./f.) *intelligent, smart*
intercambiar *to exchange*
interés (m.) *interest*
  tener interés en … *to be interested in …*
  visitar los lugares de interés *to go sightseeing*
interesante (m./f.) *interesting*
interesar *to interest*
  Me interesa/interesan … (sg./pl.) *I'm interested in …*
intermedio/intermedia (m./f.) *intermediate*
internacional (m./f.) *international*
  llamada (f.) internacional *international call*
Internet *internet*
  por Internet *online*
intersección (f.) *intersection*
investigación (f.) *research, investigation*
  trabajo (m.) de investigación *research paper*
invierno (m.) *winter*
invitación (f.) *invitation*
invitado/invitada (m./f.) *guest*
invitar *to invite*
ir *to go*
  ¿Cómo te ha ido? *How have you been?*
  ¿Cómo van las cosas? *How are things?*
  ir a … *to go to (a place), to be going to (do)*
  ir a pie/caminar *to walk*
  ir de camping *to go camping*
  ir de compras *to go shopping*
  ir de escaparates *to go window-shopping*
  ir de punta en blanco *to be dressed to the nines (lit., to go from the tip in white)*
ira (f.) *anger*
  estar rojo de la ira *to be very angry (lit., to be red with fury)*
italiano (m.) *Italian (language)*
italiano/italiana (m./f.) *Italian*
izquierda (f.) *left side*
  a la izquierda *on the left*
  Gira a la izquierda. *Turn left.*
izquierdo/izquierda (m./f.) *left*
  a mano izquierda *on the left-hand side*

J

jabón (m.) *soap*
jamón (m.) *ham*
jardín (m.) *garden*
jazz (m.) *jazz*
jeans (m. pl.) *jeans*

jefe/jefa (m./f.) *boss*
jersey (m.) *sweater*
jornada (f.) *working day*
jornal (m.) *wage*
jota (f.) *the letter j*
  no saber ni jota de … *to not have a clue about …*
joven (m./f.) *young*
jubilado/jubilada (m./f.) *retired, retired person*
juego (m.) *game*
jueves (m.) *Thursday*
juez (m.) *judge*
jugador/jugadora (m./f.) *player*
jugar *to play*
jugo (m.) *juice*
julio (m.) *July*
junio (m.) *June*
junto/junta (m./f.) *together*
juzgado (m.) *court*

K

kilo (m.) *kilo, kilogram*
kilómetro (m.) *kilometer*

L

la *the (f. sg.); it (f.), her, you (f. sg. fml.)* (direct object pronoun)
  la de ella *hers*
  la de ellas *theirs (f. pl.)*
  la de ellos *theirs (m. pl./mixed group)*
  la de él *his*
  la de usted *yours (sg. fml.)*
  la de ustedes *yours (pl.)*
labio (m.) *lip*
lado (m.) *side*
  al lado de … *next to …*
ladrón (m./f.) *thief*
lago (m.) *lake*
lámpara (f.) *lamp*
lana (f.) *wool*
langosta (f.) *lobster*
lápiz (m.) *pencil*
largo/larga (m./f.) *long*
las *the (f. pl.); them (f.), you (f. pl.)* (direct object pronoun)
lástima (f.) *pity*
  Es una lástima que … *It's a pity that …*
lata (f.) *can*

lavabo (m.) *sink, wash basin*
lavadora (f.) *washing machine*
lavaplatos (m.) *dishwasher*
lavar *to wash*
  lavar a mano *to hand wash*
  lavar en seco *to dry-clean*
  lavar la ropa *to do the laundry*
  lavar los platos *to do the dishes*
lavarse *to wash oneself*
le *(to/for) him, her, it, you* (fml. sg.) (indirect object
  pronoun)
lección (f.) *lesson*
leche (f.) *milk*
  leche en polvo *powdered milk*
lechería (f.) *dairy store*
lechuga (f.) *lettuce*
lector (m.) *reader*
  lector de CD *CD player*
  lector de CD rom *CD-ROM drive*
  lector de DVD *DVD player*
lectura (f.) *reading*
leer *to read*
lejía (f.) *bleach*
lejos *far*
  lejos de … *far from …*
lengua (f.) *tongue, language*
lentamente *slowly*
lento/lenta (m./f.) *slow*
les *(to/for) them, you* (fml. pl.) (indirect object
  pronoun)
lesión (f.) *injury*
levantar *to raise, to lift*
levantarse *to get up, to rise*
  Me levanto. *I get up.*
libra (f.) *pound*
  media libra *half pound*
libre (m./f.) *free*
librería (f.) *bookstore*
libro (m.) *book*
  libro de texto *textbook*
licenciatura (f.) *bachelor's degree*
ligero/ligera (m./f.) *light, thin*
límite (m.) *limit*
limón (m.) *lemon*
limonada (f.) *lemonade*
limpio/limpia (m./f.) *clean*
línea (f.) *line*
  línea de suscriptor/abonado digital

  (DSL) *DSL*
lino (m.) *linen*
lista (f.) *list*
listo/lista (m./f.) *ready*
  ¿Listos? *Ready?*
literatura (f.) *literature*
litro (m.) *liter*
llamada (f.) *phone call*
  hacer una llamada internacional/local/
  nacional *to make an international/local/
  national call*
llamar *to call*
  llamar por teléfono *to make a phone call*
  llamar por teléfono a … *to call … on the
  phone*
  ¿Quién lo llama? *Who's calling?*
llamarse *to be called*
  ¿Cómo se llama usted? *What's your
  name?* (fml.)
  ¿Cómo te llamas? *What's your name?* (infml.)
  Me llamo … *My name is …*
llave (f.) *key*
llegar *to arrive*
  llegar a … *to get to …, to arrive at …*
llenar *to fill*
llevar *to wear, to carry, to take, to keep*
  llevar un diario *to keep a diary*
llorar *to cry*
llover *to rain*
  Está lloviendo. *It's raining.*
lluvia (f.) *rain*
lo *it* (m.), *him, you* (m. sg. fml.) (direct object
  pronoun)
  Lo siento. *I'm sorry.*
local (m./f.) *local*
  llamada (f.) local *local call*
Londres *London*
los *the* (m. pl.); *them* (m.), *you* (m. pl.) (direct object
  pronoun)
Los Ángeles *Los Angeles*
lotería (f.) *lottery*
luego *later, then*
  Hasta luego. *I'll see you later.*
lugar (m.) *place*
  visitar los lugares de interés *to go sightseeing*
luna (f.) *moon*
lunar (m.) *mole, beauty mark*
  de lunares *polka-dotted*

lunes (m.) *Monday*
luz (f.) *light*
  apagar las luces *to turn off the lights*
  dar a luz *to give birth*
  luz de la calle *streetlight*

M

madera (f.) *wood*
  de madera *wooden*
madrastra (f.) *stepmother*
madre (f.) *mother*
madrugada (f.) *late night, early morning (from midnight till daybreak)*
  de la madrugada *in the early morning*
  Es la una y diez de la madrugada. *It's ten after one in the morning.*
maestro/maestra (m./f.) *teacher*
mágico/mágica (m./f.) *magical*
magnífico/magnífica (m./f.) *magnificent, great*
mal *bad(ly), poorly*
  estar mal *to be not doing well*
  No está mal. *It's not bad.*
mal (m.) *illness*
  estar mal del estómago *to have an upset stomach*
maleta (f.) *suitcase*
malo/mala (m./f.) *bad*
mamá (f.) *mom*
mami (f.) *mom*
mañana (f.) *morning, tomorrow*
  a las nueve de la mañana *at nine a.m.*
  de la mañana *in the morning*
  esta mañana *this morning*
  Hasta mañana. *Until tomorrow./See you tomorrow.*
manejar *handle*
mano (f.) *hand*
  a la mano *at hand*
  a mano derecha *on the right-hand side*
  a mano izquierda *on the left-hand side*
  dar la mano *to shake hands*
  estar en buenas manos *to be in good hands*
  lavar a mano *to hand wash*
manojo (m.) *handful, bunch*
mantequilla (f.) *butter*
manzana (f.) *apple, block*
mapa (m.) *map*
mar (m.) *sea, ocean*

maravilla (f.) *wonder, miracle*
marcador (m.) *scoreboard*
marcar *to mark, to dial*
  marcar un gol *to make a goal*
  marcar un número de teléfono *to dial a phone number*
marchar *to go, to leave*
mareado/mareada (m./f.) *dizzy*
mareo (m.) *sickness*
  tener mareo *to be dizzy*
marido (m.) *husband*
marino/marina (m./f.) *marine*
  azul (m./f.) **marino** *navy blue*
marrón (m./f.) *brown*
martes (m.) *Tuesday*
martini (m.) *martini*
mártir (m./f.) *martyr*
marzo (m.) *March*
mas *but*
más *more, plus (+)*
  alguien más *somebody else*
  el/la/los/las (m. sg./f. sg./m. pl./f. pl.) **más … de …** *the most … in/of …*
  Hasta más tarde. *Until later.*
  más o menos *more or less, so-so, just okay*
  más … que … *more …/-er than …*
  más tarde *later*
matemáticas (f. pl.) *mathematics*
materia (f.) *school subject*
material (m.) *material*
matrícula (f.) *registration*
  derechos (m. pl.) **de matrícula** *tuition*
matricularse *to register*
matrimonio (m.) *marriage*
mayo (m.) *May*
mayor (m./f.) *older, bigger*
  el/la/los/las (m. sg./f. sg./m. pl./f. pl.) **mayor** *the oldest, the biggest*
mazorca (f.) *corncob*
me *me* (direct object pronoun); *(to/for) me* (indirect object pronoun); *myself*
  Me aburre/aburren … (sg./pl.) *I'm bored by …*
  Me encanta/encantan … (sg./pl.) *I really like …*
  Me gusta/gustan … (sg./pl.) *I like …*
  Me gustaría … *I'd like …*
  Me interesa/interesan … (sg./pl.) *I'm interested in …*
  Me levanto. *I get up.*

Me llamo … *My name is …*
¿Me permite …? *May I please …?* (fml.)
¿Me permites …? *May I please …?* (infml.)
mecánico/mecánica (m./f.) *mechanical*
  ingeniería (f.) mecánica *mechanical*
    engineering
mediano/mediana (m./f.) *medium*
medianoche (f.) *midnight*
  a medianoche *at midnight*
medias (f. pl.) *stockings, socks*
medicamento (m.) *medication*
  tomar un medicamento *to take medication*
medicina (f.) *medicine*
médico/médica (m./f.) *doctor*
  consultorio (m.) del médico *doctor's office*
medida (f.) *measurement*
  hacer a la medida *to custom sew*
medio/media (m./f.) *half, midway*
  a las cinco y media *at five thirty*
  medianoche (f.) *midnight*
  medio tiempo (m.) *halftime*
  término (m.) medio *medium-rare*
mediodía (m.) *noon*
  a mediodía *at noon*
  Son las doce del mediodía. *It's twelve noon.*
medir *to measure*
mejilla (f.) *cheek*
mejor (m./f.) *better*
  el/la/los/las (m. sg./f. sg./m. pl./f. pl.) mejor *the best*
  Es mejor que … *It's better that …*
memoria (f.) *memory*
menor (m./f.) *younger, smaller*
  el/la/los/las (m. sg./f. sg./m. pl./f. pl.) menor *the youngest, the smallest*
menos *less, minus (-)*
  a las seis menos cuarto *at a quarter to six*
  el/la/los/las (m. sg./f. sg./m. pl./f. pl.) menos … de … *the least … in/of …*
  Es la una menos cinco. *It's five to one.* (12:55)
  más o menos *more or less, so-so, just okay*
  menos … que … *less … than …*
mensaje (m.) *message*
  dejar un mensaje después de oír la señal *to leave a message after the tone*
  mensaje instantáneo *instant message*
mente (f.) *mind*
mentir *to lie*

mercadillo (m.) *flea market*
mercado (m.) *market*
merienda (f.) *snack time*
mermelada (f.) *jam*
mes (m.) *month*
  este mes *this month*
  mes entrante *next month*
  mes pasado *last month*
  mes que viene *next month*
mesa (f.) *table*
mesera (f.) *waitress*
mesero (m.) *waiter*
metro (m.) *metro, subway*
mexicano/mexicana (m./f.) *Mexican*
México (m.) *Mexico*
mezquita (f.) *mosque*
mí *me* (after a preposition)
mi/mis (sg./pl.) *my*
microondas (m.) *microwave*
miedo (m.) *fear*
  tener miedo *to be scared/afraid*
  tener miedo de que … *to be scared/afraid that …*
miel (f.) *honey*
mientras *while*
  mientras tanto *meanwhile*
miércoles (m.) *Wednesday*
mil *one thousand*
  cien mil *hundred thousand*
  diez mil *ten thousand*
  veinte mil *twenty thousand*
millón *one million*
  un millón de casas *one million houses*
minuto (m.) *minute*
mío/mía/míos/mías (m. sg./f. sg./m. pl./f. pl.) *mine*
mirar *to watch, to look at*
  mirar la televisón *to watch television*
  Mire … *Hmm …/Look …*
mismo/misma (m./f.) *same*
  ahora mismo *right now*
mixto/mixta (m./f.) *mixed*
moda (f.) *fashion*
  de moda *in fashion, in style*
módem (m.) *modem*
moderno/moderna (m./f.) *modern*
molestarse *to be bothered*
  molestarse de que … *to be bothered that …*

momento (m.) *moment*
  en este momento *at this moment, right now*
  Un momento. *Hold on./One moment.*
monitor (m.) *monitor*
montaña (f.) *mountain*
montar *to ride*
monumento (m.) *monument*
morado/morada (m./f.) *purple*
moreno/morena (m./f.) *dark-haired, dark-skinned*
morir *to die*
Moscú *Moscow*
mostrador (m.) *counter*
mostrar *to show*
mover *to move*
móvil (m.) *mobile phone*
muchacha (f.) *girl*
muchacho (m.) *boy*
mucho *a lot, much, very*
mucho/mucha (m./f.) *a lot of*
  Mucho gusto. *It's a pleasure.*
muchos/muchas (m. pl./f. pl.) *many, a lot of*
  Muchas gracias. *Thanks a lot.*
muebles (m. pl.) *furniture*
muela (f.) *molar*
muerto/muerta (m./f.) *dead person, dead*
mujer (f.) *woman, wife*
  mujer de negocios *businesswoman*
  mujer policía *policewoman*
muletilla (f.) *filler word/phrase*
multa (f.) *fine*
mundial (m./f.) *worldwide, worldly*
  campeonato (m.) mundial *world championship*
mundo (m.) *world*
muñeca (f.) *wrist*
músculo (m.) *muscle*
museo (m.) *museum*
música (f.) *music*
  música clásica *classical music*
musical (m.) *musical*
músico (m./f.) *musician*
muy *very*

N

nacional (m./f.) *national*
  llamada (f.) nacional *national call*
nacionalidad (f.) *nationality*

nada *nothing*
  De nada. *You're welcome.*
  nada más *nothing else*
  No hay nada que … *There's nothing that …*
  No, para nada. *No, not at all.*
nadar *to swim*
nadie *nobody, no one*
  No hay nadie que … *There's no one who/that …*
naipes (m. pl.) *(playing) cards*
naranja (f.) *orange (fruit)*
nariz (f.) *nose*
  dar de narices *to fall flat on one's face*
natación (f.) *swimming*
natural (m./f.) *natural*
naturaleza (f.) *nature*
náusea (f.) *nausea, sickness*
  tener náusea(s) *to be nauseated, to have nausea*
navaja (f.) *pocket-knife*
  navaja de afeitar *razor*
necesario/necesaria (m./f.) *necessary*
  Es necesario que … *It's necessary that …*
necesitar *to need*
negar *to deny*
  negar que … *to deny that …*
negocio (m.) *business*
  hombre (m.) de negocios *businessman*
  mujer (f.) de negocios *businesswoman*
negro/negra (m./f.) *black*
  estar negro de la risa *to laugh very hard (lit., to turn black with laughter)*
  ver todo negro *to be a pessimist (lit., to see everything as black)*
nervio (m.) *nerve*
nevar *to snow*
  Está nevando. *It's snowing.*
nevera (f.) *refrigerator*
ni *nor*
  ni … ni *neither … nor*
niebla (f.) *fog*
  niebla tóxica/con humo *smog*
nieta (f.) *granddaughter*
nieto (m.) *grandson*
  nietos (pl.) *grandsons, grandchildren*
nieve (f.) *snow*
niña (f.) *young girl, female child*
ningún/ninguno/ninguna (before m. sg.

nouns/m. sg./f. sg.) *no, none*

No hay ningún ... que ... *There's no ... that/ who ...*

niño (m.) *young boy, male child*

no *not, no*

No, para nada. *No, not at all.*

noche (f.) *evening, night*

a las siete de la noche *at seven p.m.*

Buenas noches. *Good evening./Good night.*

de la noche *at night, in the evening*

esta noche *tonight*

medianoche *midnight*

Nochebuena *Christmas Eve*

por la noche *at night*

nombre (m.) *name*

normal (m./f.) *normal*

normalmente *normally*

norte (m.) *north*

nos *us* (direct object pronoun); *(to/for) us* (indirect object pronoun); *ourselves*

nosotras *we* (f. pl.)

nosotros *we* (m. pl./mixed group)

nota (f.) *note, grade*

sacar buenas/malas notas *to get good/bad grades*

tomar nota *to take note*

noticia (f.) *a piece of news*

noticias (pl.) *news*

novecientos/novecientas (m./f.) *nine hundred*

novela (f.) *novel*

novela rosa *romance novel*

noventa *ninety*

novia (f.) *girlfriend, fiancée*

noviembre (m.) *November*

novio (m.) *boyfriend, fiancé*

nube (f.) *cloud*

nublado/nublada (m./f.) *cloudy*

Está nublado. *It's cloudy.*

nuera (f.) *daughter-in-law*

nuestro/nuestra/nuestros/nuestras (m. sg./f. sg./m. pl./f. pl.) *our*

nuestro/nuestra/nuestros/nuestras (m. sg./f. sg./m. pl./f. pl.) *ours*

Nueva York *New York*

nuevamente *once again*

nueve *nine*

nuevo/nueva (m./f.) *new*

número (m.) *number*

número de teléfono *telephone number*

nunca *never*

casi nunca *seldom, almost never*

O

o *or*

más o menos *more or less, so-so, just okay*

o ... o *either ... or*

objetivo (m.) *objective, aim*

objeto (m.) *object*

obra (f.) *play (theater)*

obra dramática *drama*

obrero/obrera (m./f.) *construction worker*

occidente (m.) *west*

océano (m.) *ocean*

ochenta *eighty*

ocho *eight*

a las ocho y diez *at eight ten (8:10)*

ochocientos/ochocientas (m./f.) *eight hundred*

octubre (m.) *October*

ocupado/ocupada (m./f.) *busy*

oeste (m.) *west*

oferta (f.) *offer*

oficina (f.) *office*

oficinista (m./f.) *office worker*

ofrecer *to offer*

oír *to hear*

Ojalá que ... *I hope/wish ...*

ojo (m.) *eye*

ojo por ojo *an eye for an eye*

oler *to smell*

olvidar *to forget*

once *eleven*

onza (f.) *ounce*

ópera (f.) *opera*

operadora (f.) *operator*

operarse *to have an operation*

opuesto/opuesta (m./f.) *opposite*

oración (f.) *prayer*

ordenador (m.) *computer*

oreja (f.) *ear*

oriente (m.) *east*

os *all of you* (infml.) (direct object pronoun); *(to/for) you* (infml. pl.)(indirect object pronoun); *yourselves* (infml.)

oscuro/oscura (m./f.) *dark*

azul (m./f.) oscuro *dark blue*

verde (m./f.) oscuro *dark green*

otoño (m.) *fall*
otro/otra (m./f.) *another*

P

paciencia (f.) *patience*
  tener paciencia *to be patient*
padrastro (m.) *stepfather*
padre (m.) *father*
  padres (pl.) *fathers, parents*
paga (f.) *wage*
pagar *to pay*
  pagar en efectivo *to pay cash*
  pagar la cuenta *to check out, to pay the bill/
  check*
página (f.) *page*
  páginas (pl.) amarillas *yellow pages*
  página web *webpage*
pago (m.) *payment*
país (m.) *country*
palabra (f.) *word*
palacio (m.) *palace*
palmo (m.) *palm*
  conocer palmo a palmo *to know like the back
  of one's hand*
palo (m.) *stick*
pan (m.) *bread*
panadería (f.) *bakery*
panameño/panameña (m./f.) *Panamanian*
pantalla (f.) *screen*
pantalones (m. pl.) *pants*
pantis (m. pl.) *women's underwear*
pantuflas (f. pl.) *slippers*
pantymedias (f. pl.) *stockings*
papa (f.) *potato*
papá (m.) *dad*
papi (m.) *dad*
papaya (f.) *papaya*
papel (m.) *paper*
  papel higiénico *toilet paper*
paquete (m.) *package*
para *for, towards, in order to, intended for, by/
until a certain time*
  espacio (m.) para charla *chat room*
  No, para nada. *No, not at all.*
parada (f.) *stop, bus stop*
parado/parada (m./f.) *unemployed*
paraguas (m.) *umbrella*
Paraguay (m.) *Paraguay*

parar *to stop, to leave*
  pararse de cabeza *to go crazy, to go out of
  one's mind*
parcial (m./f.) *partial*
  a tiempo parcial *part-time*
pardo/parda (m./f.) *grayish brown*
parecer *to look like, to seem*
  ¿Qué te parece … ? *What do you think of … ?*
  ¿Qué te parece si … ? *How about if … ?*
pared (f.) *wall*
pariente (m./f.) *relative*
París *Paris*
parque (m.) *park*
parqueadero (m.) *parking lot*
parrilla (f.) *grill*
  a la parrilla *grilled*
parte (f.) *part, side*
  ¿De parte de quién? *Who's calling?*
  por otra parte *on the other hand*
  por una parte *on the one hand*
particular (m./f.) *particular*
partido (m.) *(sport) game*
  partido de béisbol *baseball game*
partir *to leave, to set off*
  partir de … *to start from …*
párvulo/párvula (m./f.) *young child*
pasado/pasada (m./f.) *spoiled*
pasado/pasada (m./f.) *past*
  año (m.) pasado *last year*
  mes (m.) pasado *last month*
  semana (f.) pasada *last week*
pasaje (m.) *ticket*
pasaporte (m.) *passport*
pasar *to pass, to forward, to go by, to happen, to
spend*
  Le paso. *I'm putting you through. (on the
  phone)*
  pasar el día *to spend the day*
  ¿Qué pasa? *How's it going?*
pasatiempos (m.) *hobby*
Pascua (f.) *Easter*
pastelería (f.) *bakery (for pastries, etc.)*
pastilla (f.) *pill*
patata (f.) *potato*
patio (m.) *backyard*
peaje (m.) *toll*
peatón (m.) *pedestrian*
pecho (m.) *breast, chest*

pediatra (m./f.) *pediatrician*
pediatría (f.) *pediatrics*
pedir *to order, to ask for*
  pedir que ... *to request that ...*
película (f.) *movie, film*
  películas (pl.) de aventuras *adventure films*
  películas de horror *horror films*
  películas de suspenso *suspense films*
  películas románticas *romantic films*
pelo (m.) *hair*
pelota (f.) *ball*
peluquería (f.) *hair salon*
pena (f.) *pain, pity*
  ¡Qué pena! *That's too bad!*
pendientes (m. pl.) *earrings*
penicilina (f.) *penicillin*
pensar *to think*
  no pensar que ... *not to think that ...*
pensión (f.) *pension*
peor (m./f.) *worse*
  el/la/los/las (m. sg./f. sg./m. pl./f. pl.) peor
   the worst
pepino (m.) *cucumber*
pequeño/pequeña (m./f.) *small*
pera (f.) *pear*
percibir *to perceive*
perder *to lose, to miss*
  perder la cabeza *to lose one's head*
Perdón. *Excuse me.*
perezoso/perezosa (m./f.) *lazy*
  ser perezoso *to be lazy*
perfecto/perfecta (m./f.) *perfect*
perfume (m.) *perfume*
periódico (m.) *newspaper*
periodista (m./f.) *journalist*
período (m.) *period*
  período de prueba *probationary period*
permitir *to allow*
  ¿Me permite ... ? *May I please ... ?* (fml.)
  ¿Me permites ... ? *May I please ... ?* (infml.)
pero *but*
perro (m.) *dog*
persona (f.) *person*
  persona extranjero *stranger*
personal (m.) *staff*
Perú (m.) *Peru*
peruano/peruana (m./f.) *Peruvian*
pesar *to weigh*

pescadería (f.) *fish shop, fish market*
pescado (m.) *fish*
pésimo/pésima (m./f.) *terrible*
peso (m.) *peso*
pestañas (f. pl.) *eyelashes*
piano (m.) *piano*
picante (m./f.) *spicy*
pie (m.) *foot*
  dedo (m.) del pie *toe*
  ir a pie *to walk*
  poner el pie en el freno *to hit the brakes*
  tener los pies en la tierra *to have both feet on*
   the ground
piel (f.) *skin*
pierna (f.) *leg*
pieza (f.) *piece*
  de dos piezas *two-piece*
pijama (m.) *pajamas*
pimienta (f.) *pepper (spice)*
pimiento (m.) *pepper (vegetable)*
pinta (f.) *spot, appearance*
pintor/pintora (m./f.) *painter*
pintura (f.) *painting*
piscina (f.) *swimming pool*
piso (m.) *floor, apartment*
placer (m.) *pleasure*
plan (m.) *plan*
plancha (f.) *iron*
planchar *to iron*
  tabla (f.) de planchar *ironing board*
planilla (f.) *form*
  planilla de impuestos *tax return*
plano (m.) *map*
plano/plana (m./f.) *flat*
planta (f.) *plant*
plantilla (f.) *staff*
plástico (m.) *plastic*
plátano (m.) *banana*
plateado/plateada (m./f.) *silver (color)*
plato (m.) *plate, dish*
  lavar los platos *to do the dishes*
  plato del día *special of the day*
  plato principal *main dish*
playa (f.) *beach*
plaza (f.) *plaza, square*
  plaza de mercado *outdoor market*
pluma (f.) *pen*
pobre (m./f.) *poor, poor person*

los pobres *the poor*
poco *little*
Hablo un poco de español. *I speak a little Spanish.*
un poco *a little*
pocos/pocas (m. pl./f. pl.) *few*
poder *can, to be able to, to have permission to*
¿Podría…? *Could you…?*
podrido/podrida (m./f.) *bad, rotten*
policía (m./f.) *police officer*
mujer (f.) policía *policewoman*
poliéster (m.) *polyester*
pollo (m.) *chicken*
polvo (m.) *dust, powder*
leche (f.) en polvo *powdered milk*
poner *to put, to place*
poner el pie en el freno *to hit the brakes*
poner en espera *to put on hold*
ponerse *to become, to turn, to put something on*
ponerse colorado *to be embarrassed (lit., to turn red)*
por *for, by, around, at, because of, due to, in place of, in exchange for, through*
por casualidad *by chance*
por desgracia *unfortunately*
¡Por Dios! *For God's sake!*
por eso *for this reason*
Por favor. *Please.*
por fin *finally, at last*
por la noche *at night*
por la radio *on the radio*
por lo tanto *therefore*
por lo visto *apparently*
por otra parte *on the other hand*
por qué *why*
por supuesto *of course*
por teléfono *on the phone*
por una parte *on the one hand*
porque *because*
portero (m.) *goalkeeper*
portugués/portuguesa (m./f.) *Portuguese*
poseer *to own, to hold*
posible (m./f.) *possible*
Es posible que… *It is possible that…*
lo antes posible *as soon as possible*
postre (m.) *dessert*
practicar *to practice, to play (sports)*
precio (m.) *price*

etiqueta (f.) con el precio *price tag*
precio económico *reasonable price*
precisamente *precisely*
preferible (m./f.) *preferable*
Es preferible que… *It's preferable that…*
preferir *to prefer*
preferir que… *to prefer that…*
pregunta (f.) *question*
preguntar *to ask*
premio (m.) *prize*
prenda (f.) *garment*
preocuparse *to worry*
No se preocupe. *Don't worry.*
preocuparse de que… *to worry that…*
preparado/preparada (m./f.) *ready, prepared*
¿Preparados? *Ready?*
presentación (f.) *presentation*
presentar *to introduce*
Te presento a… *Let me introduce you to…*
presidente/presidenta (m./f.) *president*
presión (f.) *pressure*
prestigioso/prestigiosa (m./f.) *prestigious*
primavera (f.) *spring*
primer/primero/primera (before m. sg. nouns/ m./f.) *first*
primo/prima (m./f.) *cousin*
primos (pl.) *cousins*
principal (m./f.) *main*
plato (m.) principal *main dish*
prisa (f.) *hurry*
aprisa *quickly*
tener prisa *to be in a hurry*
probador (m.) *dressing room*
probar *to try, to taste*
probarse *to try on (clothes)*
problema (m.) *problem*
producir *to produce*
producto (m.) *product*
profesión (f.) *profession*
profesional (m./f.) *professional*
profesionalmente *professionally*
profesor/profesora (m./f.) *professor*
profesorado (m.) *faculty*
programa (m.) *program*
programa de entrevistas *talk show*
programa de televisión *television program*
prohibir *to forbid, to prohibit*
prohibir que… *to forbid that/to…*

prometer *to promise*
prometido/prometida (m./f.) *fiancé(e)*
pronto *soon*
propina (f.) *tip*
proteger *to protect*
provecho (m.) *benefit*
  ¡Buen provecho! *Enjoy the meal!*
próximo/próxima (m./f.) *near, next*
  próxima semana (f.) *next week*
proyecto (m.) *project*
prueba (f.) *proof, test, probation*
  período (m.) de prueba *probationary period*
pueblo (m.) *town*
puente (m.) *bridge, long weekend*
puerta (f.) *door*
  abrir la puerta *to open the door*
pues *so, since, therefore, well, then*
  Pues, aquí estamos. *Here we are.*
  Pues bien. *Fine.*
  Pues, nada. *Not much.*
puesto (m.) *(job) position, post*
pulmones (m. pl.) *lungs*
pulsera (f.) *bracelet*
punta (f.) *tip, end*
  ir de punta en blanco *to be dressed to the nines (lit., to go from the tip in white)*
punto (m.) *point*
  en punto *exactly*
  Son las tres en punto. *It's three o'clock sharp.*
puntual (m./f.) *punctual*
púrpura (m./f.) *purple*

Q

que *which, that* (relative pronoun, conjunction)
qué *what* (question)
  ¿A qué hora es? *At what time is it?*
  ¿De qué color es ... ? *What color is ... ?*
  por qué *why*
  ¡Qué ... ! *How ... !*
  ¡Qué bien! *How nice!*
  ¿Qué hay? *What's up?/What's going on?*
  ¿Qué hora es? *What time is it?*
  ¿Qué horas son? *What time is it?*
  ¿Qué pasa? *How's it going?*
  ¡Qué pena! *That's too bad!*
  ¿Qué quiere decir eso? *What does that mean?*
  ¿Qué tal? *What's happening?*
  ¿Qué tal si ... ? *How about if ... ?*

¿Qué te parece si ... ? *How about if ... ?*
¡Yo qué sé! *How do I know!?/How should I know!?*
quedar *to remain, to retain, to fit*
  quedar empatados *to be tied*
quemado/quemada (m./f.) *burnt*
querer *to want, to love*
  querer que ... *to want that/to ...*
  ¿Qué quiere decir eso? *What does that mean?*
  Quisiera ... *I'd like ...*
  Te quiero. *I love you.*
queso (m.) *cheese*
quien/quienes (sg./pl.) *who, whom* (relative pronoun)
quién/quiénes (sg./pl.) *who, whom* (question)
  ¿De parte de quién? *Who's calling?*
  ¿De quién ... ? *Whose ... ?*
  ¿Quién lo llama? *Who's calling?*
química (f.) *chemistry*
quince *fifteen*
quinientos/quinientas (m./f.) *five hundred*

R

racimo (m.) *bunch (of grapes)*
  racimo de uvas *bunch of grapes*
radio (f.) *radio*
  por la radio *on the radio*
rampa (f.) *ramp*
rápidamente *fast, quickly*
rápido *fast, quickly*
rápido/rápida (m./f.) *fast, quick*
ratón (m.) *mouse*
raya (f.) *stripe*
  a rayas *striped*
razón (f.) *reason*
  tener razón *to be right*
realismo (m.) *realism*
realista (m./f.) *realistic*
realmente *actually*
rebaja (f.) *discount*
  comprar en rebaja *to buy on sale*
rebajado/rebajada (m./f.) *reduced*
rebanada (f.) *slice*
recepción (f.) *reception desk*
recepcionista (m./f.) *receptionist*
receso (m.) *recess*
receta (f.) *recipe*
recibir *to receive*

recoger *to pick up*
recomendar *to recommend*
  recomendar que ... *to recommend that ...*
reconocer *to recognize*
recordar *to remember*
recorrido (m.) *route*
  recorrido por autobús *tour bus trip*
recreo (m.) *recreation*
recto *straight*
  Continúa recto. *Continue straight.*
redondo/redonda (m./f.) *round*
reducir *to reduce*
referencia (f.) *reference*
refresco (m.) *soft drink, soda*
regalar *to give (a gift)*
regalo (m.) *gift*
región (f.) *region*
regional (m./f.) *regional*
registrarse *to check in*
regresar *to return*
reír *to laugh*
relación (f.) *relationship*
relámpago (m.) *lightening*
relleno (m.) *stuffing, filling*
  frase (f.) de relleno *filler phrase*
reloj (m.) *watch, clock*
repetir *to repeat*
  Repita, por favor *Repeat, please.*
representante (m.) *representative*
reserva (f.) *reservation*
reservación (f.) *reservation*
resolver *to resolve*
responder *to answer*
responsable (m./f.) *responsible*
respuesta (f.) *answer*
restaurante (m.) *restaurant*
resto (m.) *rest*
resultado (m.) *result*
retransmitir *to forward*
retrasado/retrasada (m./f.) *slow, behind*
retrasar *to delay, to postpone*
retribución (f.) *repayment*
reunión (f.) *meeting*
reunir *to gather, to meet*
revista (f.) *magazine*
rico/rica (m./f.) *rich*
río (m.) *river*
risa (f.) *laughter*

estar negro de la risa *to laugh very hard (lit., to turn black with laughter)*
roca (f.) *rock*
rodilla (f.) *knee*
rojo/roja (m./f.) *red*
  estar rojo de la ira *to be very angry (lit., to be red with fury)*
romántico/romántica (m./f.) *romantic*
ropa (f.) *clothing*
  detergente (m.) de ropa *laundry detergent*
  lavar la ropa *to do the laundry*
  tienda (f.) de ropa *clothing store*
rosa (f.) *rose*
  novela (f.) rosa *romance novel*
  ver todo color de rosa *to be an optimist, to wear rose colored glasses (lit., to see everything pink)*
rosado/rosada (m./f.) *pink*
rubio/rubia (m./f.) *blonde*
rural (m./f.) *rural*
ruso (m.) *Russian (language)*

S

sábado (m.) *Saturday*
saber (intransitive verb) *to taste*
saber (transitive verb) *to know (facts, information), to learn*
  no saber ni jota de ... *to not have a clue about ...*
  ¿Quién sabe? *Who knows?*
  ¿Sabe cómo ...? *Do you know how to ...?*
  ¡Yo qué sé! *How do I know!?/How should I know!?*
saborear *to taste*
sacar *to take out, to get*
  sacar buenas notas *to get good grades*
  sacar malas notas *to get bad grades*
saco (m.) *jacket*
sal (f.) *salt*
sala (f.) *living room*
  sala de conferencias *meeting room, conference room, lecture hall*
salado/salada (m./f.) *salty*
salario (m.) *salary*
salida (f.) *exit*
salir *to leave, to go out*
  salir de viaje *to go on a trip*
salsa (f.) *sauce, salsa*

saltar *to skip*
  saltarse el semáforo *to go through a light*
saludable (m./f.) *healthy*
saludo (m.) *greeting*
  ¡Saludos! *Hello!*
sandalias (f. pl.) *sandals*
sangre (f.) *blood*
  hacerse un examen de sangre *to take a blood test*
  ser de sangre azul *to have blue blood (lit., to be of blue blood)*
se *himself, herself, itself, yourself* (fml.), *themselves, yourselves* (fml.); *(to/for) him, her, it, you* (fml. sg./pl.), *them* (indirect object pronoun, used in place of le/les when preceding lo/la/los/las); *you, people, one* (impersonal pronoun)
secadora (f.) *dryer*
sección (f.) *section*
seco/seca (m./f.) *dry*
  lavar en seco *to dry-clean*
secretaria (m./f.) *secretary*
secreto (m.) *secret*
sed (f.) *thirst*
  tener sed *to be thirsty*
seda (f.) *silk*
seguir *to follow*
  Siga derecho. *Go straight.*
  Siga por el carril de la derecha. *Stay in the right lane.*
segundo/segunda (m./f.) *second*
  segundo año *second year*
seguridad (f.) *safety, security*
  abrocharse el cinturón de seguridad *to buckle up*
seguro (m.) *insurance*
seguro/segura (m./f.) *sure, safe*
  Seguro/Segura que sí. *I'm sure.*
seis *six*
seiscientos/seiscientas (m./f.) *six hundred*
semáforo (m.) *traffic light*
  saltarse el semáforo *to go through a light*
semana (f.) *week*
  dos días a la semana *twice a week*
  esta semana *this week*
  fin (m.) de semana *weekend*
  próxima semana *next week*
  semana pasada *last week*
  semana que viene *next week*

todas las semanas *every week*
semanal (m./f.) *weekly*
semestre (m.) *semester*
señal (f.) *signal*
  dejar un mensaje después de oír la señal *to leave a message after the tone*
senderismo (m.) *hiking*
  hacer senderismo *to go hiking*
seno (m.) *breast*
señor (m.) *Mr.*
señora (f.) *Mrs.*
sensatamente *sensibly*
sensiblemente *perceptibly*
sentar *to seat*
  estar sentado *to be seated*
sentarse *to sit down*
sentido (m.) *sense, direction*
  de sentido único *one-way*
sentir *to feel*
  Lo siento. *I'm sorry.*
  sentir que … *to regret that …*
sentirse *to feel*
septiembre (m.) *September*
ser *to be*
  Es la una. *It's one o'clock.*
  Son las tres. *It's three o'clock.*
  Son las tres en punto. *It's three o'clock sharp.*
  ser caradura *to be shameless*
serie (f.) *series*
serio/seria (m./f.) *serious*
serpiente (f.) *snake*
servicio (m.) *service*
  ¿Está incluido el servicio? *Is service included?*
servilleta (f.) *napkin*
servir *to serve*
  ¿En qué puedo servirle? *How may I help you?*
sesenta *sixty*
sesión (f.) *session*
setecientos/setecientas (m./f.) *seven hundred*
setenta *seventy*
si *if*
  ¿Qué tal si …? *How about if …?*
  ¿Qué te parece si …? *How about if …?*
sí *yes*
  ¡Claro que sí! *Of course!*
  Creo que sí. *I think so.*
  Seguro/segura que sí. *I'm sure.*

¡Yo espero que sí! *I hope so!*
sicología (f.) *psychology*
siempre *always*
siesta (f.) *nap*
siete *seven*
siglo (m.) *century*
  este siglo *this century*
significar *to mean*
silenciosamente *quietly*
silla (f.) *chair, seat*
simpático/simpática (m./f.) *friendly*
simplemente *simply, only*
sin *without*
sindicato (m.) *union*
síndrome (m.) *syndrome*
  síndrome del túnel del carpio *carpal tunnel syndrome*
síntoma (m.) *symptom*
sistema (m.) *system*
  sistema de sonido *sound system*
sitio (m.) *place*
  sitio web *website*
situación (f.) *situation*
sobre *on top of, over, above, about*
  sobre todo *especially*
sobrecocido/sobrecocida (m./f.) *overcooked*
sobremesa (f.) *after-dinner conversation*
sobrina (f.) *niece*
sobrino (m.) *nephew*
sofá (m.) *sofa, couch*
sol (m.) *sun*
  gafas (f. pl.) de sol *sunglasses*
  Hace sol. *It's sunny.*
solamente *only*
soledad (f.) *solitude*
solicitar *to apply for, to request*
solicitud (f.) *application*
sólo *merely, solely, only*
solo/sola (m./f.) *sole, only, alone*
soltero/soltera (m./f.) *single*
solución (f.) *solution*
sombrero (m.) *hat*
sonar *to sound, to ring*
soñar *to dream*
  ¡Ni lo sueñes! *Don't even dream about it!*
  soñar con ... *to dream about ...*
sonido (m.) *sound*
  sistema (m.) de sonido *sound system*

sonido (m.) *sound*
sonreír *to smile*
sopa (f.) *soup*
sorprenderse *to be surprised*
  sorprenderse de que ... *to be surprised that ...*
sorpresa (f.) *surprise*
sótano (m.) *basement*
su/sus (sg./pl.) *his, her, its, their, your* (pl./sg. fml.)
suave (m./f.) *soft*
subasta (f.) *auction*
subterráneo (m.) *subway*
suburbano/suburbana (m./f.) *suburban*
suceso (m.) *event, happening*
sucio/sucia (m./f.) *dirty*
Sudamérica *South America*
suegra (f.) *mother-in-law*
suegro (m.) *father-in-law*
sueldo (m.) *pay*
suelo (m.) *floor*
suelto/suelta (m./f.) *loose, flowing*
sueño (m.) *sleepiness, sleep*
  tener sueño *to be sleepy*
suerte (f.) *luck*
suéter (m.) *sweater*
suficiente (m./f.) *enough*
sufrir *to suffer*
sugerir *to suggest*
  sugerir que ... *to suggest that ...*
supermercado (m.) *supermarket*
supuesto (m.) *supposition*
  por supuesto *of course*
sur (m.) *south*
suscriptor/suscriptora (m./f.) *subscriber*
  línea (f.) de suscriptor digital (DSL) *DSL*
suspender *to fail, to suspend*
  suspender un examen *to fail a test*
suspenso (m.) *suspense*
  películas (f. pl.) de suspenso *suspense films*
suyo/suya/suyos/suyas (m. sg./f. sg./m. pl./f. pl.) *his, hers, theirs, yours*

T

tabla (f.) *table, board*
  tabla de planchar *ironing board*
tacón (m.) *heel*
tajada (f.) *slice*
tal *such*

¿Qué tal? *How's it going?*
¿Qué tal si … ? *How about if … ?*
tal vez *perhaps*
talla (f.) *size*
tamaño (m.) *size*
también *also, too*
tampoco *neither, not either*
tan *so (very)*
  tan … como *as … as* (comparison)
tanto *in such a manner*
  mientras tanto *meanwhile*
  por lo tanto *therefore*
tanto/tanta (m./f.) *as much, as many*
  tanto/tanta/tantos/tantas (m. sg./f. sg./m. pl./f.
    pl.) … como *as … as* (comparison)
taquilla (f.) *box office*
tarde *late*
  Hasta más tarde. *Until later.*
  más tarde *later*
  Se me hace tarde. *I'm late.*
tarde (f.) *afternoon*
  a las cuatro de la tarde *at four p.m.*
  Buenas tardes. *Good afternoon.*
  de la tarde *in the afternoon*
  esta tarde *this afternoon*
tarea (f.) *homework*
tarjeta (f.) *card*
  tarjeta de crédito *credit card*
taxi (m.) *taxi*
taxista (m./f.) *taxi driver*
taza (f.) *cup*
tazón (m.) *bowl*
te *you* (infml. sg.) (direct object pronoun);
  (to/for) you (infml. sg.) (indirect object pronoun);
  yourself (infml.)
  Te presento a … *Let me introduce you to …*
té (m.) *tea*
teatro (m.) *theater*
techo (m.) *ceiling*
teclado (m.) *keyboard*
tecnología (f.) *technology*
tejanos (m. pl.) *jeans*
telefónico/telefónica (m./f.) *(of) telephone,
  telephonic*
  cabina (f.) telefónica *telephone booth*
  guía (f.) telefónica *phone book*
teléfono (m.) *telephone*
  colgar el teléfono *to hang up the phone*

contestar el teléfono *to answer the phone*
llamar por teléfono *to make a phone call*
llamar por teléfono a … *to call … on the
  phone*
marcar un número de teléfono *to dial a
  phone number*
número (m.) de teléfono *telephone number*
televisión (f.) *television*
  mirar la televisón *to watch television*
  programa (m.) de televisión *television
    program*
televisor (m.) *television (set)*
temer *to fear, to be afraid of*
temperatura (f.) *temperature*
templo (m.) *temple*
temprano *early* (adverb)
temprano/temprana (m./f.) *early*
tendón (m.) *tendon*
tenedor (m.) *fork*
tener *to have*
  Aquí tiene. *Here you are.*
  ¿Cuántos años tiene? *How old are you* (sg.
    fml.)*/is he/is she?*
  Que tenga un buen día. *Have a nice day.*
  tener … años *to be … years old*
  tener calor *to be hot, to be warm*
  tener cansancio *to be tired*
  tener dolor de cabeza *to have a headache*
  tener dolor de garganta *to have a sore throat*
  tener fiebre *to have a fever*
  tener frío *to be cold*
  tener ganas de … *to feel like …*
  tener hambre *to be hungry*
  tener interés en … *to be interested in …*
  tener la cabeza fría *to keep a cool head*
  tener la tensión alta/baja *to have high/low
    blood pressure*
  tener los pies en la tierra *to have both feet on
    the ground*
  tener mareo *to be dizzy*
  tener miedo *to be scared*
  tener náusea(s) *to be nauseated, to have
    nausea*
  tener paciencia *to be patient*
  tener prisa *to be in a hurry*
  tener que … *to have to …*
  tener razón *to be right*
  tener sed *to be thirsty*

tener sueño *to be sleepy*
tener tos *to have a cough*
tenis (m.) *tennis*
tensión (f.) *tension*
tener la tensión alta/baja *to have high/low blood pressure*
tomar la tensión *to take the blood pressure*
tercero/tercer/tercera (m. sg./m. sg. before a m. noun/f.) *third*
tercer año *third year*
terminar *to finish*
término (m.) *term, period, point*
término medio *medium-rare*
término tres cuartos *medium*
tesis (f.) *dissertation*
tetera (f.) *teakettle*
texto (m.) *text*
libro (m.) de texto *textbook*
ti *you* (infml. sg.) (after a preposition)
tía (f.) *aunt, woman*
tiempo (m.) *time, weather*
a tiempo *on time, in time*
a tiempo completo *full-time*
a tiempo parcial *part-time*
El tiempo es bueno. *The weather is good.*
¿Cómo estás de tiempo? *Do you have time?/ How are you doing for time?*
Hace muy buen tiempo. *It's beautiful.*
medio tiempo *halftime*
tienda (f.) *store, convenience store*
tienda de antigüedades *antique store*
tienda de electrodomésticos *appliances store*
tienda de ropa *clothing store*
tienda por departamentos *department store*
Tienes que … *You have to …*
tierra (f.) *land*
tener los pies en la tierra *to have both feet on the ground*
tímido/tímida (m./f.) *shy*
tinto/tinta (m./f.) *dark red*
vino (m.) tinto *red wine*
tío (m.) *uncle, man*
típico/típica (m./f.) *typical*
tipo (m.) *type*
tiquete (m.) *ticket*
título (m.) *degree, diploma*
toalla (f.) *towel*
tobillo (m.) *ankle*

tocar *to touch, to play an instrument*
tocar el piano *to play the piano*
tocar la guitarra *to play the guitar*
todavía *still, yet*
todo (m.) *everything*
sobre todo *especially*
todo/toda (m./f.) *all, every*
todas las semanas *every week*
todo el día *all day*
todos los días *every day*
tomar *to take, to have (food and drink)*
tomar la tensión *to take the blood pressure*
tomar un medicamento *to take medication*
tomate (m.) *tomato*
tono (m.) *tone, dial tone*
tormenta (f.) *storm*
torta (f.) *cake*
tos (f.) *cough*
tener tos *to have a cough*
tostada (f.) *toast*
totalmente *absolutely*
tóxico/tóxica (m./f.) *toxic*
niebla (f.) tóxica *smog*
trabajador/trabajadora (m./f.) *hardworking*
trabajar *to work*
¿En qué trabaja? *What do you do for a living?*
trabajo (m.) *job, work*
¡Buen trabajo! *Good job!*
historial (m.) de trabajo *résumé*
trabajo de investigación *research paper*
trabajo de verano *summer job*
trabajo fijo *steady job*
traducir *to translate*
traer *to bring, to get, to take*
tráfico (m.) *traffic*
traje (m.) *suit*
traje de baño *bathing suit*
tranquilo/tranquila (m./f.) *quiet, calm*
trasladar *to transfer*
tratamiento (m.) *treatment*
tratar *to treat*
¿Cómo te trata la vida? *How's life treating you?*
tratar *to try*
tratar de … *to try … (to do something)*
trece *thirteen*
treinta *thirty*
tren (m.) *train*

estación (f.) de tren *train station*
tres *three*
trescientos/trescientas (m./f.) *three hundred*
triste (m./f.) *sad*
  Es triste que ... *It's sad that ...*
tristemente *sadly*
trotar *to jog*
trueno (m.) *thunder*
tú *you* (sg. infml.) (subject pronoun)
tu/tus (sg./pl.) *your* (sg. infml.)
túnel (m.) *tunnel*
  síndrome (m.) del túnel del carpio *carpal tunnel syndrome*
turismo (m.) *tourism*
turista (m./f.) *tourist*
tuyo/tuya/tuyos/tuyas (m. sg./f. sg./m. pl./f. pl.) *yours* (infml.)

U

último/última (m./f.) *last*
  último grito (m.) *the very latest*
un *a* (m.)
una *a* (f.), *one (o'clock)*
  Es la una. *It's one o'clock.*
  It's one o'clock.
uña (f.) *nail, claw*
unas *some* (f. pl.)
único/única (m./f.) *only, unique, single*
  de sentido (m.) único *one-way*
unido/unida (m./f.) *united*
  los Estados Unidos *the United States*
universidad (f.) *university*
uno *one*
unos *some* (m. pl.)
urbano/urbana (m./f.) *urban*
urgentemente *urgently*
Uruguay (m.) *Uruguay*
uruguayo/uruguaya (m./f.) *Uruguayan*
usar *to use, to take*
usted *you* (sg. fml.) (subject pronoun)
  el de usted (m. sg.) *yours* (sg. fml.)
  la de usted (f. sg.) *yours* (sg. fml.)
ustedes *you* (pl.) (subject pronoun)
  el de ustedes (m. sg.) *yours* (pl.) (referring to a masculine singular object)
  la de ustedes (f. sg.) *yours* (pl.) (referring to a feminine singular object)
uvas (f. pl.) *grapes*

racimo (m.) de uvas *bunch of grapes*

V

vacaciones (f. pl.) *vacation*
  de vacaciones *on vacation*
vajilla (f.) *tableware*
  detergente (m.) de vajilla *dishwashing detergent*
vale (m.) *coupon, voucher*
  ¿Cuánto vale? *How much is it?*
Vamos ... *Let's go ...*
vaqueros (m. pl.) *jeans*
variedad (f.) *variety*
varios/varias (m./f.) *several*
vaso (m.) *glass*
vecino/vecina (m./f.) *neighbor*
vegetal (m.) *vegetable*
veinte *twenty*
veinticinco *twenty-five*
veinticuatro *twenty-four*
veintidós *twenty-two*
veintinueve *twenty-nine*
veintiocho *twenty-eight*
veintiséis *twenty-six*
veintisiete *twenty-seven*
veintitrés *twenty-three*
veintiuno *twenty-one*
velocidad (f.) *speed*
vendaje (m.) *bandage*
vendedor/vendedora (m./f.) *salesman/ saleswoman*
vender *to sell*
venezolano/venezolana (m./f.) *Venezuelan*
Venezuela (f.) *Venezuela*
venir *to come, to fit (somebody)*
  año (m.) que viene *next year*
  mes (m.) que viene *next month*
  Me viene bien. *It suits me fine.*
  semana (f.) que viene *next week*
venta (f.) *sale*
ventana (f.) *window*
ver *to see*
  A ver ... *Let's see ...*
  Nos vemos. *See you. (lit., We see each other.)*
  por lo visto *apparently*
  ver todo negro *to be a pessimist (lit., to see everything as black)*
verano (m.) *summer*

trabajo (m.) de verano   *summer job*
verdad (f.)   *truth*
  Es verdad.   *That's right.*
  No es verdad que …   *It is not true that …*
  ¿verdad?   *right?*
verde (m./f.)   *green*
  contar un chiste verde   *to tell a dirty joke (lit.,*
   to tell a green joke)
  verde oscuro   *dark green*
verdura (f.)   *vegetable*
vertebral (m./f.)   *vertebral*
  columna (f.) vertebral   *backbone, spinal*
   column
vestíbulo (m.)   *hall*
vestido (m.)   *dress*
  vestido de noche   *evening dress*
vestir   *to dress (someone)*
vestirse   *to get dressed*
veterinario/veterinaria (m./f.)   *veterinarian*
vez (f.)   *time*
  a veces   *sometimes*
  dos veces por semana   *twice a week*
  una vez   *once*
  tal vez   *perhaps*
vía (f.)   *lane*
viajar   *to travel*
viaje (m.)   *travel, trip*
  Buen viaje.   *Have a good trip.*
  salir de viaje   *to go on a trip*
vida (f.)   *life*
  ¿Cómo te trata la vida?   *How's life treating*
   you?
  hoja (f.) de vida   *résumé*
viejo/vieja (m./f.)   *old*
viento (m.)   *wind*
  Hace viento.   *It's windy.*
viento (m.)   *wind*
viernes (m.)   *Friday*
vincularse   *to form links*
  vincularse con …   *to form links with …*
vinilo (m.)   *vinyl*
  disco (m.) de vinilo   *vinyl record*
vino (m.)   *wine*
  vino blanco   *white wine*
  vino tinto   *red wine*
violeta (m./f.)   *violet (color)*
violín (m.)   *violin*
visita guiada (f.)   *guided tour*

visitante (m./f.)   *visitor*
visitar   *to visit*
  visitar los lugares de interés   *to go sightseeing*
vista (f.)   *view*
  conocer de vista   *to know by sight*
vitorear   *to cheer*
vivir   *to live*
volar   *to fly*
volver   *to turn, to return*
vosotras   *you* (f. pl. infml.) (subject pronoun)
  (used in Spain)
vosotros   *you* (m. pl. infml./mixed group infml.)
  (subject pronoun) (used in Spain)
voz (f.)   *voice*
  buzón (m.) de voz   *voice mail*
vuelo (m.)   *flight*
vuelta (f.)   *turn*
  a la vuelta de la esquina   *around the corner*
vuestro/vuestra/vuestros/vuestras (m. sg./f.
  sg./m. pl./f. pl.)   *your/yours* (pl. infml.) (used in
  Spain)

W

web (f.)   *web (internet)*
  página (f.) web   *webpage*
  sitio (m.) web   *website*

Y

y   *and*
  a las ocho y diez   *at eight ten (8:10)*
  a las cinco y media   *at a half past five*
  treinta y uno   *thirty-one*
ya   *already, now, right*
  Ya está.   *That's it.*
yerno (m.)   *son-in-law*
yo   *I*

Z

zanahoria (f.)   *carrot*
zapatería (f.)   *shoe store*
zapatillas (f. pl.)   *slippers*
  zapatillas deportivas   *sneakers, tennis shoes*
zapatos (m. pl.)   *shoes*
zumo (m.)   *juice*

English-Spanish

A

a *un/una* (m./f.)
  a lot *mucho*
  a lot of *mucho/mucha* (m./f.), *muchos/muchas*
  (m. pl./f. pl.)
abdomen *abdomen* (m.)
about *de, sobre, a eso de*
  about the (m.) *del (de + el)*
  at about nine o'clock *a eso de las nueve*
  dream about … *soñar con …*
  How about if …? *¿Qué tal si …?/¿Qué te*
    parece si …?
  not have a clue about … (to) *no saber ni jota*
    de …
above *encima, sobre*
  above … *encima de …*
absolute *absoluto/absoluta* (m./f.)
absolutely *absolutamente, totalmente*
  absolutely not *en absoluto*
absurd *absurdo/absurda* (m./f.)
academic *académico/académica* (m./f.)
academy *academia* (f.)
accept (to) *aceptar*
accident *accidente* (m.)
account *cuenta* (f.)
accountant *contable* (m./f.)
across from … *enfrente de …*
actor *actor* (m.)
actress *actriz* (f.)
actually *efectivamente, realmente*
acupuncture *acupuntura* (f.)
address *dirección* (f.)
adult *adulto/adulta* (m./f.)
adventure *aventura* (f.)
  adventure films *películas* (pl.) *de aventuras*
advise (to) *aconsejar*
  advise that/to … (to) *aconsejar que …*
after … *después de …*
  after-dinner conversation *sobremesa* (f.)
  It's ten after one in the morning. *Es la una y*
    diez de la madrugada.
afternoon *tarde* (f.)
  Good afternoon. *Buenas tardes.*
  in the afternoon *de la tarde*
  this afternoon *esta tarde*

afterwards *después*
against *contra*
age *edad* (f.)
agency *agencia* (f.)
agent *agente* (m./f.)
agitated *agitado/agitada* (m./f.)
agreement *acuerdo* (m.)
aim *objetivo* (m.)
airline *aerolínea* (f.)
airplane *avión* (m.)
airport *aeropuerto* (m.)
algebra *álgebra* (f.)
all *todo/toda* (m./f.)
  all day *todo el día*
  All right. *De acuerdo.*
  No, not at all. *No, para nada.*
allergic *alérgico/alérgica* (m./f.)
allergy *alergia* (f.)
alley *callejón* (m.)
allow (to) *permitir*
almost *casi*
  almost never *casi nunca*
alone *solo/sola* (m./f.)
already *ya*
  as you already know *como ya sabes*
also *igualmente, también*
always *siempre*
a.m. *de la mañana, de la madrugada*
  at nine a.m. *a las nueve de la mañana*
American *americano/americana* (m./f.),
  estadounidense (m./f.)
amusement *diversión* (f.)
  amusement park *parque* (m.) *de diversiones*
and *y*
  and on top of that … *y encima …*
anger *ira* (f.)
ankle *tobillo* (m.)
another *otro/otra* (m./f.)
answer *respuesta* (f.)
answer (to) *responder, contestar*
  answer the phone (to) *contestar el teléfono*
answering machine *contestador* (m.)
  (automático)
antique *antigüedad* (f.)
antiques *antigüedades* (f. pl.)
  antique store *tienda* (f.) *de antigüedades*
any *cualquier*
Anything else? *¿Algo más?*

apartment *apartamento* (m.), *piso* (m.)
apology *disculpa* (f.)
apparently *por lo visto*
appeal *gracia* (f.)
appearance *pinta* (f.)
appetite *apetito* (m.)
appetizer *entrada* (f.)
apple *manzana* (f.)
application *solicitud* (f.)
apply for (to) *solicitar*
appointment *cita* (f.)
April *abril* (m.)
architect *arquitecto/arquitecta* (m./f.)
architecture *arquitectura* (f.)
area *área* (m.)
Argentina *Argentina* (f.)
Argentinian *argentino/argentina* (m./f.)
arm *brazo* (m.)
around *por, a eso de*
  around the corner *a la vuelta de la esquina*
  around town *por la ciudad*
arrive (to) *llegar*
  arrive at … (to) *llegar a …*
art *arte* (m.)
artist *artista* (m./f.)
as *como, cual/cuales* (sg./pl.)
  as … as *tan … como* (comparisons), *tanto/
    tanta/tantos/tantas* (m. sg./f. sg./m. pl./f. pl.) *…
    como* (comparisons)
  as many/much *cuanto/cuanta/cuantos/
    cuantas* (m. sg./f. sg./m. pl./f. pl.), *tanto/tanta*
    (m./f.)
  as soon as possible *lo antes posible*
  as you already know *como ya sabes*
ask (to) *preguntar*
ask for (to) *pedir*
assistant *asistente* (m./f.)
astronaut *astronauta* (m./f.)
at *a, en, por*
  arrive at … (to) *llegar a …*
  at a quarter to six *a las seis menos cuarto*
  at about nine o'clock *a eso de las nueve*
  at dawn *al amanecer*
  at dusk *al atardecer*
  at five (o'clock) *a las cinco*
  at hand *a la mano*
  at last *por fin*
  at midnight *a medianoche*

  at night *por la noche*
  at noon *a mediodía*
  at the (m.) *al (a + el)*
  at the present time *actualmente*
  at this moment *en este momento*
  At what time is it? *¿A qué hora es?*
  look at (to) *mirar*
  No, not at all. *No, para nada.*
athlete *atleta* (m./f.)
athletic *atlético/atlética* (m./f.), *deportivo/
  deportiva* (m./f.)
attach (to) *adjuntar*
  attach a file (to) *adjuntar un documento/
    archivo*
attachment *anexo* (m.), *archivo* (m.), *documento*
  (m.) *adjunto*
attend (to) *asistir*
  attend to (to) *atender*
attention *atención* (f.)
attraction *atracción* (f.)
attractive *atractivo/atractiva* (m./f.)
auction *subasta* (f.)
August *agosto* (m.)
aunt *tía* (f.)
author *autor* (m.)
automatic *automático/automático* (m./f.)
available *disponible* (m./f.)
avenue *avenida* (f.)
avocado *aguacate* (m.)
axe *hacha* (f.)

B

baby *bebé* (m./f.)
  little baby *bebito/bebita* (m./f.)
bachelor's degree *licenciatura* (f.)
back *espalda* (f.), *atrás*
  know like the back of one's hand (to) *conocer
    palmo a palmo*
backbone *columna* (f.) *vertebral*
background *historial* (m.)
backyard *patio* (m.)
bad *malo/mala* (m./f.), *podrido/podrida* (m./f.)
  It's not bad. *No está mal.*
bad(ly) *mal*
bag *bolsa* (f.)
baggy *ancho/ancha* (m./f.)
bakery *panadería* (f.), *pastelería* (f.) (*for pastries,
  etc.*)

balcony *balcón* (m.)

bald *calvo/calva* (m./f.)

ball *balón* (m.), *pelota* (f.)

banana *plátano* (m.), *banana* (f.)

band *banda* (f.), *conjunto* (m.) *(music)*

bandage *vendaje* (m.)

bank *banco* (m.)

banker *banquero/banquera* (m./f.)

bar *bar* (m.)

barbershop *barbería* (f.)

bargain *ganga* (f.)

base *base* (f.)

baseball *béisbol* (m.)

  baseball game *partido* (m.) *de béisbol*

basement *sótano* (m.)

basketball *baloncesto* (m.)

bathe (to) *bañarse*

bathing suit *traje* (m.) *de baño*

bathing trunks *bañador* (m.)

bathroom *baño* (m.)

bathtub *bañera* (f.)

be (to) *estar, ser*

  be ... years old (to) *tener ... años*

  be a pessimist (to) *ver todo negro (lit., to see
  everything as black)*

  be able to (to) *poder*

  be afraid (to) *tener miedo*

  be afraid of (to) *temer*

  be afraid that ... (to) *tener miedo de que ...*

  be an optimist (to) *ver todo color de rosa (lit.,
  to see everything pink)*

  be angry that ... (to) *enfadarse de que ...*

  be bored (to) *aburrirse*

  be bothered (to) *molestarse*

  be bothered that ... (to) *molestarse de que ...*

  be called (to) *llamarse*

  be cold (to) *tener frío*

  be dizzy (to) *tener mareo*

  be dressed to the nines (to) *ir de punta en
  blanco (lit., to go from the tip in white)*

  be embarrassed (to) *ponerse colorado (lit., to
  turn red)*

  be glad (to) *alegrarse*

  be glad that ... (to) *alegrarse de que ...*

  be going to (do) (to) *ir a ...*

  be hot (to) *tener calor*

  be hungry (to) *tener hambre*

  be in a hurry (to) *tener prisa, tener cansancio*

be in good hands (to) *estar en buenas manos*

be interested in ... (to) *tener interés en ...*

be lacking (to) *faltar*

be lazy (to) *ser perezoso*

be nauseated (to) *tener náusea(s)*

be necessary (to) *faltar*

be not doing well (to) *estar mal*

be patient (to) *tener paciencia*

be present (to) *asistir*

be right (to) *tener razón*

be scared (to) *tener miedo*

be scared that ... (to) *tener miedo de que ...*

be seated (to) *estar sentado*

be shameless (to) *ser caradura*

be sleepy (to) *tener sueño*

be surprised (to) *sorprenderse*

be surprised that ... (to) *sorprenderse de
  que ...*

be thankful (to) *agradecer*

be thirsty (to) *tener sed*

be tied (to) *quedar empatados*

be tired (to) *tener consancio*

be very angry (to) *estar rojo de la ira (lit., to
  be red with fury)*

be warm (to) *tener calor*

May you be well. *Que esté bien.*

beach *playa* (f.)

bean *fríjol* (m.)

beauty mark *lunar* (m.)

because *porque*

  because of *por*

become (to) *ponerse*

bed *cama* (f.)

bedroom *dormitorio* (m.), *alcoba* (f.), *cuarto* (m.)

beef *carne* (f.)

beer *cerveza* (f.)

before *antes*

  before ... *antes de ...*

begin (to) *empezar, comenzar*

behind *detrás, atrás, retrasado/retrasada* (m./f.)

  behind ... *detrás de ...*

believe (to) *creer*

  not believe that ... (to) *no creer que ...*

below *bajo*

belt *cinturón* (m.)

benefit *beneficio* (m.), *provecho* (m.)

best (the) *el/la/los/las* (m. sg./f. sg./m. pl./f. pl.)
mejor

bet *apuesta* (f.)
bet (to) *apostar*
  bet that … (to) *apuesto a que …*
better *mejor* (m./f.)
  It's better that … *Es mejor que …*
between *entre*
  between … and … *entre … y …*
bicycle *bicicleta* (f.)
big *gran/grande* (before sg. nouns/all other cases),
  gordo/gorda (m./f.)
  bigger *mayor* (m./f.)
  biggest (the) *el/la/los/las* (m. sg./f. sg./m. pl./f.
  pl.) *mayor*
biking *ciclismo* (m.)
bill *cuenta* (f.)
billboard *cartelera* (f.)
billiards *billar* (m.)
biology *biología* (f.)
bitter *amargo/amarga* (m./f.)
black *negro/negra* (m./f.)
bleach *lejía* (f.)
blender *batidora* (f.)
block *cuadra* (f.), *manzana* (f.)
  It's two blocks from here. *Está a dos cuadras
  de aquí.*
block (to) *bloquear*
blonde *rubio/rubia* (m./f.)
blood *sangre* (f.)
  have blue blood (to) *ser de sangre azul* (lit., to
  be of blue blood)
  have high/low blood pressure (to) *tener la
  tensión alta/baja*
  take a blood test (to) *hacerse un examen de
  sangre*
  take the blood pressure (to) *tomar la tensión*
blouse *blusa* (f.)
blue *azul* (m./f.)
  color light blue (the) *azul* (m.) *claro*
  dark blue *azul oscuro*
  have blue blood (to) *ser de sangre azul* (lit., to
  be of blue blood)
  light blue *azul claro*
  navy blue *azul marino*
  sky blue *celeste* (m./f.)
board *bordo* (m.), *tabla* (f.)
  ironing board *tabla de planchar*
  on board *a bordo*
  Welcome aboard. *Bienvenidos a bordo.*

body *cuerpo* (m.)
Bolivia *Bolivia* (f.)
Bolivian *boliviano/boliviana* (m./f.)
bone *hueso* (m.)
book *libro* (m.)
bookshelf *estante* (m.)
bookstore *librería* (f.)
booth *cabina* (f.)
bore (to) *aburrir*
  I'm bored by … *Me aburre/aburren …* (sg./pl.)
bored *aburrido/aburrida* (m./f.)
  be bored (to) *aburrirse*
boring *aburrido/aburrida* (m./f.)
boss *jefe/jefa* (m./f.)
bottle *botella* (f.), *frasco* (m.)
bowl *cuenco* (m.), *tazón* (m.)
box *caja* (f.)
box office *taquilla* (f.)
boy *chico* (m.), *muchacho* (m.)
boyfriend *novio* (m.)
bracelet *pulsera* (f.)
brain *cerebro* (m.)
brake (automobile) *freno* (m.)
  hit the brakes (to) *poner el pie en el freno*
Brazil *Brasil* (m.)
Brazilian *brasilero/brasilera* (m./f.) (adjective),
  brasileño/brasileña (m./f.) (noun)
bread *pan* (m.)
breakfast *desayuno* (m.)
breast *seno* (m.), *pecho* (m.)
bridge *puente* (m.)
bring (to) *traer*
brochure *folleto* (m.)
broom *escoba* (f.)
brother *hermano* (m.)
  brothers, brothers and sisters *hermanos* (pl.)
brother-in-law *cuñado* (m.)
brown *marrón* (m./f.)
  grayish brown *pardo/parda* (m./f.)
buckle up (to) *abrocharse el cinturón de
  seguridad*
building *edificio* (m.)
bunch *manojo* (m.)
  bunch of grapes *racimo* (m.) *de uvas*
burnt *quemado/quemada* (m./f.)
bus *autobús* (m.)
  tour bus *recorrido* (m.) *por autobús*
bus stop *parada* (f.)

business *negocio* (m.)
  businessman *hombre* (m.) *de negocios*
  businesswoman *mujer* (f.) *de negocios*
busy *ocupado/ocupada* (m./f.)
  The line is busy. *Está comunicando.*
but *pero, mas*
butcher shop *carnicería* (f.)
butter *mantequilla* (f.)
buy (to) *comprar*
  buy on sale (to) *comprar en rebaja*
by *por, en*
  by chance *por casualidad*
  by (a certain time) *para*
  go by (to) *pasar*
  I'm bored by ... *Me aburre/aburren ...* (sg./pl.)
  know by sight (to) *conocer de vista*
Bye. *Chao.*

C

cabin *cabina* (f.)
cable *cable* (m.)
café *cafetería* (f.)
cafeteria *cafetería* (f.)
cake *torta* (f.)
call (to) *llamar*
  be called (to) *llamarse*
  call ... on the phone (to) *llamar por teléfono
    a ...*
  make a phone call (to) *llamar por teléfono*
  Who's calling? *¿Quién lo llama?*
calm *tranquilo/tranquila* (m./f.)
camera *cámara* (f.)
camp *campo* (m.)
camping *cámping* (m.)
  go camping (to) *ir de cámping*
can *lata* (f.)
can *poder*
  Could you ...? *¿Podría ...?*
Canada *Canadá* (m.)
Canadian *canadiense* (m./f.)
cancel (to) *cancelar*
candidate *candidato/candidata* (m./f.)
capacity *capacidad* (f.)
car *auto* (m.), *automóvil* (m.), *carro* (m.), *coche* (m.)
card *tarjeta* (f.)
  playing cards *naipes* (m. pl.), *cartas* (f. pl.)
cardboard *cartón* (m.)
carefully *atentamente*

carnival *carnaval* (m.)
carpal tunnel syndrome *síndrome* (m.) *del túnel
del carpio*
carpenter *carpintero/carpintera* (m./f.)
carpet *alfombra* (f.)
carpus *carpio* (m.)
carrot *zanahoria* (f.)
carry (to) *llevar*
carton *bote* (m.), *cartón* (m.)
case *caso* (m.)
cash *efectivo* (m.)
  pay cash (to) *pagar en efectivo*
cash register *caja* (f.)
casual *informal* (m./f.)
cat *gato* (m.)
catch (to) *coger*
cathedral *catedral* (f.)
CD *CD* (m.)
  CD player *lector* (m.) *de CD*
  CD-ROM *CD rom* (m.)
  CD-ROM drive *lector* (m.) *de CD rom*
ceiling *techo* (m.)
cell phone *celular* (m.)
center *centro* (m.)
century *siglo* (m.)
  this century *este siglo*
chair *silla* (f.)
champagne *champaña/champán* (f./m.)
champion *campeón/campeona* (m./f.)
championship *campeonato* (m.)
chance *casualidad* (f.)
  by chance *por casualidad*
change *cambio* (m.)
change (to) *cambiar*
channel *canal* (m.)
charm *encanto* (m.)
chat *charla* (f.)
  chat room *espacio* (m.) *para charla, chat* (m.)
cheap *barato/barata* (m./f.)
check *cheque* (m.), *cuenta* (f.)
check in (to) *registrarse*
check out (to) *pagar la cuenta*
cheek *mejilla* (f.)
cheer (to) *vitorear*
cheese *queso* (m.)
chemistry *química* (f.)
chess *ajedrez* (m.)
chest *pecho* (m.)

chicken *pollo* (m.)
child (male/female) *niño/niña* (m./f.)
  child psychology *sicología* (f.) *infantil*
  children (sons and daughters) *hijos* (pl.)
  children's *infantil* (m./f.)
  young child *párvulo/párvula* (m./f.)
Chile *Chile* (m.)
Chilean *chileno/chilena* (m./f.)
chin *barbilla* (f.)
Chinese (language) *chino* (m.)
chocolate *chocolate* (m.)
choir *coro* (m.)
choose (to) *elegir, escoger*
chop *chuleta* (f.)
  lamb chop *chuleta de cordero*
Christmas Eve *Nochebuena*
church *iglesia* (f.)
cigarette *cigarrillo* (m.)
  pack of cigarettes *cajetilla* (f.) *de cigarrillos*
circus *circo* (m.)
city *ciudad* (f.)
city hall *ayuntamiento* (m.)
class *clase* (f.)
classic *clásico/clásica* (m./f.)
  classical music *música* (f.) *clásica*
classroom *aula* (m.)
claw *uña* (f.)
clean *limpio/limpia* (m./f.)
clearly *claramente, claro*
clinic *clínica* (f.)
  clinical pharmacy *farmacia* (f.) *clínica*
clock *reloj* (m.)
close *cerca*
  close to ... *cerca de ...*
close (to) *cerrar*
closet *armario* (m.)
clothing *ropa* (f.)
  clothing store *tienda* (f.) *de ropa*
cloud *nube* (f.)
cloudy *nublado/nublada* (m./f.)
  It's cloudy. *Está nublado.*
club *club* (m.)
coach *entrenador/entrenadora* (m./f.)
coal *carbón* (m.)
coca *coca* (f.)
code *código* (m.)
coffee *café* (m.)
  coffee shop *cafetería* (f.)

coffee-colored *café* (m./f.)
coffeemaker *cafetera* (f.)
coincidence *coincidencia* (f.)
  What a coincidence! *¡Qué coincidencia!*
coincidence *casualidad* (f.)
cold *frío/fría* (m./f.)
cold temperature/sensation *frío* (m.)
  be cold (to) *tener frío*
  It's cold. *Hace frío.*
colleague *colega/colega* (m./f.)
collect (to) *coleccionar*
collection *colección* (f.)
cologne *colonia* (f.)
Colombia *Colombia* (f.)
Colombian *colombiano/colombiana* (m./f.)
color *color* (m.)
  color gray (the) *gris* (m.)
  color light blue (the) *azul* (m.) *claro*
  wear rose-colored glasses (to) *ver todo color de rosa* (lit., to see everything pink)
  What color is ... ? *¿De qué color es ... ?*
column *columna* (f.)
combine (to) *combinar*
come (to) *venir*
comedy *comedia* (f.)
comfortable *cómodo/cómoda* (m./f.)
coming *entrante* (m./f.)
comma *coma* (f.)
commercial *comercial* (m./f.)
communicate (to) *comunicar*
company *compañía* (f.)
complete (to) *completar*
completely *completamente*
computer *computadora* (f.), *ordenador* (m.)
concert *concierto* (m.)
conference *conferencia* (f.)
  conference room *sala de conferencias*
congratulate (to) *felicitar*
congratulations *enhorabuena* (f.)
  Congratulations! *¡Felicitaciones!*
connect (to) *conectar*
connection *conexión* (f.)
construction worker *obrero/obrera* (m./f.)
consult (to) *consultar*
continue (to) *continuar*
  Continue straight. *Continúa recto.*
contract *contrato* (m.)
contribution *contribución* (f.)

convenience store *tienda* (f.)
cook (to) *cocinar*
cookie *galleta* (f.)
cooking *cocina* (f.)
copy *copia* (f.)
copy (to) *copiar*
corncob *mazorca* (f.)
corner *esquina* (f.)
 around the corner *a la vuelta de la esquina*
cost (to) *costar*
 How much does it cost? *¿Cuánto cuesta?*
cotton *algodón* (m.)
couch *sofá* (m.)
cough *tos* (f.)
 have a cough (to) *tener tos*
count (to) *contar*
counter *mostrador* (m.)
country *país* (m.)
coupon *vale* (m.)
course *curso* (m.), *asignatura* (f.)
court *juzgado* (m.)
cousin *primo/prima* (m./f.)
 cousins *primos* (pl.)
craft *artesanía* (f.)
credit *crédito* (m.)
 credit card *tarjeta* (f.) *de crédito*
creme *crema* (f.)
crime *delito* (m.)
cross (to) *cruzar*
cry *grito* (m.)
cry (to) *llorar*
cucumber *pepino* (m.)
cup *taza* (f.)
cupboard *aparador* (m.)
curriculum *currículum* (m.)
 CV *currículum vítae*
curtain *cortina* (f.)
custom sew (to) *hacer a la medida*
customer *cliente* (m./f.)
cycling *ciclismo* (m.)

D

dad *papá* (m.), *papi* (m.)
daily *diario/diaria* (m./f.)
dairy store *lechería* (f.)
dance (to) *bailar*
dancing *baile* (m.)
dark *oscuro/oscura* (m./f.)

dark blue *azul* (m./f.) *oscuro*
dark green *verde* (m./f.) *oscuro*
dark-skinned *moreno/morena* (m./f.)
date *fecha* (f.)
daughter *hija* (f.)
daughter-in-law *nuera* (f.)
dawn *amanecer* (m.)
 at dawn *al amanecer*
day *día* (m.)
 all day *todo el día*
 every day *todos los días*
 Have a nice day. *Que tenga un buen día.*
 special of the day *plato del día*
 spend the day (to) *pasar el día*
 this day *este día*
 working day *jornada* (f.)
dead person, dead *muerto/muerta* (m./f.)
decade *década* (f.)
December *diciembre* (m.)
decide (to) *decidir*
decision *decisión* (f.)
dedicate (to) *dedicar*
degree *grado* (m.), *título* (m.)
delay (to) *retrasar*
delete (to) *eliminar*
delicatessen *charcutería* (f.)
delicious *delicioso/deliciosa* (m./f.)
demand (to) *exigir*
demanding *exigente* (m./f.)
dentist *dentista* (m./f.)
deny (to) *negar*
 deny that ... (to) *negar que ...*
deodorant *desodorante* (m.)
department *departamento* (m.), *facultad* (f.) (at a
 college/university)
 department store *tienda* (f.) *por
 departamentos*
depend (to) *depender*
 depend on ... (to) *depender de ...*
describe (to) *describir*
description *descripción* (f.)
desert *desierto* (m.)
design *diseño* (m.)
desire *gana* (f.)
desk *escritorio* (m.)
dessert *postre* (m.)
detail *detalle* (m.)
detergent *detergente* (m.)

dishwashing detergent *detergente de vajilla*
laundry detergent *detergente de ropa*
detest (to) *detestar*
develop (to) *desarrollar*
dial (to) *marcar*
dial a phone number (to) *marcar un número de teléfono*
dial tone *tono* (m.)
diarrhea *diarrea* (f.)
diary *diario* (m.)
keep a diary (to) *llevar un diario*
die (to) *morir*
difference *diferencia* (f.)
different *diferente* (m./f.)
difficult *difícil* (m./f.)
difficult situation *apuro* (m.)
digital *digital* (m./f.)
diligently *diligentemente*
diner *cafetería* (f.)
dining room *comedor* (m.)
dinner *cena* (f.), *comida* (f.)
diploma *diploma* (m.), *título* (m.)
direct (to) *dirigir*
direction *dirección* (f.), *sentido* (m.)
dirty *sucio/sucia* (m./f.)
disaster *desastre* (m.)
discount *descuento* (m.), *rebaja* (f.)
give a discount (to) *hacer un descuento*
discuss (to) *discutir*
disease *enfermedad* (f.)
dish *plato* (m.)
do the dishes(to) *lavar los platos*
main dish *plato principal*
dishwasher *lavaplatos* (m.)
dishwashing detergent *detergente* (m.) *de vajilla*
disk *disco* (m.)
Disneyland *Disneylandia*
display window *escaparate* (m.)
dissertation *tesis* (f.)
diving *buceo* (m.)
divorce (someone) (to) *divorciarse de …*
get a divorce (to) *divorciarse*
divorced *divorciado/divorciada* (m./f.)
dizzy *mareado/mareada* (m./f.)
be dizzy (to) *tener mareo*
do (to) *hacer*
be not doing well (to) *estar mal*

Do me the favor of … *Hágame el favor de …*
do the dishes (to) *lavar los platos*
do the laundry (to) *lavar la ropa*
doctor *doctor/doctora* (m./f.), *médico/médica* (m./f.)
doctor's office *consultorio* (m.) *del médico*
document *documento* (m.)
documentary *documental* (m.)
dog *perro* (m.)
dollar *dólar* (m.)
dominate (to) *dominar*
done *hecho/hecha* (m./f.)
door *puerta* (f.)
doubt (to) *dudar*
doubt that … (to) *dudar que …*
download (to) *bajar*
drama *drama* (m.), *obra* (f.) *dramática*
dramatic *dramático/dramática* (m./f.)
draw (to) *empatar*
drawer *cajón* (m.)
dream (to) *soñar*
Don't even dream about it! *¡Ni lo sueñes!*
dream about … *soñar con …*
dress *vestido* (m.)
be dressed to the nines (to) *ir de punta en blanco* (lit., to go from the tip in white)
evening dress *vestido de noche*
dress (someone) (to) *vestir*
dressing room *probador* (m.)
drink *bebida* (f.)
drink (to) *beber*
drive (to) *conducir*
drugstore *farmacia* (f.)
drunk *borracho/borracha* (m./f.)
dry *seco/seca* (m./f.)
dry-clean (to) *lavar en seco*
dryer *secadora* (f.)
DSL *línea* (f.) *de suscriptor/abonado digital (DSL)*
due to *por*
during *durante*
dusk *atardecer* (m.)
at dusk *al atardecer*
dust *polvo* (m.)
duty *derecho* (m.)
DVD *DVD* (m.)
DVD player *lector* (m.) *de DVD*

E

each *cada* (m./f.)
ear *oreja* (f.)
early *temprano/temprana* (m./f.)
  early morning (from midnight till
    daybreak) *madrugada* (f.)
early (adverb) *temprano*
earn (to) *ganar*
earnings *ingreso* (m.)
earrings *pendientes* (m. pl.)
easily *fácilmente*
east *este* (m.), *oriente* (m.)
Easter *Pascua* (f.)
easy *fácil* (m./f.)
eat (to) *comer*
  eat dinner (to) *cenar*
economical *económico/económica* (m./f.)
economics *economía* (f.)
Ecuador *Ecuador* (m.)
Ecuadorian *ecuatoriano/ecuatoriana* (m./f.)
efficiently *eficientemente*
egg *huevo* (m.)
eight *ocho*
  at eight ten (8:10) *a las ocho y diez*
  eight hundred *ochocientos/ochocientas* (m./f.)
  twenty-eight *veintiocho*
eighteen *dieciocho, diez y ocho*
eighty *ochenta*
elbow *codo* (m.)
electric *eléctrico/eléctrica* (m./f.)
electrical *eléctrico/eléctrica* (m./f.)
  electrical appliance *electrodoméstico* (m.)
electrician *electricista/electricista* (m./f.)
electronic *electrónico/electrónica* (m./f.)
  electronics store *tienda* (f.) *de
    electrodomésticos*
elegant *elegante* (m./f.)
elementary school *colegio* (m.)
elephant *elefante* (m.)
eleven *once*
eliminate (to) *eliminar*
e-mail *correo* (m.) *electrónico, correo-e* (m.)
  e-mail address *dirección* (f.) *de correo
    electrónico*
  e-mail attachment *anexo* (m.) *al correo
    electrónico*
employee *empleado/empleada* (m./f.)

employment *empleo* (m.)
enchant (to) *encantar*
enclosed *adjunto/adjunta* (m./f.)
end *fin* (m.), *final* (m.), *punta* (f.)
engineer *ingeniero/ingeniera* (m./f.)
engineering *ingeniería* (f.)
  mechanical engineering *ingeniería mecánica*
England *Inglaterra* (f.)
English *inglés/inglesa* (m./f.)
English (language) *inglés* (m.)
  Do you speak English? (infml.) *¿Hablas inglés?*
  Do you speak English? (fml.) *¿Habla usted
    inglés?*
Enjoy the meal! *¡Buen provecho!*
enough *suficiente* (m./f.), *bastante*
enter (to) *entrar*
entertainment *entretenimiento* (m.)
entrance *entrada* (f.)
equal *igual* (m./f.)
  ... equals (=) ... *... es igual a ...*
erase (to) *borrar*
especially *sobre todo*
even *hasta*
evening *noche* (f.)
  evening dress *vestido* (m.) *de noche*
  Good evening. *Buenas noches.*
  in the evening *de la noche*
  this evening *esta noche* (f.)
event *suceso* (m.)
every *todo/toda* (m./f.), *cada* (m./f.)
  every day *todos los días*
  every week *todas las semanas*
everything *todo* (m.)
  How is everything going? *¿Cómo va todo?*
ex- *ex*
exact *exacto/exacta* (m./f.), *en punto*
  Exactly. *Exacto.*
exceed (to) *exceder*
excellent *excelente* (m./f.)
exception *excepción* (f.)
exchange (to) *cambiar, intercambiar*
  in exchange for *por*
exciting *emocionante* (m./f.)
excuse *disculpa* (f.)
excuse (to) *disculpar*
  Excuse me. *Disculpa./Disculpe.* (infml./fml.)/
    Perdón.
exercise *ejercicio* (m.)

exit *salida* (f.)
expense *gasto* (m.)
expensive *caro/cara* (m./f.), *costoso/costosa* (m./f.)
experience *experiencia* (f.)
explanation *explicación* (f.)
extra *extra* (m./f.)
  extra hours *horas* (f. pl.) *extras*
extraordinary *extraordinario/extraordinaria*
  (m./f.)
extroverted *extrovertido/extrovertida* (m./f.)
eye *ojo* (m.)
  an eye for an eye *ojo por ojo*
eyebrow *ceja* (f.)
eyeglasses *gafas* (f. pl.)
  wear rose-colored glasses (to) *ver todo color*
    de rosa (lit., to see everything pink)
eyelashes *pestañas* (f. pl.)

F

face *cara* (f.)
  face the circumstances (to) *dar la cara*
factory *fábrica* (f.)
faculty *profesorado* (m.)
fail (to) *suspender*
  fail a test (to) *suspender un examen*
fall *otoño* (m.)
fall (to) *caer*
  fall flat on one's face (to) *dar de narices*
fame *fama* (f.)
familiar *familiar* (m./f.)
family *familia* (f.)
  (of) family *familiar* (m./f.)
famous *famoso/famosa* (m./f.)
fan *aficionado/aficionada* (m./f.), *hincha* (m./f.)
fantastic *fantástico/fantástica* (m./f.)
far *lejos*
  far from … *lejos de …*
farmer *granjero/granjera* (m./f.)
fashion *moda* (f.)
  in fashion *de moda*
fast (adjective) *rápido/rápida* (m./f.)
fast (adverb) *rápidamente, rápido*
fasten (to) *abrochar*
fat *gordo/gorda* (m./f.)
father *padre* (m.)
father-in-law *suegro* (m.)
fatigue *consancio* (m.)
favor *favor* (m.)

  Do me the favor of … *Hágame el favor de …*
favorite *favorito/favorita* (m./f.)
fax machine *fax* (m.)
fear *miedo* (m.)
fear (to) *temer*
February *febrero* (m.)
feel (to) *sentir, sentirse*
  feel like … (to) *tener ganas de …*
fees *honorarios* (m. pl.)
festive *festivo/festiva* (m./f.)
fever *fiebre* (f.)
  have a fever (to) *tener fiebre*
few *pocos/pocas* (m. pl./f. pl.)
fiancé(e) *prometido/prometida* (m./f.)
field *campo* (m.)
fifteen *quince*
fifty *cincuenta*
file *archivo* (m.), *carpeta* (f.), *documento* (m.)
filing cabinet *armario* (m.)
fill (to) *llenar*
filler phrase *frase* (f.) *de relleno*
  filler word/phrase *muletilla* (f.)
filling *relleno* (m.)
film *película* (f.)
  adventure films *películas* (pl.) *de aventuras*
  horror films *películas de horror*
  romantic films *películas románticas*
  suspense films *películas de suspenso*
finally *por fin*
finance *finanzas* (f. pl.)
find (to) *encontrar*
  find (something) (to) *dar con*
fine (adjective) *estupendo/estupenda* (m./f.)
  Fine. *Pues bien.*
  I'm fine. *Estoy bien.*
fine (noun) *multa* (f.)
finger *dedo* (m.)
finish (to) *acabar, terminar*
first *primer/primero/primera* (before m. sg.
  nouns/m./f.)
fish *pescado* (m.)
  fish shop/market *pescadería* (f.)
fit (to) *quedar*
  fit (somebody) (to) *venir*
  It suits me fine. *Me viene bien.*
five *cinco*
  at a half past five *a las cinco y media*
  at five (o'clock) *a las cinco*

five hundred *quinientos/quinientas* (m./f.)
forty-five *cuarenta y cinco*
  It's five to one. (12:55) *Es la una menos cinco.*
twenty-five *veinticinco*
fixed *fijo/fija* (m./f.)
flat *plano/plana* (m./f.)
flea market *mercadillo* (m.)
flight *vuelo* (m.)
floor *suelo* (m.), *piso* (m.)
flower *flor* (f.)
flowing *suelto/suelta* (m./f.)
fly (to) *volar*
fog *niebla* (f.)
follow (to) *seguir*
food *comida* (f.)
fool *bobo/boba* (m./f.)
foot *pie* (m.)
  have both feet on the ground (to) *tener los pies en la tierra*
football *fútbol americano*
for *por, para*
  For God's sake! *¡Por Dios!*
  for this reason *por eso*
forbid (to) *prohibir*
  forbid that/to … (to) *prohibir que …*
forehead *frente* (f.)
foreign *extranjero/extranjera* (m./f.)
forest *bosque* (m.)
forget (to) *olvidar*
fork *tenedor* (m.)
form *planilla* (f.)
  form links (to) *vincularse*
  form links with … (to) *vincularse con …*
forty *cuarenta*
  forty-five *cuarenta y cinco*
forward (to) *retransmitir, pasar*
fossil *fósil* (m.)
four *cuatro*
  at four p.m. *a las cuatro de la tarde*
  four hundred *cuatrocientos/cuatrocientas* (m./f.)
  twenty-four *veinticuatro*
fourteen *catorce*
free *gratis, libre* (m./f.)
freeway *autopista* (f.), *autovía* (f.), *carretera* (f.)
French *francés/francesa* (m./f.)
French (language) *francés* (m.)
  I speak French fluently. *Domino el francés.*

frequency *frecuencia* (f.)
frequent *frecuente* (m./f.)
frequently *frecuentemente, con frecuencia*
Friday *viernes* (m.)
fried *frito/frita* (m./f.)
friend *amigo/amiga* (m./f.)
friendly *simpático/simpática* (m./f.)
from *de, desde*
  across from … *enfrente de …*
  far from … *lejos de …*
  from the (m.) *del (de + el)*
  from … through … *de … a …*
  It's two blocks from here. *Está a dos cuadras de aquí.*
  start from … (to) *partir de …*
  Where are you from? *¿De dónde eres?*
fruit *fruta* (f.)
full *completo/completa* (m./f.)
  full-time *a tiempo completo*
fun *divertido/divertida* (m./f.)
  have fun (to) *divertirse*
function (to) *funcionar*
funny *gracioso/graciosa* (m./f.)
furnished *amueblado/amueblada* (m./f.)
furniture *muebles* (m. pl.)
future *futuro* (m.)

G

gallery *galería* (f.)
game *juego* (m.), *partido* (m.) *(sport)*
garage *garaje* (m.)
garden *jardín* (m.)
garment *prenda* (f.)
gas station *gasolinera* (f.)
gather (to) *reunir*
gel *gel* (m.)
generally *generalmente*
generous *generoso/generosa* (m./f.)
gentleman *caballero* (m.)
geography *geografía* (f.)
German *alemán/alemana* (m./f.)
German (language) *alemán* (m.)
get (to) *sacar, traer*
  get a divorce (to) *divorciarse*
  get angry (to) *enfadarse*
  get dressed (to) *vestirse*
  get good/bad grades (to) *sacar buenas/malas notas*

get married (to) *casarse*
get to ... (to) *llegar a ...*
get up (to) *levantarse, despertarse*
  I get up. *Me levanto.*
gift *regalo* (m.)
girl *chica* (f.), *muchacha* (f.)
girlfriend *novia* (f.)
give (to) *dar*
  give (a gift) (to) *regalar*
  give a discount (to) *hacer un descuento*
  give birth (to) *dar a luz*
  give thanks (to) *dar (las) gracias*
glass *vaso* (m.)
gloves *guantes* (m. pl.)
go (to) *ir, marchar*
  be going to (do) (to), go to (a place) (to) *ir a ...*
  go by (to) *pasar*
  go camping (to) *ir de cámping*
  go crazy (to), go out of one's mind (to) *pararse de cabeza*
  go hiking (to) *hacer excursionismo, hacer senderismo*
  go on a trip (to) *salir de viaje*
  go out (to) *salir*
  go shopping (to) *ir de compras*
  go sightseeing (to) *visitar los lugares de interés*
  Go straight. *Siga derecho.*
  go through a light (to) *saltarse el semáforo*
  go to bed (to) *acostarse*
  go window-shopping (to) *ir de escaparates*
  go with ... (to) *combinar con ...*
  How's it going? *¿Qué pasa?*
  What's going on? *¿Qué hay?*
goal *gol* (m.)
  score a goal (to) *anotar/hacer/marcar un gol*
goalkeeper *portero* (m.)
God *Dios* (m.)
  For God's sake! *¡Por Dios!*
gold (color) *dorado/dorada* (m./f.)
good *buen/bueno/buena* (before m. sg. nouns/ m./f.)
  be in good hands (to) *estar en buenas manos*
  Good afternoon. *Buenas tardes.*
  Good evening./Good night. *Buenas noches.*
  Good job! *¡Buen trabajo!*
  Good morning. *Buenos días.*
  Have a good trip. *Buen viaje.*

  It's good that ... *Es bueno que ...*
  The weather is good. *El tiempo es bueno.*
Good-bye. *Adiós.*
  say good-bye (to) *despedirse*
grace *gracia* (f.)
grade *nota* (f.)
  grades *calificaciones* (f. pl.)
  get good/bad grades (to) *sacar buenas/malas notas*
graduate (to) *graduarse*
gram *gramo* (m.)
grandchildren *nietos* (pl.)
granddaughter *nieta* (f.)
grandfather *abuelo* (m.)
grandmother *abuela* (f.)
grandparents *abuelos* (pl.)
grandson *nieto* (m.)
grapes *uvas* (f. pl.)
  bunch of grapes *racimo* (m.) *de uvas*
graphic *gráfico/gráfica* (m./f.)
grass *césped* (m.)
gray *gris* (m./f.)
  gray (the color) *gris* (m.)
great *gran/grande* (before sg. nouns/all other cases), *magnífico/magnífica* (m./f.)
  Great! *¡Estupendo!*
green *verde* (m./f.)
  dark green *verde oscuro*
greeting *saludo* (m.)
grill *parrilla* (f.)
  grilled *a la parrilla*
grill (to) *asar*
guava *guayaba* (f.)
guest *invitado/invitada* (m./f.)
guidebook *guía* (f.)
guided tour *visita guiada* (f.)
guitar *guitarra* (f.)
  play the guitar (to) *tocar la guitarra*
gymnasium *gimnasio* (m.)
gymnastics *gimnasia* (f.)

H

hail (to) *granizar*
  It's hailing. *Está granizando.*
hair *pelo* (m.)
hair salon *peluquería* (f.)
half *medio/media* (m./f.)
  at a half past five *a las cinco y media*

halftime *medio tiempo* (m.)
hall *vestíbulo* (m.)
ham *jamón* (m.)
hand *mano* (f.)
 at hand *a la mano*
 be in good hands (to) *estar en buenas manos*
 hand wash (to) *lavar a mano*
 know like the back of one's hand (to) *conocer palmo a palmo*
 on the left-hand side *a mano izquierda*
 on the one hand *por una parte*
 on the other hand *por otra parte*
 on the right-hand side *a mano derecha*
 shake hands (to) *dar la mano*
handbag *bolso* (m.), *cartera* (f.)
handful *manojo* (m.)
handle *manejar*
hang (to) *colgar*
 hang up the phone (to) *colgar el teléfono*
happen (to) *pasar*
 What's happening? *¿Qué tal?*
happening *suceso* (m.)
happily *felizmente*
happy *alegre* (m./f.), *contento/contenta* (m./f.), *feliz* (m./f.)
hard *duro/dura* (m./f.)
hardworking *trabajador* (m./f.)
hat *sombrero* (m.)
have (to) *tener, haber, tomar (food and drink)*
 Do you have time? *¿Cómo estás de tiempo?*
 have a cough (to) *tener tos*
 have a fever (to) *tener fiebre*
 Have a good trip. *Buen viaje.*
 have a headache (to) *tener dolor de cabeza*
 Have a nice day. *Que tenga un buen día.*
 have a sore throat (to) *tener dolor de garganta*
 have an operation (to) *operarse*
 have an upset stomach (to) *estar mal del estómago*
 have blue blood (to) *ser de sangre azul (lit., to be of blue blood)*
 have both feet on the ground (to) *tener los pies en la tierra*
 have fun (to) *divertirse*
 have high/low blood pressure (to) *tener la tensión alta/baja*
 have just ... (done something) (to) *acabar de ...*

have lunch (to) *almorzar*
have nausea (to) *tener náusea(s)*
have permission to (to) *poder*
have to ... (to) *tener que ...*
 How have you been? *¿Cómo te ha ido?*
 not have a clue about ... (to) *no saber ni jota de ...*
 What time do you have? *¿Qué hora tiene?*
 You have to ... *Tienes que ...*
he *él*
head *cabeza* (f.), *cabecera* (f.)
 have a headache (to) *tener dolor de cabeza*
 keep a cool head (to) *tener la cabeza fría*
 lose one's head (to) *perder la cabeza*
headphones *audífonos* (m. pl.)
healthy *saludable* (m./f.)
hear (to) *oír*
heart *corazón* (m.)
heat *calor* (m.)
heel *tacón* (m.)
height *alto* (m.)
Hello. *Hola.*
 Hello! *¡Saludos!*
 Hello? (on the phone) *¿Aló?/¿Dígame?*
help *ayuda* (f.)
 How may I help you? *¿En qué puedo servirle?*
 Thank you for your help. *Le agradezco su ayuda.*
help (to) *ayudar*
 Can you help me? *¿Puede ayudarme?*
her (before a noun) *su/sus* (sg./pl.)
 her (direct object pronoun) *la*
 (to/for) her (indirect object pronoun) *le, se (used in place of le when preceding lo/la/los/las)*
herb *hierba* (f.)
here *aquí*
 Here is ... *Aquí está ...*
 Here you are. *Aquí tiene.*
 Here we are. *Pues, aquí estamos.*
 It's two blocks from here. *Está a dos cuadras de aquí.*
hers *suyo/suya/suyos/suyas* (m. sg./f. sg./m. pl./f. pl.), *el de ella* (m. sg.), *la de ella* (f. sg.)
herself *se*
hey (filler word) *che (Argentina), oye*
hide-and-seek *escondidas* (f. pl.)
high *alto/alta* (m./f.)
 have high blood pressure (to) *tener la tensión*

alta

highway *autopista* (f.), *autovía* (f.), *carretera* (f.)

hiking *excursionismo* (m.), *senderismo* (m.)

  go hiking (to) *hacer excursionismo, hacer senderismo*

hill *cerro* (m.), *colina* (f.)

him (direct object pronoun) *lo*

  (to/for) him (indirect object pronoun) *le, se (used in place of le when preceding lo/la/los/las)*

himself *se*

hip *cadera* (f.)

his *suyo/suya/suyos/suyas* (m. sg./f. sg./m. pl./f. pl.), *el de él* (m. sg.), *la de él* (f. sg.)

  his (before a noun) *su/sus* (sg./pl.)

history *historia* (f.)

Hmm… *Mire…*

hobby *afición* (f.), *pasatiempos* (m.)

hockey *hockey* (m.)

hold (to) *poseer*

  Hold on. *Un momento.*

  Hold on, please. *Espere, por favor.*

  put on hold (to) *poner en espera*

holiday *fiesta* (f.), *día* (m.) *festivo*

homeopathy *homeopatía* (f.)

homework *tarea* (f.)

honest *honesto/honesta* (m./f.)

honey *miel* (f.)

hope (to) *esperar*

  hope that … (to) *esperar que …*

  I hope … *Ojalá que …*

  I hope so! *¡Yo espero que sí!*

horror *horror* (m.)

  horror films *películas* (f. pl.) *de horror*

horse *caballo* (m.)

horseback riding *equitación* (f.)

hospital *hospital* (m.)

hot *caliente* (m./f.)

  be hot (to) *tener calor*

  It's hot. *Hace calor.*

hotel *hotel* (m.)

hour *hora* (f.)

  extra hours *horas* (pl.) *extras*

house *casa* (f.)

how *cómo*

  Do you know how to …? *¿Sabe cómo …?*

  How …! *¡Qué …!*

  How about if …? *¿Qué tal si … ?/¿Qué te parece si … ?*

How are things? *¿Cómo van las cosas?*

How are you doing for time? *¿Cómo estás de tiempo?*

How are you? *¿Cómo está usted?* (fml.)/*¿Cómo estás (tú)?* (infml.)

How do I know!?/How should I know!? *¡Yo qué sé!*

How do you say "…" in …? *¿Cómo se dice "…" en …?*

How have you been? *¿Cómo te ha ido?*

How is everything going? *¿Cómo va todo?*

how many *cuántos/cuántas* (m. pl./f. pl.)

How may I help you? *¿En qué puedo servirle?*

how much *cuánto/cuánta* (m./f.)

How much does it cost? *¿Cuánto cuesta?*

How much is it? *¿Cuánto es?/¿Cuánto vale?*

How nice! *¡Qué bien!*

How old are you (sg. fml.)/is he/is she? *¿Cuántos años tiene?*

How's it going? *¿Qué pasa?*

How's life treating you? *¿Cómo te trata la vida?*

learn how to … (to) *aprender a …*

huge *enorme* (m./f.)

human *humano/humana* (m./f.)

  human body *cuerpo* (m.) *humano*

hundred *cien/ciento* (before a noun/before a number except mil)

  eight hundred *ochocientos/ochocientas* (m./f.)

  five hundred *quinientos/quinientas* (m./f.)

  four hundred *cuatrocientos/cuatrocientas* (m./f.)

  hundred thousand *cien mil*

  nine hundred *novecientos/novecientas* (m./f.)

  one hundred and three dollars *ciento tres dólares*

  one hundred people *cien personas*

  one hundred percent *cien por ciento*

  seven hundred *setecientos/setecientas* (m./f.)

  six hundred *seiscientos/seiscientas* (m./f.)

  three hundred *trescientos/trescientas* (m./f.)

  two hundred *doscientos/doscientas* (m./f.)

hunger *hambre* (f.)

hunting *caza* (f.)

hurricane *huracán* (m.)

hurry *prisa* (f.)

  be in a hurry (to) *tener prisa*

husband *esposo* (m.), *marido* (m.)
hygienic *higiénico/higiénica* (m./f.)

I

I *yo*
ice *hielo* (m.)
ice cream *helado* (m.)
 ice cream parlor *heladería* (f.)
idea *idea* (f.)
ideal *ideal* (m./f.)
idiot *bobo/boba* (m./f.)
if *si*
 How about if … ? *¿Qué tal si … ?/¿Qué te parece si … ?*
illness *enfermedad* (f.), *mal* (m.)
imagine (to) *imaginar*
immediate *inmediato/inmediata* (m./f.)
immediately *inmediatamente, de inmediato*
important *importante* (m./f.)
impossible *imposible* (m./f.)
 It is impossible that … *Es imposible que …*
impressive *impresionante* (m./f.)
in *en*
 be in a hurry (to) *tener prisa*
 be in good hands (to) *estar en buenas manos*
 be interested in … (to) *tener interés en …*
 check in (to) *registrarse*
 in exchange for *por*
 in fashion *de moda*
 in front *delante*
 in front of … *delante de …/enfrente de …*
 in love *enamorado/enamorada* (m./f.)
 in order to *para*
 in place of *por*
 in style *de moda*
 in the afternoon *de la tarde*
 in the early morning *de la madrugada*
 in the evening *de la noche*
 in the morning *de la mañana*
incentive *incentivo* (m.)
include (to) *incluir*
 Is service included? *¿Está incluido el servicio?*
information *información* (f.)
 information center *centro* (m.) *de información*
ingredient *ingrediente* (m.)
inherit (to) *heredar*
injury *lesión* (f.)

inside *dentro*
 inside of … *dentro de …*
insist (to) *insistir*
 insist that … (to) *insistir en que …*
instantaneous *instantáneo/instantánea* (m./f.)
instant message *mensaje* (m.) *instantáneo*
insurance *seguro* (m.)
intelligent *inteligente* (m./f.)
intended for *para*
interest *interés* (m.)
interest (to) *interesar*
 be interested in … (to) *tener interés en …*
 I'm interested in … (to) *Me interesa/ interesan …* (sg./pl.)
interesting *interesante* (m./f.)
intermediate *intermedio/intermedia* (m./f.)
international *internacional* (m./f.)
 international call *llamada* (f.) *internacional*
internet *Internet*
intersection *cruce* (m.), *intersección* (f.)
interview *entrevista* (f.)
interview (to) *entrevistar*
introduce (to) *presentar*
 Let me introduce you to … *Te presento a …*
investigation *investigación* (f.)
invitation *invitación* (f.)
invite (to) *invitar*
iron *plancha* (f.)
iron (to) *planchar*
 ironing board *tabla* (f.) *de planchar*
it (direct object pronoun) *lo/la* (m./f.)
 (to/for) it (indirect object pronoun) *le, se (used in place of le when preceding lo/la/los/las)*
 That's it. *Ya está.*
It is … *Es …/Está …*
 It's a pity that … *Es una lástima que …*
 It's a pleasure. *Mucho gusto.*
 It's beautiful. (weather) *Hace muy buen tiempo.*
 It's better that … *Es mejor que …*
 It's cloudy. *Está nublado.*
 It's cold. *Hace frío.*
 It's five to one. (12:55) *Es la una menos cinco.*
 It's good that … *Es bueno que …*
 It's hailing. *Está granizando.*
 It's hot. *Hace calor.*
 It's impossible that … *Es imposible que …*
 It's necessary that … *Es necesario que …*

It's necessary to ... *Hay que ...*
It's not bad. *No está mal.*
It's not true that ... *No es cierto que ...*
It's one o'clock. *Es la una.*
It's possible that ... *Es posible que ...*
It's preferable that ... *Es preferible que ...*
It's raining. *Está lloviendo.*
It's sad that ... *Es triste que ...*
It's snowing. *Está nevando.*
It's sunny. *Hace sol.*
It's ten after one in the morning. *Es la una y diez de la madrugada.*
It's three o'clock sharp. *Son las tres en punto.*
It's three o'clock. *Son las tres.*
It's twelve noon. *Son las doce del mediodía.*
It's two blocks from here. *Está a dos cuadras de aquí.*
It's windy. *Hace viento.*
Italian *italiano/italiana* (m./f.)
Italian (language) *italiano* (m.)
its *su/sus* (sg./pl.)
itself *se*

J

jacket *americana* (f.), *chaqueta* (f.), *saco* (m.)
jam *mermelada* (f.)
January *enero* (m.)
jar *frasco* (m.)
jazz *jazz* (m.)
jealous *celoso/celosa* (m./f.)
jeans *jeans* (m. pl.), *tejanos* (m. pl.), *vaqueros* (m. pl.)
job *trabajo* (m.), *empleo* (m.)
  Good job! *¡Buen trabajo!*
  summer job *trabajo de verano*
  steady job *trabajo fijo*
jog (to) *trotar*
joke *chiste* (m.)
  tell a dirty joke (to) (lit., to tell a green joke) *contar un chiste verde*
journalist *periodista* (m./f.)
judge *juez* (m.)
juice *jugo* (m.), *zumo* (m.)
July *julio* (m.)
June *junio* (m.)

K

keep (to) *llevar, guardar*
  keep a cool head (to) *tener la cabeza fría*

keep a diary (to) *llevar un diario*
key *llave* (f.)
keyboard *teclado* (m.)
kid *crío/cría* (m./f.)
kilo, kilogram *kilo* (m.)
kilometer *kilómetro* (m.)
kind *clase* (f.)
  all kinds *toda clase*
kiss (to) *besar*
kitchen *cocina* (f.)
knee *rodilla* (f.)
knife *cuchillo* (m.)
know (to) *saber* (facts, information), *conocer* (people, places)
  as you already know *como ya sabes*
  Do you know how to ...? *¿Sabe cómo ...?*
  How do I know!?/How should I know!? *¡Yo qué sé!*
  know by sight (to) *conocer de vista*
  know like the back of one's hand (to) *conocer palmo a palmo*
  make known (to) *dar a conocer*
  not have a clue about ... (to) *no saber ni jota de ...*
  not know (to) *desconocer*
  Who knows? *¿Quién sabe?*

L

label *etiqueta* (f.)
lake *lago* (m.)
lamb *cordero/cordera* (m./f.)
  lamb chop *chuleta* (f.) *de cordero*
lamp *lámpara* (f.)
lamppost *farola* (f.)
land *tierra* (f.)
lane *carril* (m.), *vía* (f.)
  Stay in the right lane. *Siga por el carril de la derecha.*
language *idioma* (m.), *lengua* (f.)
large *gran/grande* (before sg. nouns/all other cases)
last *último/última* (m./f.)
  at last *por fin*
  last month *mes* (m.) *pasado*
  last night *anoche*
  last week *semana* (f.) *pasada*
  last year *año* (m.) *pasado*
late *tarde*

I'll see you later. *Hasta luego.*
I'm late. *Se me hace tarde.*
late night (from midnight) *madrugada* (f.)
later *más tarde, luego*
Until later. *Hasta más tarde.*
very latest (the) *último grito* (m.)
laugh (to) *reír*
  laugh very hard (to) (lit., to turn black with laughter) *estar negro de la risa*
laughter *risa* (f.)
laundry detergent *detergente* (m.) *de ropa*
law *derecho* (m.)
lawn *césped* (m.)
lawyer *abogado/abogada* (m./f.)
lazy *perezoso/perezosa* (m./f.)
  be lazy (to) *ser perezoso*
learn (to) *aprender, saber*
  learn how to ... (to) *aprender a ...*
  I'm learning Spanish. *Estoy aprendiendo español.*
least ... in/of ... (the) *el/la/los/las* (m. sg./f. sg./m. pl./f. pl.) *menos ... de ...*
leather *cuero* (m.)
leave (to) *dejar, marchar, parar, partir, salir*
  leave a message after the tone (to) *dejar un mensaje después de oír la señal*
lecture *conferencia* (f.)
  lecture hall *sala* (f.) *de conferencias*
left side *izquierda* (f.)
  on the left *a la izquierda*
  Turn left. *Gira a la izquierda.*
left-hand *izquierdo/izquierda* (m./f.)
  on the left-hand side *a mano izquierda*
leg *pierna* (f.)
lemon *limón* (m.)
lemonade *limonada* (f.)
less *menos*
  least ... in/of ... (the) *el/la/los/las* (m. sg./f. sg./m. pl./f. pl.) *menos ... de ...*
  less ... than ... *menos ... que ...*
  more or less *más o menos*
lesson *lección* (f.)
Let's go ... *Vamos ...*
Let's see ... *A ver ...*
letter *cartas* (f. pl.)
lettuce *lechuga* (f.)
library *biblioteca* (f.)
lie (to) *mentir*

life *vida* (f.)
  How's life treating you? *¿Cómo te trata la vida?*
lift (to) *levantar*
light *luz* (f.)
  turn off the lights (to) *apagar las luces*
light *claro/clara* (m./f.), *ligero/ligera* (m./f.)
  light blue *azul* (m./f.) *claro*
lightening *relámpago* (m.)
like *como*
like (to) *(se) gustar*
  I like ... *Me gusta/gustan ...* (sg./pl.)
  I really like ... *Me encanta/encantan ...* (sg./pl.)
  I'd like ... *Me gustaría ...*
  like (it) that ... (to) *gustar que ...*
  What would you like? *¿Qué desea?*
likewise *igualmente*
limit *límite* (m.)
line *cola* (f.), *fila* (f.), *línea* (f.)
  stand in line (to) *hacer una cola/fila*
  The line is busy. *Está comunicando.*
linen *lino* (m.)
lip *labio* (m.)
list *lista* (f.)
  list of plays *cartelera* (f.)
listen to (to) *escuchar*
liter *litro* (m.)
literature *literatura* (f.)
little *poco*
  a little *un poco*
  I speak a little Spanish. *Hablo un poco de español.*
live (to) *vivir*
  What do you do for a living? *¿En qué trabaja?*
living room *sala* (f.)
loan *crédito* (m.), *préstamo* (m.)
lobster *langosta* (f.)
local *local* (m./f.)
  local call *llamada* (f.) *local*
London *Londres*
long *largo/larga* (m./f.)
  long weekend *puente* (m.)
look at (to) *mirar*
look for (to) *buscar*
look like (to) *parecer*
look up (to) *consultar*
loose *suelto/suelta* (m./f.)
Los Angeles *Los Ángeles*

Glossary **319**

lose (to) *perder*
  lose one's head (to) *perder la cabeza*
lottery *lotería* (f.)
love (to) *querer, amar*
  I love you. *Te quiero.*
  I'd love to! *¡Me encantaría!*
  in love *enamorado/enamorada* (m./f.)
low-cost *económico/económica* (m./f.)
low-cut *escotado/escotada* (m./f.)
lower (to) *bajar*
LP *disco de vinilo* (m.)
luck *suerte* (f.)
lunch *almuerzo* (m.)
  have lunch (to) *almorzar*
lungs *pulmones* (m. pl.)

M

made *hecho/hecha* (m./f.)
magazine *revista* (f.)
magical *mágico/mágica* (m./f.)
magnificent *magnífico/magnífica* (m./f.)
mailbox *buzón* (m.)
main *principal* (m./f.)
  main dish *plato* (m.) *principal*
major *carrera* (f.), *especialidad* (f.)
major in … (to) *especializarse en …*
  make (to) *hacer*
  **make an international/local/national call
  (to)** *hacer una llamada internacional/local/
  nacional*
  make known (to) *dar a conocer*
man *hombre* (m.), *tío* (m., colloquial)
manager *gerente* (m.)
manner *forma* (f.)
many *muchos/muchas* (m. pl./f. pl.)
  how many *cuántos/cuántas* (m. pl./f. pl.)
map *mapa* (m.), *plano* (m.)
March *marzo* (m.)
marine *marino/marina* (m./f.)
mark (to) *marcar*
market *mercado* (m.)
  flea market *mercadillo*
marriage *matrimonio* (m.)
married *casado/casada* (m./f.)
marry (someone) (to) *casarse con*
  get married (to) *casarse*
martini *martini* (m.)
martyr *mártir* (m./f.)

marvelous *estupendo/estupenda* (m./f.)
master (to) *dominar*
master's degree *maestría* (f.), *especialización* (f.)
match (to) *combinar*
material *material* (m.)
mathematics *matemáticas* (f. pl.)
matter (to) *importar*
  It doesn't matter. *No importa.*
May *mayo* (m.)
May I please … ? (fml.) *¿Me permite … ?*
  (fml.)/*¿Me permites … ?* (infml.)
  May you be well. *Que esté bien.*
mayor *alcalde* (m.)
me (after a proposition) *mí*
  me (direct object pronoun) *me*
  (to/for) me (indirect object pronoun) *me*
mean (to) *significar*
  What does that mean? *¿Qué quiere decir eso?*
meanwhile *mientras tanto*
measure (to) *medir*
measurement *medida* (f.)
meat *carne* (f.)
mechanical *mecánico/mecánica* (m./f.)
  mechanical engineering *ingeniería* (f.)
  mecánica
medication *medicamento* (m.)
  take medication (to) *tomar un medicamento*
medicine *medicina* (f.)
  medicine cabinet *botiquín* (m.)
medium *mediano/mediana* (m./f.), *término* (m.)
  tres cuartos (cooked meat)
  medium-rare *término* (m.) *medio*
meet (to) *conocer, reunirse*
  meet (somebody) (to) *conocer (a alguien),
  encontrarse con*
  meet up with (to) *encontrar*
  Pleased to meet you. *Gusto en conocerlo/la.*
meeting *reunión* (f.), *conferencia* (f.)
  meeting room *sala* (f.) *de conferencias*
memory *memoria* (f.)
menu *carta* (f.)
merely *sólo*
message *mensaje* (m.)
  instant message *mensaje instantáneo*
  leave a message after the tone (to) *dejar un
  mensaje después de oír la señal*
metro *metro* (m.)
Mexican *mexicano/mexicana* (m./f.)

Mexico *México* (m.)

microwave *microondas* (m.)

midnight *medianoche* (f.), *media noche* (f.)

  at midnight *a medianoche*

midway *medio/media* (m./f.)

milk *leche* (f.)

  powdered milk *leche en polvo*

  skim milk *leche descremada*

million *millón*

  one million houses *un millón de casas*

mind *mente* (f.)

  go out of one's mind (to) *pararse de cabeza*

mine *mío/mía/míos/mías* (m. sg./f. sg./m. pl./f. pl.)

minus (-) *menos*

minute *minuto* (m.)

miracle *maravilla* (f.)

mirror *espejo* (m.)

misfortune *desgracia* (f.)

miss (to) *perder, faltar*

mixed *mixto/mixta* (m./f.)

mobile phone *móvil* (m.)

modem *módem* (m.)

modern *moderno/moderna* (m./f.)

molar *muela* (f.)

mole *lunar* (m.)

mom *mamá* (f.), *mami* (f.)

moment *momento* (m.)

  at this moment *en este momento*

  One moment. *Un momento.*

Monday *lunes* (m.)

money *dinero* (m.)

monitor *monitor* (m.)

month *mes* (m.)

  last month *mes pasado*

  next month *mes entrante, mes que viene*

  this month *este mes*

monument *monumento* (m.)

moon *luna* (f.)

more *más*

  more or less *más o menos*

  more …/-er than … *más … que …*

moreover *además*

morning *mañana* (f.)

  early morning (from midnight till daybreak) *madrugada* (f.)

  Good morning. *Buenos días.*

  in the early morning *de la madrugada*

  in the morning *de la mañana*

It's ten after one in the morning. *Es la una y diez de la madrugada.*

this morning *esta mañana*

Moscow *Moscú*

mosque *mezquita* (f.)

most … in/of … (the) *el/la/los/las* (m. sg./f. sg./m. pl./f. pl.) *más … de …*

mother *madre* (f.)

mother-in-law *suegra* (f.)

mountain *montaña* (f.)

mouse *ratón* (m.)

mouth *boca* (f.)

move (to) *mover*

movie *película* (f.)

  movie listing *cartelera de cine*

  movie theater *cine* (m.)

Mr. *señor* (m.), *don* (m.)

Mrs. *señora* (f.), *doña* (f.)

much *mucho*

  how much *cuánto/cuánta* (m./f.)

municipal building *ayuntamiento* (m.), *alcaldía* (f.)

muscle *músculo* (m.)

museum *museo* (m.)

music *música* (f.)

  classical music *música clásica*

musical *musical* (m.)

musician *músico* (m.)

must *deber*

my *mi/mis* (sg./pl.)

myself *me*

N

nail *uña* (f.)

name *nombre* (m.)

  My name is … *Me llamo …*

  What's your name? *¿Cómo se llama usted?* (fml.)/*¿Cómo te llamas?* (infml.)

nap *siesta* (f.)

napkin *servilleta* (f.)

narrow *angosto/angosta* (m./f.), *estrecho/estrecha* (m./f.)

national *nacional* (m./f.)

  national call *llamada* (f.) *nacional*

nationality *nacionalidad* (f.)

natural *natural* (m./f.)

nature *naturaleza* (f.)

nausea *náusea* (f.)

be nauseated/have nausea (to) *tener
náusea(s)*

navy blue *azul* (m./f.) *marino*

near *cerca, próximo/próxima* (m./f.)

near ... *cerca de ...*

necessary *necesario/necesaria* (m./f.)

be necessary (to) *faltar*

It's necessary that ... *Es necesario que ...*

It's necessary to ... *Hay que ...*

neck *cuello* (m.)

necklace *collar* (m.)

need (to) *necesitar*

needle *aguja* (f.)

neighbor *vecino/vecina* (m./f.)

neighborhood *barrio* (m.)

neither *tampoco*

neither ... nor *ni ... ni*

nephew *sobrino* (m.)

nerve *nervio* (m.)

never *nunca*

almost never *casi nunca*

new *nuevo/nueva* (m./f.)

news *noticias* (pl.)

a piece of news *noticia* (f.)

newspaper *periódico* (m.)

New York *Nueva York*

next *próximo/próxima* (m./f.)

next month *mes* (m.) *que viene*

next to ... *al lado de ...*

next week *próxima semana* (f.)*, semana* (f.)
que viene

next year *año* (m.) *que viene*

nice *bonito/bonita* (m./f.)

Have a nice day. *Que tenga un buen día.*

How nice! *¡Qué bien!*

niece *sobrina* (f.)

night *noche* (f.)

at night *de la noche*

Good night. *Buenas noches.*

last night *anoche*

late night (from midnight) *madrugada* (f.)

nine *nueve*

at about nine o'clock *a eso de las nueve*

at nine a.m. *a las nueve de la mañana*

be dressed to the nines (to) *ir de punta en
blanco* (lit., to go from the tip in white)

nine hundred *novecientos/novecientas* (m./f.)

twenty-nine *veintinueve*

nineteen *diecinueve, diez y nueve*

ninety *noventa*

no *no, ningún/ninguno/ninguna* (before m. sg.
nouns/m. sg./f. sg.)

no one *nadie*

No, not at all. *No, para nada.*

There's no ... that/who ... *No hay ningún ...
que ...*

There's no one who/that ... *No hay nadie
que ...*

nobody *nadie*

There's no one who/that ... *No hay nadie
que ...*

none *ningún/ninguno/ninguna* (before m. sg.
nouns/m. sg./f. sg.)

noon *mediodía* (m.)

at noon *a mediodía*

It's twelve noon. *Son las doce del mediodía.*

nor *ni*

neither ... nor *ni ... ni*

normal *normal* (m./f.)

normally *normalmente*

north *norte* (m.)

nose *nariz* (f.)

not *no*

absolutely not *en absoluto*

be not doing well (to) *estar mal*

It's not bad. *No está mal.*

No, not at all. *No, para nada.*

not either *tampoco*

note *nota* (f.)

take note (to) *tomar nota*

notebook *cuaderno* (m.)

nothing *nada*

nothing else *nada más*

There's nothing that ... *No hay nada que ...*

novel *novela* (f.)

romance novel *novela rosa*

November *noviembre* (m.)

now *ahora, ya*

right now *ahora mismo*

nowadays *hoy en día*

number *número* (m.)

telephone number *número de teléfono*

O

object *objeto* (m.)

objective *objetivo* (m.)

ocean océano (m.), *mar* (m.)
October octubre (m.)
of *de*
  because of *por*
  in place of *por*
  of course *por supuesto*
  Of course! *¡Claro que sí!*
  of the (m.) *del (de + el)*
  of which (relative pronoun) *cuyo/cuya/cuyos/*
   cuyas (m. sg./f. sg./m. pl./f. pl.)
  on top of *sobre*
  outside of … *fuera de …*
  Yes, of course. *Sí, claro.*
offer oferta (f.)
offer (to) *ofrecer*
office oficina (f.), *despacho* (m.), *estudio* (m.),
  consultorio (m.)
  doctor's office *consultorio del médico*
  office worker *oficinista* (m./f.)
often *con frecuencia*
oil aceite (m.)
(just) okay *más o menos*
old viejo/vieja (m./f.), *antiguo/antigua* (m./f.)
  be … years old (to) *tener … años*
  How old are you (sg. fml.)/is he/is
   she? *¿Cuántos años tiene?*
  older mayor (m./f.)
  oldest (the) *el/la/los/las* (m. sg./f. sg./m. pl./f.
   pl.) *mayor*
on *en*
  buy on sale (to) *comprar en rebaja*
  depend on … (to) *depender de …*
  go on a trip (to) *salir de viaje*
  Hold on, please. *Espere, por favor.*
  Hold on. *Un momento.*
  on board *a bordo*
  on the left *a la izquierda*
  on the left-hand side *a mano izquierda*
  on the one hand *por una parte*
  on the other hand *por otra parte*
  on the phone *por teléfono*
  on the radio *por la radio*
  on the right *a la derecha*
  on the right-hand side *a mano derecha*
  on the sidewalk *por el andén*
  on time *a tiempo*
  on top of *sobre*
  on vacation *de vacaciones*

put on hold (to) *poner en espera*
put something on (to) *ponerse*
try on (clothes) (to) *probarse*
once again *nuevamente*
one *uno*
  It's five to one. (12:55) *Es la una menos cinco.*
  It's one o'clock. *Es la una.*
  no one *nadie*
  on the one hand *por una parte*
  one (o'clock) *una*
  One moment. *Un momento.*
  once *una vez*
  once again *nuevamente*
  one-piece enterizo/enteriza (m./f.)
  one-way de sentido (m.) *único*
  thirty-one *treinta y uno*
  twenty-one *veintiuno*
one (impersonal pronoun) *se*
onion cebolla (f.)
online *por Internet, en línea*
only (adjective) único/única (m./f.), *solo/sola*
  (m./f.)
only (adverb) *solamente, sólo, simplemente*
open (to) *abrir*
  open the door (to) *abrir la puerta*
opera ópera (f.)
operator operadora (f.)
opposite opuesto/opuesta (m./f.)
or *o*
  either … or *o … o*
  more or less *más o menos*
orange (color) anaranjado/anaranjada (m./f.)
orange (fruit) naranja (f.)
order (to) *pedir*
  in order to *para*
ounce onza (f.)
our nuestro/nuestra/nuestros/nuestras (m. sg./f.
  sg./m. pl./f. pl.)
ours nuestro/nuestra/nuestros/nuestras (m. sg./f.
  sg./m. pl./f. pl.)
ourselves *nos*
outbound journey ida (f.)
outdoor market *plaza de mercado*
outside (adverb) *afuera, fuera*
  outside of … *fuera de …*
outside (noun) exterior (m.)
outskirts afueras (f. pl.)
oven horno (m.)

over *sobre*
overcoat *abrigo* (m.)
overcooked *sobrecocido/sobrecocida* (m./f.)
overtime *horas* (f. pl.) *extras*
owe (to) *deber*
own (to) *poseer*

P

package *paquete* (m.)
packet *cajetilla* (f.)
  pack of cigarettes *cajetilla de cigarrillos*
page *página* (f.)
  yellow pages *páginas* (pl.) *amarillas*
  webpage *página web*
pain *dolor* (m.), *pena* (f.)
painter *pintor/pintora* (m./f.)
painting *pintura* (f.), *cuadro* (m.)
pajamas *pijama* (m.)
palace *palacio* (m.)
palm *palmo* (m.)
Panamanian *panameña/panameño* (m./f.)
pants *pantalones* (m. pl.)
papaya *papaya* (f.)
paper *papel* (m.)
  research paper *trabajo* (m.) *de investigación*
Paraguay *Paraguay* (m.)
Pardon me? *¿Cómo?*
parents *padres* (pl.)
Paris *París*
park *parque* (m.)
parking lot *parqueadero* (m.)
part *parte* (f.)
partial *parcial* (m./f.)
particular *particular* (m./f.)
part-time *a tiempo parcial*
party *fiesta* (f.)
pass (to) *aprobar, pasar*
  pass a course (to) *aprobar un curso*
  pass a test (to) *aprobar un examen*
passport *pasaporte* (m.)
past *pasado/pasada* (m./f.)
  at a half past five *a las cinco y media*
  at a quarter past six *a las seis y cuarto*
pastry *dulce* (m.)
path *camino* (m.)
patience *paciencia* (f.)
  be patient (to) *tener paciencia*
patterned, with a pattern *estampado/*

  estampada (m./f.)
pay *sueldo* (m.)
pay (to) *pagar*
  pay cash (to) *pagar en efectivo*
payment *pago* (m.)
pear *pera* (f.)
pedestrian *peatón* (m.)
pediatrician *pediatra* (m./f.)
  regular pediatrician *pediatra* (m./f.) *de cabecera*
pediatrics *pediatría* (f.)
pen *bolígrafo* (m.), *pluma* (f.)
pencil *lápiz* (m.)
penicillin *penicilina* (f.)
pension *pensión* (f.)
people *gente* (f.)
people (impersonal pronoun) *se*
pepper *pimienta* (f.) (spice), *pimiento* (m.) (vegetable)
perceive (to) *percibir*
percent *por ciento*
perceptibly *sensiblemente*
perfect *perfecto/perfecta* (m./f.)
perfume *perfume* (m.)
perhaps *tal vez*
period *período* (m.)
period *término* (m.)
permanent *fijo/fija* (m./f.)
person *persona* (f.)
Peru *Perú* (m.)
Peruvian *peruano/peruana* (m./f.)
peso *peso* (m.)
pharmacist *farmacéutico/farmacéutico* (m./f.)
pharmacy *farmacia* (f.)
philosophy *filosofía* (f.)
phone book *guía* (f.) *telefónica*
phone call *llamada* (f.)
  make an international/local/national call (to) *hacer una llamada internacional/local/nacional*
photograph *foto* (f.)
photography *fotografía* (f.)
phrase *frase* (f.)
physics *física* (f.)
piano *piano* (m.)
pick up (to) *recoger, coger, buscar*
picture *foto* (f.), *cuadro* (m.)
  take a picture (to) *hacer una foto*

piece *pieza* (f.)
  one-piece *enterizo/enteriza* (m./f.)
  two-piece *de dos piezas*
pig *cerdo/cerda* (m./f.)
piglet *chanchito/chanchita* (m./f.)
pill *pastilla* (f.)
pink *rosado/rosada* (m./f.)
pity *lástima* (f.), *pena* (f.)
  It's a pity that… *Es una lástima que…*
place *lugar* (m.), *sitio* (m.)
  in place of *por*
place (to) *poner*
plaid *a cuadros*
plan *plan* (m.)
plant *planta* (f.)
plastic *plástico* (m.)
plate *plato* (m.)
play (to) *jugar, practicar (sports), tocar (instrument)*
  play sports (to) *hacer deporte*
  play the piano (to) *tocar el piano*
  play the guitar (to) *tocar la guitarra*
play (theater) *obra* (f.)
player *jugador/jugadora* (m./f.)
plaza *plaza* (f.)
pleasant *agradable* (m./f.)
please (to) *gustar*
  Pleased to meet you. *Encantado./Encantada.* (said by a man/said by a woman)/*Gusto en conocerlo/la.*
  Please. *Por favor.*
pleasure *placer* (m.), *gusto* (m.)
  It's a pleasure. *Mucho gusto.*
plumber *fontanero/fontanera* (m./f.)
plus (+) *más*
p.m. *de la tarde, de la noche*
  at four p.m. *a las cuatro de la tarde*
  at seven p.m. *a las siete de la noche*
pocket-knife *navaja* (f.)
point *punto* (m.), *término* (m.)
police officer *policía* (m./f.)
  policewoman *mujer* (f.) *policía*
polka-dot *de lunares*
polyester *poliéster* (m.)
pond *estanque* (m.)
pool *piscina* (f.)
poor, poor person *pobre* (m./f.)
  poor (the) *los pobres*

poorly *mal*
pork *cerdo* (m.), *carne* (f.) *de cerdo*
Portuguese *portugués/portuguesa* (m./f.)
position (job) *puesto* (m.)
possible *posible* (m./f.)
  as soon as possible *lo antes posible*
  It is possible that… *Es posible que…*
post (job) *puesto* (m.)
postage stamp *estampilla* (f.)
post office *correo* (m.)
postpone (to) *retrasar*
potato *papa* (f.), *patata* (f.)
pound *libra* (f.)
  half pound *media libra*
powder *polvo* (m.)
  powdered milk *leche* (f.) *en polvo*
practice (to) *practicar*
prayer *oración* (f.)
precisely *precisamente*
prefer (to) *preferir*
  prefer that… (to) *preferir que…*
preferable *preferible* (m./f.)
  It's preferable that… *Es preferible que…*
pregnant *embarazada* (f.)
prepared *preparado/preparada* (m./f.)
presentation *presentación* (f.)
president *presidente/presidenta* (m./f.)
pressure *presión* (f.)
  have high/low blood pressure (to) *tener la tensión alta/baja*
prestigious *prestigioso/prestigiosa* (m./f.)
pretty *bonito/bonita* (m./f.)
prevent (to) *impedir*
price *precio* (m.)
  price tag *etiqueta* (f.) *con el precio*
  reasonable price *precio económico*
printer *impresora* (f.)
prison *cárcel* (f.)
prize *premio* (m.)
probation *prueba* (f.)
  probationary period *período* (m.) *de prueba*
problem *problema* (m.)
produce (to) *producir*
product *producto* (m.)
profession *profesión* (f.)
professional *profesional* (m./f.)
professionally *profesionalmente*
professor *profesor/profesora* (m./f.)

program *programa* (m.)
  television program *programa de televisión*
prohibit (to) *prohibir*
project *proyecto* (m.)
promise (to) *prometer*
proof *prueba* (f.)
protect (to) *proteger*
psychology *sicología* (f.)
punctual *puntual* (m./f.)
purchase *compra* (f.)
purple *morado/morada* (m./f.), *púrpura* (m./f.)
put (to) *poner*
  I'm putting you through. (on the phone) *Lo paso.*
  put on hold (to) *poner en espera*
  put something on (to) *ponerse*

Q

qualification *cualificación* (f.)
qualified *cualificado/cualificada* (m./f.)
quarter *cuarto* (m.)
  at a quarter past six *a las seis y cuarto*
  at a quarter to six *a las seis menos cuarto*
question *pregunta* (f.)
questionnaire *cuestionario* (m.)
quick *rápido/rápida* (m./f.)
quickly *rápidamente, rápido, aprisa*
quiet *tranquilo/tranquila* (m./f.)
quietly *silenciosamente*
quite, quite a lot *bastante*

R

radio *radio* (f.)
  on the radio *por la radio*
railroad *ferrocarril* (m.)
rain *lluvia* (f.)
rain (to) *llover*
  It's raining. *Está lloviendo.*
raincoat *gabardina* (f.)
raise (to) *levantar*
ramp *rampa* (f.)
rash *brote* (m.)
razor *navaja* (f.) *de afeitar*
read (to) *leer*
reader *lector* (m.)
reading *lectura* (f.)
ready *listo/lista* (m./f.), *preparado/preparada* (m./f.)

Ready? *¿Listos?/¿Preparados?*
realism *realismo* (m.)
realistic *realista* (m./f.)
Really? *No me digas.*
reason *razón* (f.)
reasonable price *precio* (m.) *económico*
receive (to) *recibir*
reception desk *recepción* (f.)
receptionist *recepcionista* (m./f.)
recess *receso* (m.)
recipe *receta* (f.)
recognize (to) *reconocer*
recommend (to) *recomendar*
  recommend that … (to) *recomendar que …*
record *registro* (m.), *historial* (m.), *disco* (m.)
record (to) *anotar*
recreation *recreo* (m.)
red *rojo/roja* (m./f.), *colorado/colorada* (m./f.)
  red wine *vino* (m.) *tinto*
reduce (to) *reducir*
reduced *rebajado/rebajada* (m./f.)
reference *referencia* (f.)
refrigerator *nevera* (f.)
regain strength (to) *coger fuerzas* (f. pl.)
regarding … *en cuanto a …*
region *región* (f.)
regional *regional* (m./f.)
register (to) *matricularse*
registration *matrícula* (f.)
regret that … (to) *sentir que …*
relationship *relación* (f.)
relative *pariente* (m./f.)
remain (to) *quedar*
remember (to) *recordar*
rent (to) *alquilar*
repayment *retribución* (f.)
repeat (to) *repetir*
  Repeat, please. *Repita, por favor*
reply to (to) *contestar*
report *informe* (m.)
  report card *calificaciones* (f. pl.)
representative *representante* (m.)
request (to) *solicitar*
  request that … (to) *pedir que …*
research *investigación* (f.)
  research paper *trabajo* (m.) *de investigación*
reservation *reserva* (f.), *reservación* (f.)
resolve (to) *resolver*

responsible *responsable* (m./f.)
rest *resto* (m.)
rest (to) *descansar*
restaurant *restaurante* (m.)
result *resultado* (m.)
résumé *historial* (m.) *de trabajo, currículum vítae, hoja* (f.) *de vida*
retain (to) *quedar*
retired, retired person *jubilado/jubilada* (m./f.)
return (to) *regresar, volver*
rice *arroz* (m.)
rich *rico/rica* (m./f.)
ride (to) *montar*
right *derecho* (m.), *ya*
   be right (to) *tener razón*
   right? *¿verdad?*
   on the right *a la derecha*
   on the right-hand side *a mano derecha*
   right now *en este momento, ahora mismo*
   right side *derecha* (f.)
   right-side *derecho/derecha* (m./f.)
   That's right. *Es verdad./Así es.*
   Turn right. *Gira a la derecha.*
ring *anillo* (m.)
ring (to) *sonar*
rise (to) *levantarse*
river *río* (m.)
robe *albornoz* (m.), *bata* (f.), *deshabillé* (m.)
rock *roca* (f.)
romance novel *novela* (f.) *rosa*
romantic *romántico/romántica* (m./f.)
   romantic films *películas* (f. pl.) *románticas*
room *alcoba* (f.), *cuarto* (m.), *habitación* (f.)
rose *rosa* (f.)
   wear rose-colored glasses (to) *ver todo color de rosa* (lit., to see everything pink)
rotten *podrido/podrida* (m./f.)
rough *agitado/agitada* (m./f.)
round *redondo/redonda* (m./f.)
route *recorrido* (m.)
run (to) *correr*
rural *rural* (m./f.)
Russian (language) *ruso* (m.)

S

sack *bolsa* (f.)
sad *triste* (m./f.)
   It's sad that … *Es triste que …*

sadly *tristemente*
safe *seguro/segura* (m./f.)
safety *seguridad* (f.)
salad *ensalada* (f.)
salary *salario* (m.)
sale *venta* (f.)
   buy on sale (to) *comprar en rebaja*
salesman/saleswoman *vendedor/vendedora* (m./f.)
salsa *salsa* (f.)
salt *sal* (f.)
salty *salado/salada* (m./f.)
same *mismo/misma* (m./f.)
   The same to you. *Igualmente.*
sand *arena* (f.)
sandals *sandalias* (f. pl.)
Saturday *sábado* (m.)
sauce *salsa* (f.)
save (to) *ahorrar, guardar*
say (to) *decir*
   How do you say " … " in … ? *¿Cómo se dice " … " en … ?*
   say good-bye (to) *despedirse*
scarf *bufanda* (f.)
scary *espantoso/espantosa* (m./f.)
schedule *horario* (m.)
scholarship *beca* (f.)
school *escuela* (f.), *academia* (f.)
   school subject *materia* (f.)
science *ciencia* (f.)
scoreboard *marcador* (m.)
scream *grito* (m.)
scream (to) *gritar*
screen *pantalla* (f.)
sculpture *escultura* (f.)
sea *mar* (m.)
season *estación* (f.)
seat *silla* (f.)
seat (to) *sentar*
   be seated (to) *estar sentado*
second *segundo/segunda* (m./f.)
   second year *segundo año*
secondary school *colegio* (m.)
secret *secreto* (m.)
secretary *secretaria* (m./f.)
section *sección* (f.)
security *seguridad* (f.)
see (to) *ver*

I'll see you later. *Hasta luego.*
Let's see … *Vamos …/A ver …*
See you. *Nos vemos. (lit., We see each other.)*
See you soon. *Hasta pronto.*
See you tomorrow. *Hasta mañana.*
seem (to) *parecer*
seldom *casi nunca*
sell (to) *vender*
semester *semestre* (m.)
send (to) *enviar*
sense *sentido* (m.)
sensibly *sensatamente*
September *septiembre* (m.)
series *serie* (f.)
serious *grave* (m./f.), *serio/seria* (m./f.)
serve (to) *servir, atender*
service *servicio* (m.)
  Is service included? *¿Está incluido el servicio?*
session *sesión* (f.)
set off (to) *partir*
seven *siete*
  at seven p.m. *a las siete de la noche*
  seven hundred *setecientos/setecientas* (m./f.)
  twenty-seven *veintisiete*
seventeen *diecisiete, diez y siete*
seventy *setenta*
several *varios/varias* (m./f.)
sewing *costura* (f.)
shake hands (to) *dar la mano*
shampoo *champú* (m.)
shave (to) *afeitar*
  shave (oneself) (to) *afeitarse*
shaving cream *crema de afeitar*
she *ella*
sheet (of paper) *hoja* (f.)
shelf *estante* (m.)
shirt *camisa* (f.)
shoes *zapatos* (m. pl.)
  shoe store *zapatería* (f.)
  tennis shoes *zapatillas* (f. pl.) *deportivas*
  What shoe size do you wear? *¿Qué número calza?*
shop (to) *comprar*
shopping mall *centro* (m.) *comercial*
short *bajo/baja* (m./f.), *corto/corta* (m./f.)
shoulder *hombro* (m.)
shout (to) *gritar*
show (to) *mostrar, dar*

shower *ducha* (f.)
shrimp *camarón* (m.), *gamba* (f.)
shy *tímido/tímida* (m./f.)
siblings *hermanos* (pl.)
sick *enfermo/enferma* (m./f.)
sickness *mareo* (m.), *náusea* (f.)
side *lado* (m.), *parte* (f.)
  on the left-hand side *a mano izquierda*
  on the right-hand side *a mano derecha*
sidewalk *andén* (m.), *acera* (f.)
  on the sidewalk *por el andén/la acera*
signal *señal* (f.)
signature *firma* (f.)
silk *seda* (f.)
silver (color) *plateado/plateada* (m./f.)
simply *simplemente*
since *desde, pues*
sing (to) *cantar*
singer *cantante* (m./f.)
single *único/única* (m./f.), *soltero/soltera* (m./f.)
sink *lavabo* (m.), *fregadero* (m.) (kitchen)
sister *hermana* (f.)
sister-in-law *cuñada* (f.)
sit down (to) *sentarse*
situation *situación* (f.)
six *seis*
  at a quarter past six *a las seis y cuarto*
  at a quarter to six *a las seis menos cuarto*
  six hundred *seiscientos/seiscientas* (m./f.)
  twenty-six *veintiséis*
sixteen *dieciséis, diez y seis*
sixty *sesenta*
size *talla* (f.), *tamaño* (m.)
  What shoe size do you wear? *¿Qué número calza?*
ski (to) *esquiar*
skill *destreza* (f.), *cualificación* (f.)
skimmed *descremado/descremada* (m./f.)
  skim milk *leche* (f.) *descremada*
skin *piel* (f.)
skip (to) *saltar*
skirt *falda* (f.)
sky *cielo* (m.)
  sky blue *celeste* (m./f.)
sleep *sueño* (m.)
  be sleepy (to) *tener sueño*
sleep (to) *dormir*
sleepiness *sueño* (m.)

slice rebanada (f.), *tajada* (f.)

slippers *chinelas* (f. pl.), *pantuflas* (f. pl.),
zapatillas (f. pl.)

slow *lento/lenta* (m./f.), *retrasado/retrasada*
(m./f.)

slowly *despacio, lentamente*
Speak more slowly, please. *Hable más
despacio, por favor.*

small *pequeño/pequeña* (m./f.)
smaller *menor* (m./f.)
smallest (the) *el/la/los/las* (m. sg./f. sg./m. pl./f.
pl.) *menor*

smart *inteligente* (m./f.)

smell (to) *oler*

smile (to) *sonreír*

smog *niebla* (f.) *tóxica/con humo*

smoke (to) *fumar*

smoked *ahumado/ahumada* (m./f.)

snack time *merienda* (f.)

snake *serpiente* (f.)

sneakers *zapatillas* (f. pl.) *deportivas*

snow *nieve* (f.)

snow (to) *nevar*
It's snowing. *Está nevando.*

so *así, pues*
I hope so! *¡Yo espero que sí!*
I think so. *Creo que sí.*
so-so *más o menos*
So ... *Así que ...*
so to speak *por así decir*

so (very) *tan*

soap *jabón* (m.)

soccer *fútbol* (m.)

socks *calcetines* (m. pl.), *medias* (f. pl.)

soda *refresco* (m.)

sofa *sofá* (m.)

soft *suave* (m./f.)

soft drink *refresco* (m.)

sole *solo/sola* (m./f.)

solely *sólo*

solitude *soledad* (f.)

solution *solución* (f.)

some *unos/unas* (m. pl./f. pl.), *algún/alguno/
alguna* (before m. sg. nouns/m. sg./f. sg.), *algunos/
algunas* (m. pl./f. pl.)

somebody, someone *alguien*
somebody else *alguien más*

something *algo, algún/alguno/alguna* (before

m. sg. nouns/m. sg./f. sg.), *algunos/algunas* (m.
pl./f. pl.)

sometimes *a veces*

somewhat *algo*

son *hijo* (m.)

song *canción* (f.)

son-in-law *yerno* (m.)

soon *pronto*
as soon as possible *lo antes posible*
See you soon. *Hasta pronto.*

(I'm) sorry. *Lo siento.*

sound *sonido* (m.)
sound system *sistema* (m.) *de sonido*

sound (to) *sonar*

soup *sopa* (f.)

sour *agrio/agria* (m./f.), *cortado/cortada* (m./f.),
amargo/amarga (m./f.)

south *sur* (m.)

South America *Sudamérica*

space *espacio* (m.)

Spain *España* (f.)

Spanish *español/española* (m./f.)

Spanish (language) *español* (m.)
I'm learning Spanish. *Estoy aprendiendo
español.*
I speak a little Spanish. *Hablo un poco de
español.*

speak (to) *hablar*
Do you speak English? (fml.) *¿Habla usted
inglés?*
Do you speak English? (infml.) *¿Hablas inglés?*
I speak a little Spanish. *Hablo un poco de
español.*
I speak French fluently. *Domino el francés.*
so to speak *por así decir*
Speak more slowly, please. *Hable más
despacio, por favor.*
speak to ... (to) *hablar con ....*

specialization *especialización* (f.)

specialize (to) *especializarse*

special of the day *plato del día*

specialty *especialidad* (f.)

spectator *espectador/espectadora* (m./f.)

speed *velocidad* (f.)

spend (to) *pasar*
spend the day (to) *pasar el día*

spicy *condimentado/condimentada* (m./f.),
picante (m./f.)

spinal column *columna* (f.) *vertebral*
spoiled *pasado/pasada* (m./f.)
spoon *cuchara* (f.)
sport *deporte* (m.)
  person who plays sports *deportista* (m./f.)
spot *pinta* (f.)
spring *primavera* (f.)
spy *espía* (m./f.)
square *cuadro* (m.), *plaza* (f.)
stadium *estadio* (m.)
staff *personal* (m.), *plantilla* (f.)
stairs *escaleras* (f. pl.)
stamp collecting *filatelia* (f.)
stand in line (to) *hacer una cola/fila*
star *estrella* (f.)
start (to) *comenzar*
  start ... (doing something) (to) *comenzar a ...*
  start from ... (to) *partir de ...*
state *estado* (m.)
station *estación* (f.)
  train station *estación de tren, estación de ferrocarril*
Stay in the right lane. *Siga por el carril de la derecha.*
steady job *trabajo* (m.) *fijo*
stepdaughter *hijastra* (f.)
stepfather *padrastro* (m.)
stepmother *madrastra* (f.)
stepson *hijastro* (m.)
stick *palo* (m.)
still *todavía*
stockings *pantymedias* (f. pl.), *medias* (f. pl.)
stomach *estómago* (m.)
  have an upset stomach (to) *tener mal de estómago*
stop *alto* (m.), *parada* (f.)
  Stop! *¡Alto!*
stop (to) *parar, cesar*
  stop ... (doing something) (to) *cesar de ...*
store *tienda* (f.)
  antique store *tienda de antigüedades*
  clothing store *tienda de ropa*
  convenience store *tienda* (f.)
  department store *tienda por departamentos*
  electronics store *tienda de electrodomésticos*
  store clerk *dependiente/dependienta* (m./f.)
storm *tormenta* (f.)

stove *cocina* (f.)
straight *recto, derecho*
  Continue straight. *Continúa recto.*
  Go straight. *Siga derecho.*
strange *extraño/extraña* (m./f.)
stranger *extranjero/extranjera* (m.)
street *calle* (f.)
streetlight *luz* (f.) *de la calle*
strength *fuerza* (f.)
  regain strength (to) *coger fuerzas* (f. pl.)
stressing, stressful *estresante* (m./f.)
stripe *raya* (f.)
striped *a rayas*
strong *fuerte* (m./f.)
student *estudiante/estudiante* (m./f.), *alumno/alumna* (m./f.)
study *estudio* (m.)
  studies *estudios* (pl.)
study (to) *estudiar*
stuffing *relleno* (m.)
style *estilo* (m.)
  in style *de moda*
subject *asignatura* (f.)
submit (to) *entregar*
subscriber *abonado/abonada* (m./f.)
suburban *suburbano/suburbana* (m./f.)
subway *subterráneo* (m.), *metro* (m.)
success *éxito* (m.)
such *tal*
suede *gamuza* (f.)
suffer (to) *sufrir*
sugar *azúcar* (m.)
suggest (to) *sugerir*
  suggest that ... (to) *sugerir que ...*
suit *traje* (m.)
suitcase *maleta* (f.)
summer *verano* (m.)
  summer job *trabajo* (m.) *de verano*
sun *sol* (m.)
  It's sunny. *Hace sol.*
Sunday *domingo* (m.)
sunglasses *gafas* (f. pl.) *de sol*
supermarket *supermercado* (m.)
supporter *hincha* (m./f.)
supposition *supuesto* (m.)
sure *seguro/segura* (m./f.)
  I'm sure. *Seguro/segura que sí.*
surprise *sorpresa* (f.)

be surprised (to) *sorprenderse*
be surprised that ... (to) *sorprenderse de que ...*
suspend (to) *suspender*
suspense *suspenso* (m.)
  suspense films *películas* (f. pl.) *de suspenso*
sweater *suéter* (m.), *jersey* (m.)
sweet (adjective) *dulce* (m./f.)
sweet (noun) *dulce* (m.)
swell (to) *hincharse*
swim (to) *nadar*
swimming *natación* (f.)
  swimming pool *piscina* (f.)
switchboard *centralita* (f.)
symptom *síntoma* (m.)
syndrome *síndrome* (m.)
  carpal tunnel syndrome *síndrome del túnel del carpio*
system *sistema* (m.)
  sound system *sistema de sonido*

T

table *mesa* (f.), *tabla* (f.)
tableware *vajilla* (f.)
tag *etiqueta* (f.)
  price tag *etiqueta con el precio*
tail *cola* (f.)
take (to) *tomar, traer, coger, usar, llevar*
  take a bath (to) *bañarse*
  take a blood test (to) *hacerse un examen de sangre*
  take a picture (to) *hacer una foto*
  take a shower (to) *ducharse*
  take a test (to) *hacer un examen, presentarse a un examen*
  Take care. *Que estés bien.*
  take care of (to) *atender*
  take into acount (to) *tener en cuenta*
  take medication (to) *tomar un medicamento*
  take out (to) *sacar*
  take the blood pressure (to) *tomar la tensión*
talented *dotado/dotada* (m./f.)
talk (to) *hablar*
talk show *programa* (m.) *de entrevistas*
tall *alto/alta* (m./f.)
taste *gusto* (m.)
taste (to) *saborear, probar, saber*
tax *impuesto* (m.)

tax return *planilla* (f.) *de impuestos*
taxi *taxi* (m.)
  taxi driver *taxista* (m./f.)
tea *té* (m.)
teacher *maestro/maestra* (m./f.)
teakettle *tetera* (f.)
team *equipo* (m.)
technology *tecnología* (f.)
teenager *adolescente* (m.)
telephone *teléfono* (m.)
  answer the phone (to) *contestar el teléfono*
  call ... on the phone (to) *llamar por teléfono a ...*
  dial a phone number (to) *marcar un número de teléfono*
  hang up the phone (to) *colgar el teléfono*
  make a phone call (to) *llamar por teléfono*
  on the phone *por teléfono*
  telephone booth *cabina* (f.) *telefónica*
  telephone number *número* (m.) *de teléfono*
telephonic *telefónico/telefónica* (m./f.)
television *televisión* (f.)
  television program *programa* (m.) *de televisión*
  television set *televisor* (m.)
  watch television (to) *mirar la televisón*
tell (to) *contar, decir*
  tell a dirty joke (to) *contar un chiste verde (lit., to tell a green joke)*
  tell time (to) *dar la hora*
temperature *temperatura* (f.)
temple *templo* (m.)
ten *diez*
  at eight ten (8:10) *a las ocho y diez*
  It's ten after one in the morning. *Es la una y diez de la madrugada.*
  ten thousand *diez mil*
tendon *tendón* (m.)
tennis *tenis* (m.)
  tennis shoes *zapatillas* (f. pl.) *deportivas*
tension *tensión* (f.)
term *término* (m.)
terrible *pésimo/pésima* (m./f.)
test *examen* (m.), *prueba* (f.)
  fail a test (to) *suspender un examen*
  pass a test (to) *aprobar un examen*
  take a blood test (to) *hacerse un examen de sangre*

take a test (to) *hacer un examen, presentarse a un examen*

text *texto* (m.)

textbook *libro* (m.) *de texto*

than *que*

less ... than ... *menos ... que ...*

more ... /-er than ... *más ... que ...*

thanks *gracias* (pl.)

be thankful (to) *agradecer*

give thanks (to) *dar (las) gracias*

Thanks a lot. *Muchas gracias.*

Thank you. *Gracias.*

Thank you for your help. *Le agradezco su ayuda.*

that (demonstrative) *ese/esa* (m. sg./f. sg.) (*near the listener*), *aquel/aquella* (m. sg./f. sg.) (*far from the speaker and the listener*)

that (one) *ése/ésa* (m. sg./f. sg.) (*near the listener*)

that (one) over there *aquél/aquélla* (m. sg./f. sg.) (*far from the speaker and the listener*)

that (one, thing) (neuter) *eso* (m.) (*near the listener*)

that (one, thing) over there (neuter) *aquello* (m.) (*far from the speaker and the listener*)

That's it. *Ya está.*

That's right. *Es verdad./Así es.*

That's too bad! *¡Qué pena!*

that (conjunction, relative pronoun) *que*

the *el/la/los/las* (m. sg./f. sg./m. pl./f. pl.)

of the (m.) /from the (m.) /about the (m.) *del (de + el)*

to the (m.) /at the (m.) *al (a + el)*

theater *teatro* (m.)

their *su/sus* (sg./pl.)

theirs (m./f.) *suyo/suya/suyos/suyas* (m. sg./f. sg./m. pl./f. pl.)

theirs (f. pl.) *el de ellas* (m. sg.), *la de ellas* (f. sg.)

theirs (m. pl./mixed group) *el de ellos* (m. sg.), *la de ellos* (f. sg.)

them (direct object pronoun) *los/las* (m./f.)

(to/for) them (indirect object pronoun) *les, se* (used in place of les when preceding lo/la/los/las)

themselves *se*

then *entonces, luego, pues*

Until then. *Hasta entonces.*

there *ahí, allí*

There is ... /There are ... *Hay ...*

There's no ... that/who ... *No hay ningún ...*

que ...

There's no one who/that ... *No hay nadie que ...*

There's nothing that ... *No hay nada que ...*

therefore *por lo tanto, pues*

these *estos/estas* (m. pl./f. pl.)

these (ones) *éstos/éstas* (m. pl./f. pl.)

they *ellos/ellas* (m. pl. & mixed group/f. pl.)

thick *espeso/espesa* (m./f.)

thief *ladrón* (m./f.)

thin *delgado/delgada* (m./f.), *ligero/ligera* (m./f.)

thing *cosa* (f.)

How are things? *¿Cómo van las cosas?*

think (to) *creer, pensar*

Don't you think? *¿No crees?*

I think so. *Creo que sí.*

not think that ... (to) *no pensar que ...*

What do you think of ... ? *¿Qué te parece ... ?*

third *tercero/tercer/tercera* (m. sg./m. sg. before a noun/f. sg.)

third year *tercer año*

thirst *sed* (f.)

be thirsty (to) *tener sed*

thirteen *trece*

thirty *treinta*

thirty-one *treinta y uno*

thirty percent off *treinta por ciento de descuento*

this *este/esta* (m. sg./f. sg.)

this (one) *éste/ésta* (m. sg./f. sg.)

this (one, thing) (neuter) *esto* (m.)

this afternoon *esta tarde*

this day *este día*

this evening *esta noche* (f.)

those *aquellos/aquellas* (m. pl./f. pl.) (*far from the speaker and the listener*)

those (ones) over there *aquéllos/aquéllas* (m. pl./f. pl.) (*far from the speaker and the listener*)

thousand *mil*

hundred thousand *cien mil*

ten thousand *diez mil*

twenty thousand *veinte mil*

three *tres*

It's three o'clock. *Son las tres.*

It's three o'clock sharp. *Son las tres en punto.*

one hundred and three dollars *ciento tres dólares*

three hundred *trescientos/trescientas* (m./f.)

twenty-three *veintitrés*

throat *garganta* (f.)

have a sore throat (to) *tener dolor de garganta*

through *por*

from ... through ... *de ... a ...*

go through a light (to) *saltarse el semáforo*

I'm putting you through. (on the phone) *Lo paso.*

thunder *trueno* (m.)

Thursday *jueves* (m.)

ticket *billete* (m.), *boleto* (m.), *pasaje* (m.), *tiquete* (m.), *entrada* (f.)

tie *corbata* (f.)

tie (to) *empatar*

tied *empatado/empatada* (m./f.)

be tied (to) *quedar empatados*

tight *ajustado/ajustada* (m./f.)

time *hora* (f.), *tiempo* (m.), *vez* (f.)

at the present time *actualmente*

At what time is it? *¿A qué hora es?*

Do you have time?/How are you doing for time? *¿Cómo estás de tiempo?*

full-time *a tiempo completo*

on time, in time *a tiempo*

overtime *horas* (f. pl.) *extras*

part-time *a tiempo parcial*

tell time (to) *dar la hora*

What time is it? *¿Qué hora es?/¿Qué horas son?*

What time do you have? *¿Qué hora tiene?*

tingling feeling *cosquilleo* (m.)

tip *propina* (f.), *punta* (f.)

tired *cansado/cansada* (m./f.)

be tired (to) *tener cansancio*

to *a, con*

in order to *para*

It's five to one. (12:55) *Es la una menos cinco.*

to the (m.) *al (a + el)*

toast *tostada* (f.)

today *hoy*

toe *dedo del pie*

together *junto/junta* (m./f.)

toilet *inodoro* (m.)

toilet paper *papel* (m.) *higiénico*

toll *peaje* (m.)

tomato *tomate* (m.)

tomorrow *mañana* (f.)

Until tomorrow./See you tomorrow. *Hasta mañana.*

tone *tono* (m.), *señal* (f.)

leave a message after the tone (to) *dejar un mensaje después de oír la señal*

tongue *lengua* (f.)

tonight *esta noche*

too *también*

too much, too many *demasiado/demasiada* (m./f.)

tooth *diente* (m.)

touch (to) *tocar*

tour bus trip *recorrido por autobús*

tourism *turismo* (m.)

tourist *turista* (m./f.)

toward(s) *hacia, para*

towel *toalla* (f.)

town *ciudad* (f.), *pueblo* (m.)

around town *por la ciudad*

toxic *tóxico/tóxica* (m./f.)

traffic *tráfico* (m.)

go through a traffic light (to) *saltarse el semáforo*

traffic jam *embotellamiento* (m.)

traffic light *semáforo* (m.)

train *tren* (m.), *ferrocarril* (m.)

train station *estación* (f.) *de tren, estación* (f.) *de ferrocarril*

transfer (to) *trasladar*

translate (to) *traducir*

travel *viaje* (m.)

travel (to) *viajar*

treat (to) *tratar*

How's life treating you? *¿Cómo te trata la vida?*

treatment *tratamiento* (m.)

tree *árbol* (m.)

trip *viaje* (m.)

go on a trip (to) *salir de viaje*

Have a good trip. *Buen viaje.*

true *cierto/cierta* (m./f.)

It is not true that ... *No es cierto que ...*

truth *verdad* (f.)

try (to) *tratar, probar*

try ... (to do something) (to) *tratar de ...*

try on (clothes) (to) *probarse*

T-shirt *camiseta* (f.)

Tuesday *martes* (m.)

tuition *derechos* (m. pl.) *de matrícula*

tuna *atún* (m.)

tunnel *túnel* (m.)

turn *vuelta* (f.)
turn (to) *doblar, girar, volver, ponerse*
 turn around (to) *dar la vuelta*
 Turn left. *Gira a la izquierda.*
 turn off (to) *apagar*
 turn off the lights (to) *apagar las luces*
 Turn right. *Gira a la derecha.*
twelve *doce*
 It's twelve noon. *Son las doce del mediodía.*
twenty *veinte*
 twenty-eight *veintiocho*
 twenty-five *veinticinco*
 twenty-four *veinticuatro*
 twenty-nine *veintinueve*
 twenty-one *veintiuno*
 twenty-seven *veintisiete*
 twenty-six *veintiséis*
 twenty-three *veintitrés*
 twenty-two *veintidós*
two *dos*
 twenty-two *veintidós*
 twice a week *dos veces por semana*
 two hundred *doscientos/doscientas* (m./f.)
 two-piece *de dos piezas*
type *tipo* (m.)
typical *típico/típica* (m./f.)

U

ugly *feo/fea* (m./f.)
umbrella *paraguas* (m.)
uncle *tío* (m.)
uncomfortable *incómodo/incómoda* (m./f.)
under *bajo*
undergarments (men's) *calzones* (m. pl.)
underneath *debajo*
 underneath ... *debajo de ...*
underpants (men's) *calzoncillos* (m. pl.)
undershirt *camisilla* (f.), *camiseta* (f.)
understand (to) *comprender, entender*
underwear (women's) *bombachas* (f. pl.), *bragas*
 (f. pl.), *calzoncitos* (m. pl.), *pantis* (m. pl.)
unemployed *parado/parada* (m./f.)
unfortunately *desafortunadamente, por desgracia*
unfriendly *antipático/antipática* (m./f.)
union *sindicato* (m.)
unique *único/única* (m./f.)
united *unido/unida* (m./f.)
United States (the) *los Estados Unidos*

university *universidad* (f.)
 university course *carrera* (f.)
unpleasant *desagradable* (m./f.)
until *hasta, para*
 Till then. *Hasta entonces.*
 Until later. *Hasta más tarde.*
 Until then. *Hasta entonces.*
 Until tomorrow. *Hasta mañana.*
urban *urbano/urbana* (m./f.)
urgently *urgentemente*
Uruguay *Uruguay* (m.)
Uruguayan *uruguayo/uruguaya* (m./f.)
us (direct object pronoun); (to/for) us (indirect
 object pronoun) *nos*
use (to) *usar*
 use for the first time (to) *estrenar*

V

vacation *vacaciones* (f. pl.)
 on vacation *de vacaciones*
variety *variedad* (f.)
vegetable *vegetal* (m.), *verdura* (f.)
Venezuela *Venezuela* (f.)
Venezuelan *venezolano/venezolana* (m./f.)
vertebral *vertebral* (m./f.)
very *muy, mucho*
veterinarian *veterinario/veterinaria* (m./f.)
view *vista* (f.)
village *aldea* (f.)
vinyl *vinilo* (m.)
 vinyl record *disco* (m.) *de vinilo*
violet (color) *violeta* (m./f.)
violin *violín* (m.)
visit (to) *visitar*
visitor *visitante* (m./f.)
voice *voz* (f.)
 voice mail *buzón* (m.) *de voz*
voucher *vale* (m.)

W

wage *paga* (f.), *jornal* (m.)
wait *espera* (f.)
wait (to) *esperar*
waiter *camarero* (m.), *mesero* (m.)
waitress *camarera* (f.), *mesera* (f.)
wake up (to) *despertarse*
walk (to) *andar, caminar, ir a pie/caminar*
wall *pared* (f.)

wallet *cartera* (f.)
want (to) *querer, desear*
  want that/to … (to) *querer que …*
wish (to) *desear*
  I wish … *Ojalá que …*
  wish that … (to) *desear que …*
wash (to) *lavar*
  hand wash (to) *lavar a mano*
  wash oneself (to) *lavarse*
wash basin *lavabo* (m.)
washing machine *lavadora* (f.)
watch *reloj* (m.)
watch (to) *mirar*
  watch television (to) *mirar la televisón*
water *agua* (f.)
  mineral water *agua mineral*
  water (the) *el agua*
  waters (the) *las aguas*
way *camino* (m.), *forma* (f.)
  one-way *de sentido* (m.) *único*
we *nosotros* (m. pl./mixed group), *nosotras* (f. pl.)
weak *débil* (m./f.)
wear (to) *llevar, calzar (shoes)*
  wear rose-colored glasses (to) *ver todo color de rosa (lit., to see everything pink)*
  What shoe size do you wear? *¿Qué número calza?*
weather *tiempo* (m.)
  The weather is good. *El tiempo es bueno.*
web (on the computer) *web* (f.)
  webpage *página* (f.) *web*
  website *sitio* (m.) *web*
Wednesday *miércoles* (m.)
week *semana* (f.)
  every week *todas las semanas*
  last week *semana pasada*
  next week *próxima semana, semana que viene*
  this week *esta semana*
  twice a week *dos días a la semana*
weekend *fin* (m.) *de semana*
  long weekend *puente* (m.)
weekly *semanal* (m./f.)
weigh (to) *pesar*
Welcome. *Bienvenido./Bienvenida.* (m./f.) (to a man/to a woman)
  You're welcome. *De nada.*
well *bien, pues*
  be not doing well (to) *estar mal*

May you be well. *Que esté bien.*
  well-done *bien asada*
west *oeste* (m.), *occidente* (m.)
what *qué, cuál/cuáles* (sg./pl.)
  At what time is it? *¿A qué hora es?*
  What a coincidence! *¡Qué coincidencia!*
  What color is …? *¿De qué color es …?*
  What do you do for a living? *¿En qué trabaja?*
  What do you think of …? *¿Qué te parece …?*
  What does that mean? *¿Qué quiere decir eso?*
  What shoe size do you wear? *¿Qué número calza?*
  What time do you have? *¿Qué hora tiene?*
  What time is it? *¿Qué hora es?/¿Qué horas son?*
  What would you like? *¿Qué desea?*
  What?/Pardon me? *¿Cómo?*
  What's going on? *¿Qué hay?*
  What's happening? *¿Qué tal?*
  What's up?/What's going on? *¿Qué hay?*
  What's your name? *¿Cómo se llama usted?* (fml.)/*¿Cómo te llamas?* (infml.)
when *cuándo* (question), *cuando* (relative adverb)
where *dónde* (question), *donde* (relative adverb)
  Where are you from? *¿De dónde eres?*
which *cuál/cuáles* (sg./pl.) (question), *cual/cuales* (sg./pl.) (relative pronoun)
  of which (relative pronoun) *cuyo/cuya/cuyos/cuyas* (m. sg./f. sg./m. pl./f. pl.)
while *mientras*
white *blanco/blanca* (m./f.)
  white wine *vino* (m.) *blanco*
who *quién/quiénes* (sg./pl.) (question), *quien/quienes* (sg./pl.) (relative pronoun)
  Who knows? *¿Quién sabe?*
  Who's calling? *¿De parte de quién?/¿Quién lo llama?*
whole *entero/entera* (m./f.)
  whole milk *leche* (f.) *entera*
whom (question) *quién/quiénes* (sg./pl.)
  whom (relative pronoun) *quien/quienes* (sg./pl.)
whose (relative pronoun) *cuyo/cuya/cuyos/cuyas* (m. sg./f. sg./m. pl./f. pl.)
  Whose …? *¿De quién …?*
why *por qué*
wide *ancho/ancha* (m./f.)
wife *esposa* (f.), *mujer* (f.)
win (to) *ganar*
  I hope they win! *¡Ojalá que ganen!*

wind *viento* (m.)
  It's windy. *Hace viento.*
window *ventana* (f.)
  display window *escaparate* (m.)
wine *vino* (m.)
  red wine *vino tinto*
  white wine *vino blanco*
wineglass *copa* (f.)
  glass of wine *copa de vino*
winter *invierno* (m.)
wish *deseo* (m.)
with *con*
  with you *contigo*
without *sin*
woman *mujer* (f.), *tía* (f.)
  businesswoman *mujer de negocios*
  policewoman *mujer policía*
wonder *maravilla* (f.)
wonderful *estupendo/estupenda* (m./f.)
wood *madera* (f.)
wooden *de madera*
wool *lana* (f.)
word *palabra* (f.)
work *trabajo* (m.)
work (to) *trabajar, funcionar*
  What do you do for a living? *¿En qué trabaja?*
working day *jornada* (f.)
world *mundo* (m.)
  world championship *campeonato* (m.) *mundial*
worldly *mundial* (m./f.)
worldwide *mundial* (m./f.)
worry (to) *preocuparse*
  Don't worry. *No se preocupe.*
  worry that … (to) *preocuparse de que …*
worse *peor* (m./f.)
worst (the) *el/la/los/las* (m. sg./f. sg./m. pl./f. pl.)
  peor
wrist *muñeca* (f.)
write (to) *escribir*
  write down (to) *anotar*
writer *escritor/escritora* (m./f.)
wrong *equivocado/equivocada* (m./f.)
  wrong number *número* (m.) *equivocado*

Y

year *año* (m.)
  be … years old (to) *tener … años*
  fifties (the) *los años cicuenta*

last year *año pasado*
next year *año que viene*
second year *segundo año*
third year *tercer año*
this year *este año*
yellow *amarillo/amarilla* (m./f.)
  yellow pages *páginas* (f. pl.) *amarillas*
yes *sí*
yesterday *ayer*
yet *todavía*
you (after a proposition) *ti* (infml. sg.)
you (direct object pronoun) *lo/la/te/los/las/os* (m. sg. fml./f. sg. fml./sg. infml./m. pl./f. pl./pl. infml)
you (impersonal pronoun) *se*
(to/for) you (indirect object pronoun) *le/les* (fml. sg./pl.), *se* (fml. sg./pl.) (used in place of le/les when preceding lo/la/los/las), *te/os* (infml. sg./pl.)
you (subject pronoun) *usted/tú/ustedes/vosotros/vosotras* (sg. fml./sg. infml./pl./m. pl. & mixed group infml. used in Spain/f. pl. infml. used in Spain)
young *joven* (m./f.)
  young boy *niño* (m.)
  young child *párvulo/párvula* (m./f.)
  young girl *niña* (f.)
  younger *menor* (m./f.)
  youngest (the) *el/la/los/las* (m. sg./f. sg./m. pl./f. pl.) *menor*
your (pl. fml. & infml.) *su/sus* (sg./pl.)
  your (pl. infml.) *vuestro/vuestra/vuestros/vuestras* (m. sg./f. sg./m. pl./f. pl.) (used in Spain)
  your (sg. fml.) *su/sus* (sg./pl.)
  your (sg. infml.) *tu/tus* (sg./pl.)
yours (pl. fml. & infml.) *suyo/suya/suyos/suyas* (m. sg./f. sg./m. pl./f. pl.), *el de ustedes* (m. sg.), *la de ustedes* (f. sg.)
  yours (pl. infml.) *vuestro/vuestra/vuestros/vuestras* (m. sg./f. sg./m. pl./f. pl.) (used in Spain)
  yours (sg. fml.) *suyo/suya/suyos/suyas* (m. sg./f. sg./m. pl./f. pl.), *el de usted* (m. sg.), *la de usted* (f. sg.)
  yours (sg. infml.) *tuyo/tuya/tuyos/tuyas* (m. sg./f. sg./m. pl./f. pl.) (infml.)
yourself *se/te* (fml./infml.)
yourselves *se/os* (fml./infml.)
youth hostel *hostal* (m.)

Z

zero *cero*